breakfast

THE MOST IMPORTANT BOOK ABOUT THE

~~MOST IMPORTANT~~ MEAL OF THE DAY
Best

breakfast

THE MOST IMPORTANT BOOK ABOUT THE BEST MEAL OF THE DAY

THE EDITORS OF  CRISPY

FOREWORD BY
HUGH ACHESON

Oxmoor House.

CONTENTS

WHEN YOU WAKE UP IN THE MORNING, POOH,

WHAT'S THE FIRST THING YOU SAY TO YOURSELF?

PIGLET

WHAT'S FOR BREAKFAST?

WHAT DO YOU SAY, PIGLET?

POOH

I SAY, I WONDER WHAT'S GOING TO HAPPEN EXCITING TODAY?

PIGLET

IT'S THE SAME THING.

POOH

—A. A. MILNE

FOREWORD
BY HUGH ACHESON

Breakfast is the meal that many of us have lost track of. It has become a ritualized trough of oat bars, Go–Gurts, caffeine, and maybe an overripe banana. My workday mornings are usually hurried episodes of coffee and cereal, a sustenance function rather than an enjoyable repast. It is a justified adaptation to how we conduct our busy lives, and how convenient it is to just make your body kind of operational. Yet it feels like such a ruinous choice, missing the whole point of eating, which should be soulful and nourishing. Alas, I miss the beauty of the morning meal.

I grew up in a household with too many picky soft scrambled egg enthusiasts, so I do know a fair bit about the breakfast hour. But, I also have a father who balanced that culinary quest for egg custard perfection with bread, not toasted, but obliterated to the darkest hues of burnt. He would eat it without complaint, and still never come clean about whether he really liked it or if he was refusing to atone for his culinary massacres. He also cooked us burnt rice and fish sticks, but not really much in the way of breakfast. I do love him immensely, just not for the food he made us.

Somewhere along the line I, and many more, just gave up and left fantastic breakfasts for restaurant brunches. It was an abandonment of a way of life,
cramming our simple breakfasts into Carnation powders, and the more formal ones into long lines at brunches to eat food made by exhausted line cooks working the shift they abhor. And just so you know, brunch is just breakfast and lunch crammed into an XXL shirt that says "Is it Mimosa Time?".

Hell, we even leave toast to the professionals now, albeit beautiful toast that is a monument to fresh jammed fruit and whipped ricotta. But it is toast (I am winking at you, Jessica Koslow). It is time to reclaim our breakfast roots. It is time to dutch dutch baby.

With this book—compiled, tested, and written by morning meal geniuses—you can break the code to beautiful sunrise meals. Get your spatula out, bring those eggs to room temp, crisp some potatoes, make some waffles, and stay in your kitchen. (If you live in NYC you need to empty the oven of the towels and linens you store in the unused device.) It is time to cook. It is time to say no to brunch lines and oat bars. Get the crossword and a pencil, make some beautiful coffee or complex tea, one that tells a story that you can tell me, put on some Archie Shepp, and craft a memorable meal that will change your morning life.

Let's take time to make some real breakfasts of champions.

INTRODUCTION

Here's a thing I've never told anyone: I want to shrink down to the size of a pea and run around a breakfast buffet. I want to swim in orange juice and spit it into the air like a fountain and catch it in my mouth. I want to lay out on a warm pancake like a seal basking on a beach. I'd slowly roll over and lick the pat of butter, and then roll back into basking position. I'd tunnel into the pancake like a sugar-crazed badger.

Then I'd move on to the meats. Compared to tiny me, each bacon strip would be as tall as a lamppost. I'd have to gnaw at them like a cartoon woodchuck attacking a tree, from the bottom up. I'd hollow out four sausage patties and place them around my body like tires and roll down a hill of corned beef hash. There'd be sausage links, and I'd take two under my arms and jump into a bowl of cereal and use them as floaties. A slice of fried Taylor Ham, curved like a toilet plunger, would be a trampoline, and I'd bounce off it and land in a plate of potatoes.

I'd stomp into a hash brown, breaking through to its mushy center, which would squish between my toes. I'd break off two crispy pieces and strap them to my feet like skis, swoosh down a fork, and launch off its ketchup-slick prongs into a mound of home fries. The bits of green pepper and onion in the home fries would be so greasy they'd escape my grip like slimy fish. I'd rest for a moment on a latke.

Next there'd be a giant platter of eggs. I'd go straight to sunny-side up and sit in the yolk like it's a hot tub. I'd put on a Denver omelet like a cape. I'd strip the delicate white off a poached egg and wear it as a skin suit like Buffalo Bill in *The Silence of the Lambs*. I'd look at myself in a reflective can of brown bread and say, "Would you eat me? I'd eat me."

A fruit salad would be like massive colorful rock formations—a juicy Cappadocia. I'd scale strawberries, wedging my feet into their seeds for safety. I'd do parkour (or what I imagine parkour to be) along the ridges of sliced apple, cantaloupe, and honeydew. Wait! Pause. What sort of sadistic cheapskate loaded my fantasy fruit salad with lowly honeydew? Moving on...

Generously buttered toast would tower over me like a brownstone. I'd run into a warm black currant scone linebacker-style and come out the other end with gooey currant stuck to my hands and face. There would be muffins, and croissants, and kouign-amann, and Danish, and babka, and doughnuts, and bagels, and rugelach, and morning buns, and mini rhubarb galettes that are still big compared to me, and regular-size rhubarb galettes for me to run around in like baseball fields.

OK, that's about it. Thanks for reading all that. This being a breakfast book, it's one of the few places I could share it. Why do I have this fantasy? Probably because I'm the editor of the breakfast site Extra Crispy. I frequently have breakfast on the brain in a professional capacity, and it has worked its way into my psyche in strange ways. For over two years we've been publishing a wide variety of essays, recipes, and videos that celebrate the morning meal. This book is comprised of stories and recipes, along with original photographs and other new work by our brilliant, breakfast-obsessed contributors. Call it a whimsical breakfast jamboree. Or if you're feeling literal, call it a breakfast cookbook with essays. Keep it on your coffee table, or in your breakfast nook. And if you don't have a breakfast nook, call your contractor right now and demand one. Even if you live in a tiny apartment and if you were to add a breakfast nook your entire house would basically be the nook, get that nook. This book is absolutely nook-worthy! Happy breakfasting!

RYAN GRIM, EDITOR, EXTRA CRISPY

CHAPTER ONE

BUILDING BLOCKS

OF
BREAKFAST

Why Do We Eat Eggs for Breakfast?

BY EILEEN REYNOLDS

Poached or scrambled, fried or boiled, tenderly Instagrammed or inhaled via McMuffin, eggs are the undisputed workhorse of the American breakfast. But when did eggs become so heavily associated with morning appetites? Do you ever wonder why we eat eggs for breakfast?

The question is best tackled in two parts, and the first is easy. We eat eggs because they are a miracle. People have eaten eggs in almost all cultures and eras of human history. As the editors of *Lucky Peach* put it in *All About Eggs*, "eggs are what humans have in common."

The same can't be said for breakfast, which is where answering the second part of the question gets complicated. Whereas much of the world has long taken a strictly utilitarian approach to breakfast—in many places the go-to remains a warm (often caffeinated)

A SHORT HISTORY OF EGGS FOR BREAKFAST

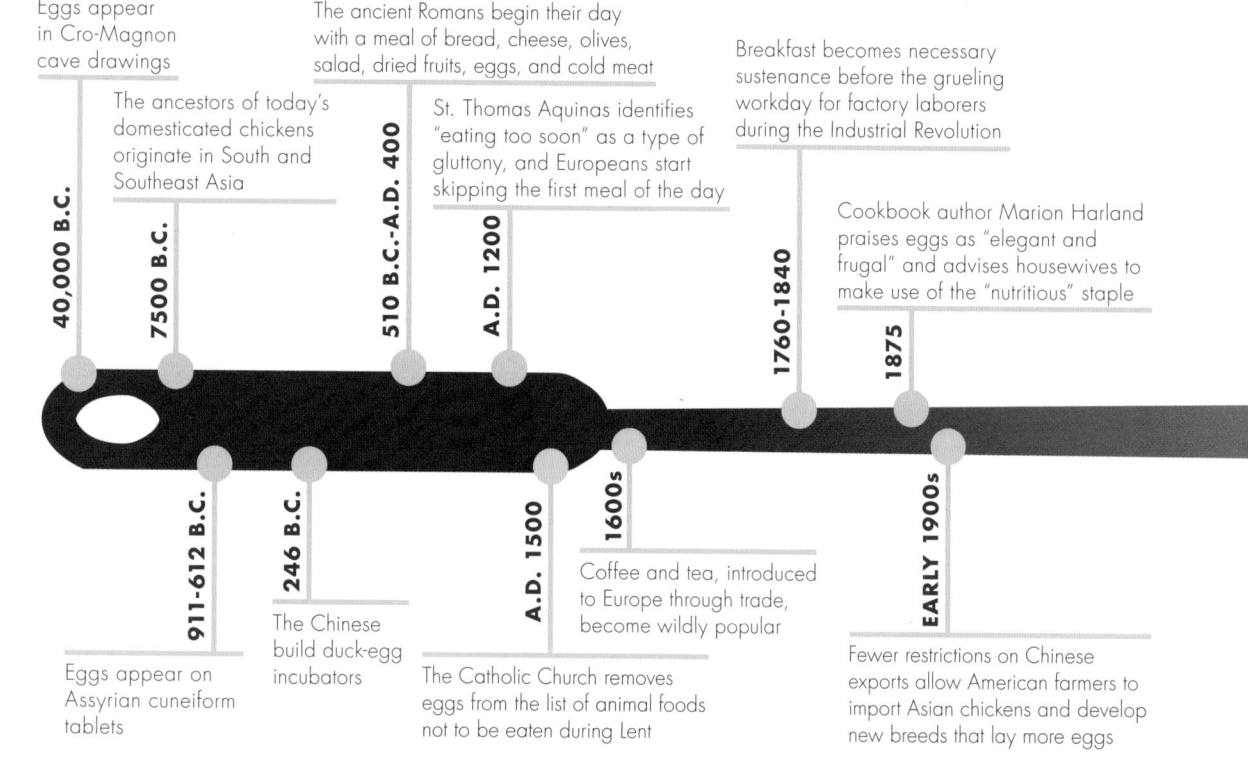

40,000 B.C. Eggs appear in Cro-Magnon cave drawings

7500 B.C. The ancestors of today's domesticated chickens originate in South and Southeast Asia

911-612 B.C. Eggs appear on Assyrian cuneiform tablets

246 B.C. The Chinese build duck-egg incubators

510 B.C.-A.D. 400 The ancient Romans begin their day with a meal of bread, cheese, olives, salad, dried fruits, eggs, and cold meat

A.D. 1200 St. Thomas Aquinas identifies "eating too soon" as a type of gluttony, and Europeans start skipping the first meal of the day

A.D. 1500 The Catholic Church removes eggs from the list of animal foods not to be eaten during Lent

1600s Coffee and tea, introduced to Europe through trade, become wildly popular

1760-1840 Breakfast becomes necessary sustenance before the grueling workday for factory laborers during the Industrial Revolution

1875 Cookbook author Marion Harland praises eggs as "elegant and frugal" and advises housewives to make use of the "nutritious" staple

EARLY 1900s Fewer restrictions on Chinese exports allow American farmers to import Asian chickens and develop new breeds that lay more eggs

liquid plus a grain—in parts of the West, whether and what to eat upon waking has been known to occasion a moral panic. Is a substantial breakfast good or bad for body, mind, and spirit? The American iteration of that debate came to center around eggs in particular and has been shaped by two centuries of ever-evolving attitudes toward health, virtue, and class.

Ancient Romans appear to have begun their day with an energy-boosting meal that involved some combination of bread, cheese, olives, salad, dried fruits, eggs, and cold meat left over from the night before. But by the Middle Ages, Europeans had downsized from the Romans' three meals to just two per day, nixing the early morning nibble.

There were some exceptions: Children, the elderly, and sick people got a pass, and laborers who needed calories for the workday would've eaten bread, cheese, and ale. But the healthy and well-to-do either abstained or lied about their boorish breakfast habits, possibly getting their fix inside bedchambers with only servants as witnesses.

In time, the prohibition softened. By the late 1500s, Queen Elizabeth I was known to eat a breakfast of ale and oatcakes. Coffee and tea—introduced to Europe through trade in the seventeenth century—became wildly popular, and the Church ultimately loosened breakfast restrictions most people were already ignoring anyway.

Coincidentally, the fifteenth and sixteenth centuries were a boom time for egg recipes, when those who couldn't afford meat could nonetheless raise hens on very little land, and the Church removed eggs from the list of animal foods not to be eaten during Lent.

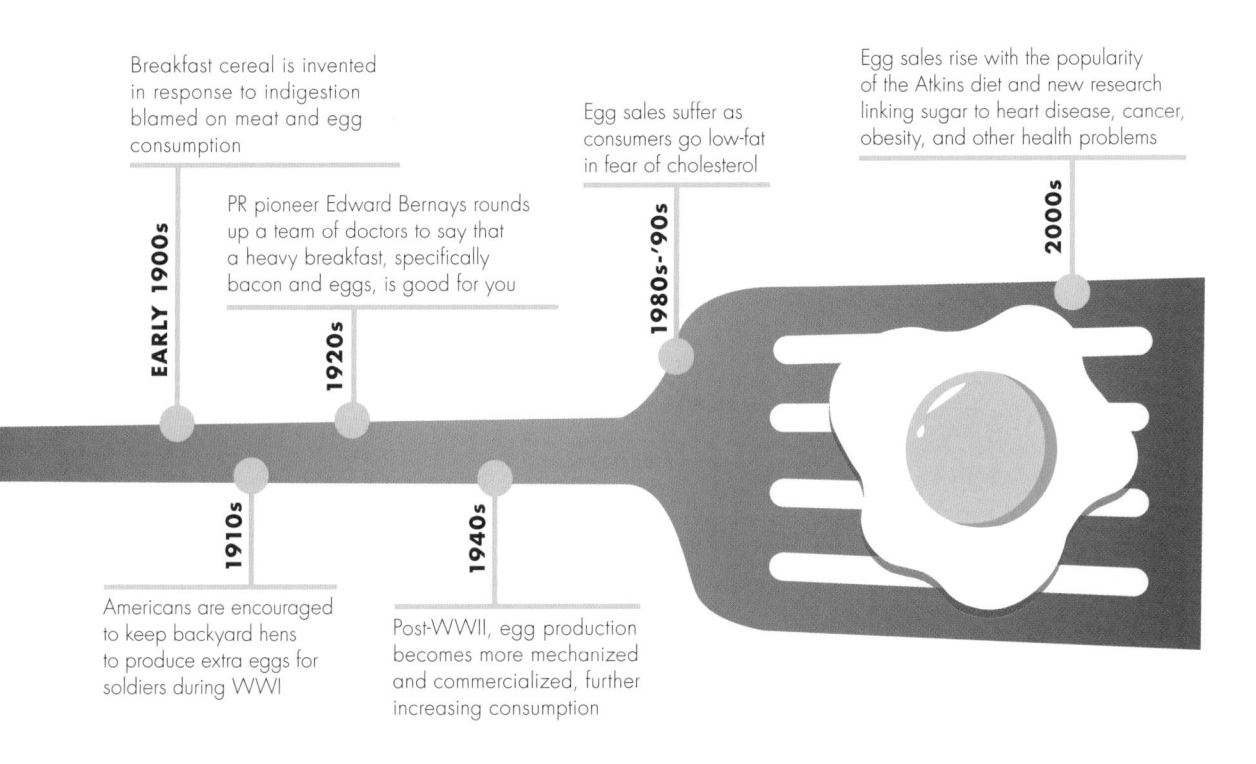

EARLY 1900s Breakfast cereal is invented in response to indigestion blamed on meat and egg consumption

1920s PR pioneer Edward Bernays rounds up a team of doctors to say that a heavy breakfast, specifically bacon and eggs, is good for you

1980s-'90s Egg sales suffer as consumers go low-fat in fear of cholesterol

2000s Egg sales rise with the popularity of the Atkins diet and new research linking sugar to heart disease, cancer, obesity, and other health problems

1910s Americans are encouraged to keep backyard hens to produce extra eggs for soldiers during WWI

1940s Post-WWII, egg production becomes more mechanized and commercialized, further increasing consumption

PEOPLE HAVE EATEN EGGS IN ALMOST ALL CULTURES AND ERAS OF HUMAN HISTORY.

It wasn't until the Industrial Revolution that breakfast really came into its own as a distinct and openly celebrated meal. For factory laborers, sustenance before the workday was more essential than ever, and for the rich—thanks to plentiful household help, easily transported ingredients, newfangled gadgets, and, eventually, electricity—breakfast provided an opportunity to show off newfound wealth. In England and America, the wealthy made omelets and built breakfast parlors— entire elegantly appointed rooms to stage the multicourse meal orchestrated by a bevy of servants. And the brand-new middle class imitated those habits with their own attempts at morning excess.

Eggs were useful in that endeavor. One surprised English visitor to the Midwestern prairie in the 1850s, at the height of this American breakfast golden age, described a particularly extravagant morning feast of "hot and cold bread of different sorts, including corn bread, little seed cakes, pancakes, preserves and blackberry syrup in large soup tureens, hot beef steaks, roast and boiled chickens, and various sorts of cold meat." This was essentially dinner for breakfast, a spread that would make eggs Benedict, invented in New York a few decades later, seem like a light snack by comparison.

A predictable consequence of all that conspicuous breakfast consumption was chronic indigestion, known at the time as "dyspepsia," Abigail Carroll writes in *Three Squares: The Invention of the American Meal*. While popular wisdom held that the condition was caused by eating underbaked bread, some physicians theorized that it could be cured by replacing meats and eggs with a lighter meal of grains. Hence, breakfast cereal was born, and eggs would have to fight for their place at the table like never before.

Luckily, they had public relations pioneer (and nephew of Sigmund Freud) Edward Bernays in their corner. Hired by the Beech-Nut Packing Company to help deal with a surplus of bacon in the 1920s, he scored a major victory for team fat by rounding up a group of doctors to say just the opposite of what the cereal evangelists had concluded. A heavy breakfast—specifically bacon and eggs—was good for you. The widely publicized "study" helped permanently cement the pairing as the ideal American breakfast.

Eggs had other boosters, too. Between 1850 and 1900, Diane Toops explains in *Eggs: A Global History*, loosened restrictions on exports from China meant that American farmers could import Asian chickens, leading to the development of new breeds that laid more and tastier eggs. Almost all farmers began raising chickens for eggs to eat or sell, and during World War I, Americans were encouraged to keep hens that would produce extra eggs for soldiers. After World War II, egg production became increasingly mechanized and commercialized, further increasing consumption. Diners may also have contributed to their popularity with 24-hour breakfast menus that emphasized what we now consider iconic egg dishes.

Of course, eggs would later suffer in the great cholesterol scare of the low-fat 1980s and '90s—only to rise again more recently with the popularity of the Atkins diet and new research linking sugar to heart disease, cancer, obesity, and other twenty-first-century specters. And so the debate marches on, with scientific experts marshaling the moral authority once held exclusively by institutions like the Church.

Whether we slurp them in secret shame, like medieval nobility; proudly proclaim them a cure-all, like master propagandist Edward Bernays; or refuse to eat them at all, such public stances only strengthen the link between eggs and breakfast. It's the intensity of the argument that allows their continued dominance over our mornings.

WHAT'S THE DIFFERENCE BETWEEN

BROWN & WHITE EGGS?

Some people might prefer white chicken eggs because they look cleaner, while others buy brown eggs because they seem more "natural." But it turns out that the difference between the two is negligible. An egg tastes like an egg no matter the color of the shell.

According to the United States Department of Agriculture, there is no nutritional difference between white and brown eggs.

White eggs, contrary to popular belief, are not bleached. The color depends on the kind of chicken that is laying the egg, and it usually corresponds with the color of the chicken's earlobe.

There are even blue and green eggs, laid by Araucana chickens in South America, and yes, those eggs have the same nutritional content as brown and white eggs. (Araucana chickens do not, however, have blue earlobes, but red ones.)

The taste of brown and white eggs is also comparable. Experts from *Consumer Reports* conducted a blind study comparing the taste of brown and white eggs. They tasted basically the same, so don't believe anyone who says they can tell the difference.

You aren't crazy for thinking that brown eggs are more expensive than white ones. That has less to do with the quality of the egg than the type of chicken. Brown eggs are a little more expensive because the breed of hens that lays brown eggs tends to be bigger and are therefore more expensive to care for.

5 EASY WAYS TO MAKE THE BEST SCRAMBLED EGGS OF YOUR LIFE

BY CAROLINE LANGE

Scrambled eggs may be one of the first things we learn to cook as kids, but they aren't one of the first things we master. We've all encountered dry or watery or (gulp) browned scrambled eggs that could have been avoided with just a little bit of effort.

The art of scrambled eggs is a delicate one, but a few very small shifts in technique can take a C-grade skill set to an A and ensure you a lifetime of perfectly pleasing scrambled eggs—provided you're the person rocking the skillet. Here are a few tips to get you started on your path to scrambled-egg excellence:

SEASON THE BEATEN RAW EGGS, NOT THE COOKED ONES.

This is a matter of debate. Some say this breaks down the eggs, rendering them watery; others believe this makes them moister. I say that it simply seasons the eggs more uniformly, and since scrambled eggs should be served right away, there's not too much opportunity for any wateriness to occur.

START IN A COLD PAN.

You know how a hot pan can set a thin layer of the eggs the moment they're poured in? That interrupts your scramble's potential for ultimate creaminess by cooking one portion of the eggs faster than all the rest. Instead, start the eggs in a cold pan (with a pat of butter) and set it on a low flame. Then go to work, stirring regularly, knowing that your eggs are cooking through at an even rate.

COOK BACON FIRST, THEN COOK YOUR EGGS IN THE SAME PAN.

Because your eggs will be creeeeeeamy and flecked in the nicest way with bacon fat (and will taste, you know, like bacon). You could also do this with fat that renders from cooking breakfast sausage. If you're not a meat eater, use a generous amount of olive oil or, preferably, butter. Use a pat that's not quite a tablespoon per two or three eggs. Never start in a dry pan.

ADD A LITTLE LEMON JUICE BEFORE—OR AFTER—COOKING.

Sounds strange, right? Reserve your judgment. A wee bit of acid encourages the egg's proteins to hook up and be creamy and tender. You don't need much juice—just about ½ teaspoon per two to three eggs. You can also add a touch of lemon juice just before serving. A teeny squeeze of lemon juice brightens a pile of buttery scrambled eggs.

TAKE THE PAN OFF THE HEAT AT LEAST A MINUTE BEFORE THE EGGS LOOK "DONE" TO YOU.

In fact, even if you like your eggs on the dry side, they should look almost wet. Both the pan you scramble the eggs in and the eggs themselves will hold heat even after they're off the flame. This is called carryover cooking, and it means that your eggs can go from runny to dry in the time it takes you to refill your coffee cup. When the scramble looks two hairs softer than you'd usually like it, take it off the heat, grab a plate, and they'll be just right.

FOUR WAYS TO UPGRADE YOUR FRIED EGGS

BY DAWN PERRY

I used to know a woman who started every workday of her adult life with a fried egg on toast. I admired the commitment to actually eating breakfast, but I'm not one for that predictable of a routine. The only way I could eat a fried egg every day is if I changed it up somehow. You too? You've come to the right place.

We've all heard the trick about using bacon grease to fry eggs but how many people actually fry up rashers on a weekday morning? (Actually, if you've made your way to this book, probably a lot of you.) But there's a lot you can do to jazz up a fried egg, whether it's going on toast or not.

Here are some ideas for upgrading your eggs not because you have to, but because you can.

EGGS FRIED IN BREADCRUMBS

Still dog-eared in my copy of *The Zuni Cafe Cookbook* is Judy Rodgers's recipe for Fried Eggs in Breadcrumbs. While that recipe has always been in the back of my head I've never actually made it. But that's the thing about the best recipes: They inspire without requiring one to follow them to a T.

Here's how you do it: Heat a tablespoon or two of oil in your cast-iron skillet or favorite egg pan (I know you have one). When it's shimmering and hot, add a nice, even layer of breadcrumbs. They can be panko, Progresso, or your very own fresh homemade. Scootch them together so they're roughly the size of a fried egg, about 4–5 inches across. Crack an egg on top and cook to your liking—until the white is set for sunny-side up, or flip for over medium. For extra credit you can add some chopped fresh herbs to the crumbs.

EGGS FRIED IN FLAVORED OIL

The pimentón fried egg is one of the Canal House gals' great contributions to food. You heat a tablespoon of oil (per egg) in a hot skillet, add a pinch of smoked paprika (per egg), and swirl around until fragrant. Crack the egg in there and fry to your liking, spooning some of the auburn oil over and around. That's a great idea, especially alongside a split, toasted baguette rubbed with garlic and tomato.

Just as easy would be adding a pinch of Madras curry powder (per egg) and serving with warm, buttered naan. Try some whole cumin seed cut with a bit of sesame seeds for an egg with texture. A little Chinese five-spice powder would be nice if the egg were destined for a bowl of leftover steamed rice, topped with sliced scallions and a little chili oil.

What else? Fresh herbs certainly work. Pop a sprig of marjoram or thyme, or a couple fresh sage leaves, in the oil until sizzling, push them to the edge of the skillet, then add the egg. That fried herb sprig infuses the oil and makes for a very nice Instagram photo, too. And don't forget the old workhorses shallot and garlic. A few slices of either—or both—would make a delightfully savory egg if that's your a.m. inclination.

FRICO FRIED EGGS

I have recently found that my most honest cravings tend toward the kids' menu, so it's no surprise this egg, fried on top of a layer of crispy melted cheese, is my favorite. It's a similar approach to Eggs Fried in Breadcrumbs: Heat a tablespoon of oil until shimmering, add about two tablespoons of shredded or grated cheese (per egg) to the center of the skillet. When it starts to melt, crack an egg on top. Fry to desired doneness and flip as you like. I prefer yellow cheddar for this (like I said, kids' menu) but Parmesan, pecorino, or Gruyère are all great choices. I just had a vision of one of these beauties floating on top of a bowl of tomato soup, but perhaps that's more of a brunch dish. Your call.

DEEP-FRIED EGGS

I admit this is not really weekday-morning friendly but I have to include it. No secrets, no special tricks, it's just a deep-fried egg. Heat a couple of inches of neutral-flavored oil—that's canola, vegetable, safflower, etc.—in a heavy-bottomed medium pot to about 350°F (but I know none of you are going to dig out the thermometer for this so just heat over medium until a little piece of bread dropped in the oil sizzles, but doesn't go crazy).

For safety's sake, crack an egg into a small bowl, and then gently tip it into the hot oil. This will prevent a hot oil splash, and your mom thanks you for taking caution. Fry the egg until golden, using a slotted spoon to gently coax the white together like a poached egg. Use that same slotted spoon to transfer the fried egg to a paper towel–lined plate, and season with salt and pepper. Serve however you like, toast or no toast, but the Deep-Fried Egg is a great way to slay new sleepover buddies as well as hangovers.

AND IF YOU JUST WANT A SIMPLE EGG ON TOAST, FRIED TO YOUR LIKING, BY ALL MEANS, DO YOUR THING. I JUST WANT YOU TO BE INFORMED AND EAT BREAKFAST.

THE PERI🥚DIC

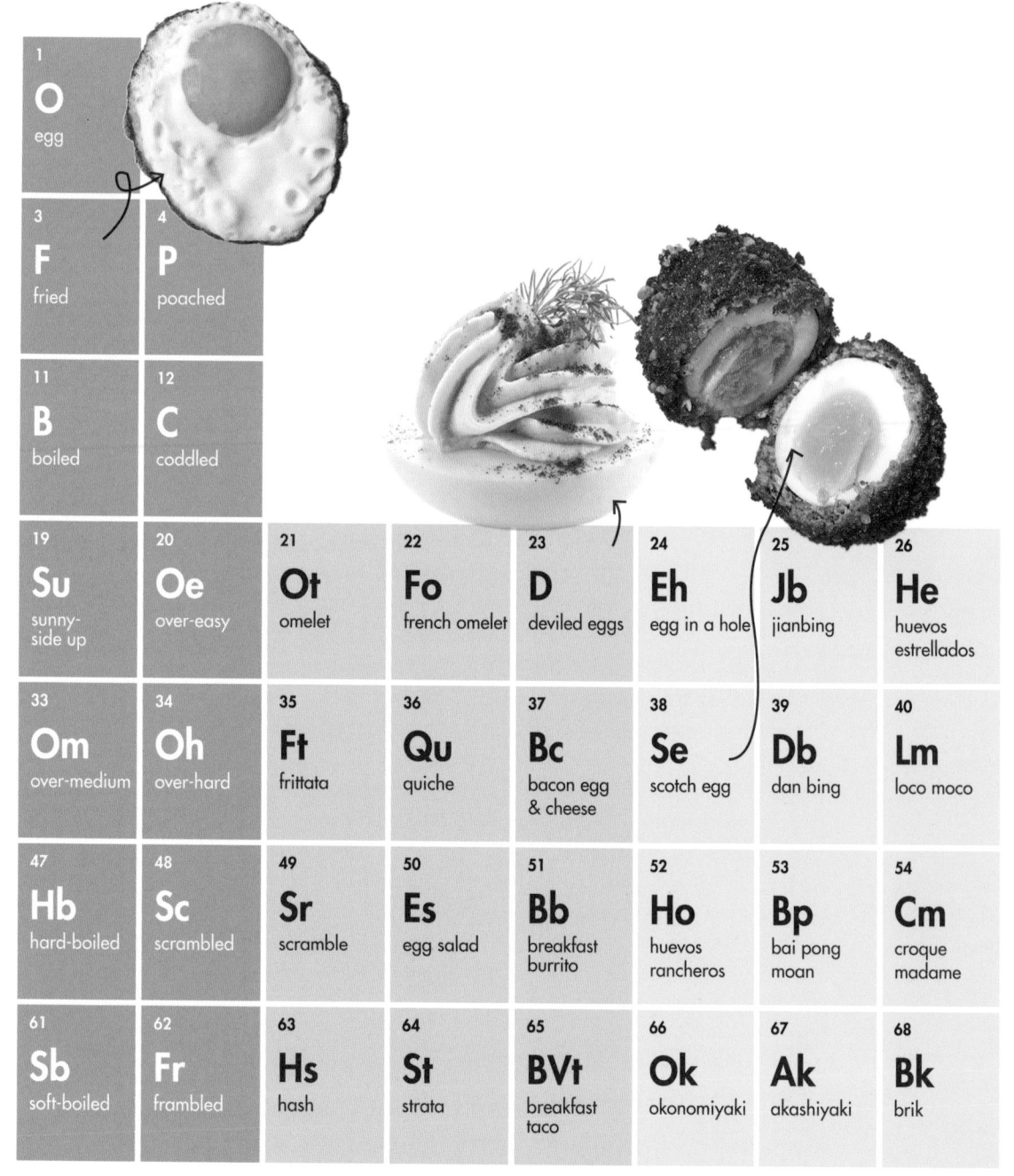

1 O egg							
3 **F** fried	**4** **P** poached						
11 **B** boiled	**12** **C** coddled						
19 **Su** sunny-side up	**20** **Oe** over-easy	**21** **Ot** omelet	**22** **Fo** french omelet	**23** **D** deviled eggs	**24** **Eh** egg in a hole	**25** **Jb** jianbing	**26** **He** huevos estrellados
33 **Om** over-medium	**34** **Oh** over-hard	**35** **Ft** frittata	**36** **Qu** quiche	**37** **Bc** bacon egg & cheese	**38** **Se** scotch egg	**39** **Db** dan bing	**40** **Lm** loco moco
47 **Hb** hard-boiled	**48** **Sc** scrambled	**49** **Sr** scramble	**50** **Es** egg salad	**51** **Bb** breakfast burrito	**52** **Ho** huevos rancheros	**53** **Bp** bai pong moan	**54** **Cm** croque madame
61 **Sb** soft-boiled	**62** **Fr** frambled	**63** **Hs** hash	**64** **St** strata	**65** **BVt** breakfast taco	**66** **Ok** okonomiyaki	**67** **Ak** akashiyaki	**68** **Bk** brik

TABLE ◯F EGGS

| 2 **Kg** kogel mogel | | 75 **Cu** egg custard | 76 **To** french toast |

| 5 **Er** egg butter | 6 **Eb** eggs and brains | 7 **Tg** tamagoyaki | 8 **Sf** soufflé | 9 **On** onsen tamago | 10 **Cw** chawanmushi | 77 **Ta** egg tart | 78 **Pn** pastel de nata |

| 13 **Cr** creamed eggs | 14 **Mn** menemen | 15 **Rf** rafanata | 16 **Gp** gyeran-ppang | 17 **Bg** baghali ghatogh | 18 **Ds** egg drop soup | 79 **Cp** custard pie | 80 **Pv** pavlova |

| 27 **Bl** balut | 28 **Mz** matzo brei | 29 **So** spanish omelet | 30 **Ba** banitsa | 31 **Ef** eggs florentine | 32 **Ce** century egg | 81 **Zb** zabaglione | 82 **Me** meringue |

2
3

| 41 **Kj** kedgeree | 42 **Bj** egg bhurji | 43 **Eg** eggah | 44 **Ep** egg puffs | 45 **Be** eggs benedict | 46 **Pk** pickled egg |

| 55 **Cu** egg curry | 56 **Mi** migas | 57 **Hf** hangtown fry | 58 **Sd** shirred eggs | 59 **Sa** eggs sardou | 60 **Te** tea egg |

| 69 **Sk** steak and eggs | 70 **Mh** machacado con huevo | 71 **Fy** egg foo young | 72 **Co** egg in a cloud | 73 **Sh** shakshuka | 74 **Vb** virgin boy egg |

KEY

■ = Basic Eggs
■ = Familiar Faves
□ = Fried
  = Boiled
  = Scrambled
■ = Omelets
■ = Baked
■ = Poached
■ = Preserved
■ = Steamed
■ = Sweets

THE ONLY WAY TO MAKE PERFECTLY POACHED EGGS

BY JISELLE BASILE

When you go to brunch, you're guaranteed a perfect poached egg. It's quite the opposite experience when you poach eggs at home. Chances are, you've probably worked your way through a dozen eggs with no signs of success. It's no surprise if you're trying the plastic-wrap trick. Boiling water in direct contact with plastic is not the healthiest thing, and when you try to fish out the poached egg, it's stuck to the cling wrap. After that so-called hack fails, you try making a poached egg in a microwave. But that's cheating—in a weird way—because it's not actually a poached egg. Forget those methods and return to tradition.

The only foolproof method to poach an egg is the old-fashioned way, over the stove with a pot of simmering water. Of course there's still room for mistakes here, but we'll run through what can go wrong in hopes that you do it right every single time after. It takes a few tries to learn how long to cook the egg (depending on your taste) and how to get the swirl going. Practice makes perfect, and we believe in you.

WRONG

Your water has come to a boil, but it's too hot. The temperature of the water is a very important factor in poaching. It might seem like boiling water would be the best option. So, you're probably thinking: The hotter the water, the faster the egg will cook. The faster the egg cooks, the less time there is for a broken yolk. This isn't necessarily true. You want to make sure that the water is just shy of boiling. Let's call it "a light simmer." If you have a thermometer, make sure the temperature is 160°F to 180°F. If you don't have a thermometer, don't sweat it. Just look for small bubbles around the edges of the pot—that's the sweet spot.

WRONG

The temperature is perfect, yet you crack the egg right into the water. EHHHH! The whites become watery and separate from the yolk while cooking. But regardless of how fresh your egg is, with this method, wispy whites will always appear. If you crack the egg directly into the water, the yolk will drop to the bottom and you'll have a bunch of wispy whites floating around aimlessly in the pot.

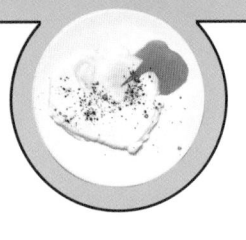

THE RIGHT WAY TO POACH EGGS

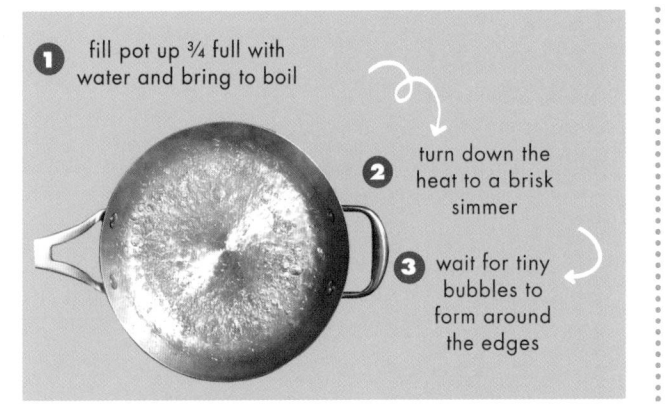

1 fill pot up ¾ full with water and bring to boil

2 turn down the heat to a brisk simmer

3 wait for tiny bubbles to form around the edges

with a spoon, make a gentle whirlpool in the middle of the pot

4

5

6 break egg into a small bowl then drop into the middle

8

7 cook for two minutes

watch the whites swirl around the yolk

9 P-E-R-F-E-C-T-I-O-N

You Should Soft-Boil Eggs for 375 Seconds

It may seem weird to call for a soft-boiled egg cooking time down to the second, but bear in mind that the temperature difference between a creamy yolk and a solid one is a mere 8°F. If you like your yolks only thickened, without any slightly set parts on the edges, boil them for 6 minutes. Egg yolks cook faster than egg whites, so we call for cold eggs. Cold yolks cook slower, because they are insulated in the shells by the whites.

2 quarts water
2 cold large eggs

¼ teaspoon kosher salt
¼ teaspoon freshly ground pepper

1. Bring 2 quarts water to a boil in a medium saucepan over medium-high. Gently add the eggs, straight from the fridge. The boil will halt for a moment as the water temperature drops. When boiling resumes, adjust heat as needed so the eggs don't bounce hard on the bottom of the pan, cracking the shells. Cook 6 minutes and 15 seconds for thick, creamy yolks that have just barely begun to set around the edges.

2. Meanwhile, fill a medium bowl with ice and water. The second the eggs are done, pull them out with a slotted spoon, and plunge them into the ice bath. Let stand 2 minutes. Cut off tops or crack the eggs, and remove the shells gently; soft-cooked eggs are wobbly and fragile. Sprinkle evenly with salt and pepper after cutting so the yolks get seasoned, too.

THE BOILED EGG TIMELINE

Gently place your eggs in a pot of boiling water. Set a timer and watch for desired doneness. Once the eggs are done, place them in an ice bath to stop the cooking.

HOW TO MAKE BACON FOR A CRAP-TON OF PEOPLE

BY ALLISON ROBICELLI

People will defend brunch until the end, even if—or maybe because—it leaves us in a drunkish, hazy state by 3 p.m. on Sunday afternoon, $15 poorer following a plate of mediocre eggs and potatoes we could have made, better and cheaper, ourselves. Take as proof the comments section on the now-infamous *New York Times* op-ed, "Brunch Is for Jerks." Everyone who responded did so with passion. Half the commenters were bemused at these entitled millennials with their "conspicuous consumption." The other half were folks angrily channeling the hollering, be-muscled Gerard Butler in *300*: This is brunch! And we love it.

I am somewhere between the two parties: I'm an early riser, so by the time standard brunch rolls around anywhere between noon and 4 p.m., I've already had breakfast and elevenses and possibly lunch, too. But I do love the idea of it, a lazy morning(ish) meal with all your people and nowhere to go. I actually don't think we host brunch at home often enough—maybe because the prospect of poaching eggs or making bacon for a crowd can feel totally overwhelming, especially if you are anticipating coinciding a hangover with your brunch prep. Going out and spending the cash feels like the easier option.

Making a zillion slices of bacon couldn't be easier, or more efficient.

In fact, bacon is one of the few things that actually, blessedly, somehow becomes easier to make when you want to cook for a whole gang of folks than it is when you're just making it for yourself. (If only more things were like this.)

As I see it, there's no reason to ever make bacon any other way, and it might make you feel so jazzed you'll be inspired to plot ahead to bring next weekend's brunch plans home. Here is how to do it:

Plan for about 1 pound of bacon for every 3 to 4 people. You can fit about a pound of bacon on a half sheet pan (aka about the size of your garden-variety cookie sheet). Preheat the oven to 400°F and line a rimmed (it really needs to be rimmed) sheet pan with foil. I like to fold up the edges just slightly, which helps keep the bacon fat contained and your pan clean. Arrange the bacon in a single layer, keeping some room between the slices but not getting too fussy about it.

When the oven is hot, slide in the bacon and let it cook: 15 minutes for cooked and golden but not particularly crisp, 20 to 25 minutes for extra crispy. Remove to a paper towel-lined dish and serve. Carefully remove the foil with the bacon fat, either crumpling up the whole thing and throwing it away or pouring off the fat into a jar or ramekin to save for frying eggs, sautéeing Brussels sprouts, or DIY bacon candles.

How to Make Candied Bacon

Candied bacon is sweet, salty, sticky, and crispy all at once. It's sensory overload in all the best ways. Eat a tray of it in downtown Tokyo while listening to acid jazz and looking through a kaleidoscope and you'll explode *Scanners*-style from overstimulation.

The best way to harness the flavor power of candied bacon is to crumble it over sweets. Banana bread, scones, doughnuts (and just about anything else you might find in a bakery display) come to new life when paired with candied bacon. Bring a tray to brunch this weekend and prepare to be greeted as a hero.

10 thick-cut bacon slices (about 10 ounces)

¾ cup packed light brown sugar, divided

1 teaspoon coarsely ground black pepper, divided

1. Preheat oven to 375°F. Line a rimmed baking sheet with aluminum foil. Place a wire rack coated with cooking spray inside prepared baking sheet. Arrange bacon slices in a single layer on rack, leaving a little space between slices. Sprinkle evenly with 6 tablespoons of the brown sugar and ½ teaspoon of the pepper. Bake in preheated oven 20 minutes.

2. Remove baking sheet from oven, and carefully turn bacon slices. Sprinkle evenly with remaining 6 tablespoons brown sugar and ½ teaspoon pepper. Return to oven, and bake until crisp and just beginning to darken, 18 to 22 minutes. (Don't be afraid to push the time. Even if the bacon slices burn a little bit on the tips, the sugary, fatty goodness will counteract any bitterness.)

3. Transfer bacon slices to a sheet of parchment paper. Let stand until firm, 10 to 15 minutes.

BY ALLISON ROBICELLI

We all know hash, but ask yourself, do you really know hash? Must it have potatoes? Onions? Should it be firm with a slight bit of a bite, or an amorphous blob of food? Must there be meat? Is there a size requirement for foodstuff particles?

Hash is everything—and nothing. Hash has rules, yet there are no rules. Hash is a comforting dish that nourishes your soul and a hodgepodge of random crap you found in the back of the fridge. Here are some tips for making hash perfectly every time.

CAST-IRON PAN

You can use a regular skillet, but cast iron is best. Put that baby on high heat while you're doing your prep. Get a little high-heat oil ready, too, like canola or grapeseed. Olive oil is useless here.

ONIONS AND POTATOES

Some say that the only nonnegotiable ingredients in hash are onions and potatoes, which is sort of silly because that's home fries. Most recipes have you start by sautéing onions, but this is wrong and dumb. The potatoes need time over high heat to crisp. Throw the onions in first and they're going to burn. Put your chopped onions off to the side and focus.

Here is the moment when hash can seem like a chore. Potatoes need to be parcooked before they are fried, and I only find myself making hash on the occasion where my fridge contains soggy leftover french fries. If leftover

HASH IS A COMFORTING DISH THAT NOURISHES YOUR SOUL AND A HODGEPODGE OF RANDOM CRAP YOU FOUND IN THE BACK OF THE FRIDGE.

fries aren't handy, go frozen with hash browns or tater tots, thawed to ensure maximum crisp. To achieve that, allow oil to heat in the pan first until it just starts to smoke. If you don't, it'll get sucked into the potatoes, resulting in sad hash.

If you don't have potatoes, sub in another fibrous, hearty vegetable like cauliflower, Brussels sprouts, or various roots and tubers. Is it technically hash? I'm not passionate enough about this subject to fight you on it, but I'm sure there's someone on the internet who can.

Once your potatoes/whatever get crisp to your liking, reduce the heat to medium and add the onions. Let 'em go for a minute or two to let their sugars cook up nice before you add the following:

COOKED MEAT

The point of hash is to use up leftovers, so chop up whatever you had the night before and toss it in. If you want corned beef hash, head to the deli section and ask them to cut you some slices on maximum thickness. You can do that with anything there, like bologna, which would also be excellent. If you want to use raw meat, cook it before you start.

OTHER STUFF

I don't know what else is in your fridge. If it looks like it would go well with potatoes and onions, chop it up and throw it in there.

SEASONING

Throw in spice blends like Old Bay, poultry seasoning, blackening spice, barbecue rubs, or your own. Let cook for about a minute to help toast the spices.

YOU DESERVE A BETTER BREAKFAST BURRITO

BY ALLISON ROBICELLI

What is the essential nature of a breakfast burrito? What separates it from a regular burrito? Can't any burrito eaten before noon be considered a breakfast burrito? Is there a rule that eggs must be involved? What if I don't like eggs?

The hard truth: I cannot tell you how to make a breakfast burrito. To perpetuate this myth of "eggs, meat, cheese, potatoes" as an ideal is deceitful and wrong. A breakfast burrito should be a cabinet of curiosities: a hodgepodge of ingredients nestled in a warm tortilla cocoon where it will not be subjected to judgmental eyes. Build the breakfast burrito of your dreams—not what Big Corporate Burrito wants you to do.

CARBS

Carbs wrapped in carbs may feel excessive, but their role is important. Without some starch to suck up all the liquids oozing from various fillings, a burrito becomes a soggy mess. The popular choice is some sort of processed potato product: mainly shredded hash browns or tater tots. Unwritten rules state that rice is meant for afternoon burritos, but not in my book! Microwaved leftover rice gives you the perfect base for a drip-proof breakfast burrito.

PROTEIN

There's nothing wrong with the eggs + bacon/sausage/ham combo if it's your thing. What you must be mindful of is scrambling your eggs. You already know that any egg that looks done in the pan is overdone thanks to residual heat. In a burrito, you've got the residual heat and all the other hot stuff, so err on the side of "really runny." Or, if you're not digging in right away, toss the eggs raw with the hot fillings and let them cook inside the tortilla.

VEGETABLES

You should probably add some so you can say you had a healthy breakfast. Leftovers are good, as is keeping guacamole or fresh salsa on hand for mindless assembly.

CHEESE

There is not a single cheese that is wrong for a burrito, because cheese is never wrong. It's a total impossibility.

ASSEMBLY

Put all your components into a bowl, mix them, then plop into your tortilla and roll it up just like they do at Chipotle. It won't look sexy on the inside, but mixing will allow the starch and cheese to glue everything together and make every bite even, which is the number one problem in modern burrito-ing. No more hot sauce oozing out. It's going to be a good morning indeed.

HOW TO MAKE A COPYCAT
TACO BELL BREAKFAST CRUNCHWRAP

1 scramble the eggs and set aside

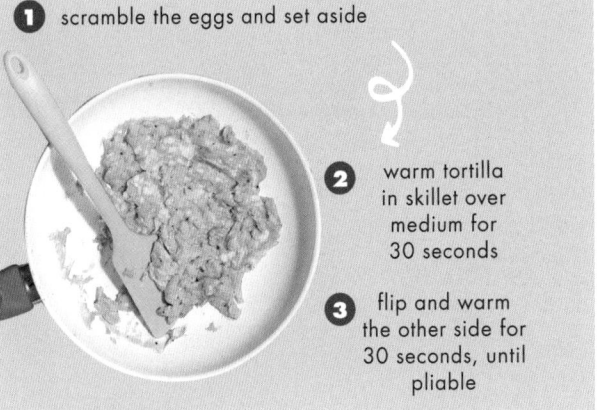

2 warm tortilla in skillet over medium for 30 seconds

3 flip and warm the other side for 30 seconds, until pliable

4 make a creamy sauce with mayo, paprika, sliced jalapeños, and cumin. smear on warm tortilla

5 add a cooked hash brown, shredded cheese, crumbled bacon, and scrambled eggs

6 fold the sides of the tortilla towards the center

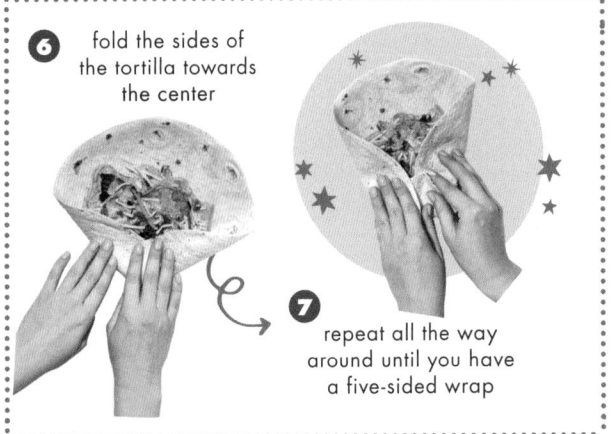

7 repeat all the way around until you have a five-sided wrap

8 toast the wrap in an oiled skillet over medium for about 40 seconds. flip and toast the other side, 40 seconds, until slightly browned

9 cut and serve with salsa

Instant Pot Burrito

A breakfast burrito is like a meaty, cheesy, eggy little payload of love that you detonate upon yourself, and an Instant Pot can streamline the process. Just sauté a few ingredients, set the cooking cycle with the touch of a button, walk away, and boom—you've mostly achieved burritos. All that's left is the assembly.

8 large eggs

½ cup whole milk

½ teaspoon kosher salt

¼ teaspoon black pepper

1 tablespoon extra-virgin olive oil

5 ounces fresh Mexican chorizo

1 cup chopped yellow onion (from 1 onion)

1 cup chopped poblano chile (from 1 large poblano)

½ cup water

4 ounces pre-shredded Mexican cheese blend (about 1 cup)

4 large flour tortillas

½ cup pico de gallo

½ cup loosely packed fresh cilantro leaves

4 teaspoons hot sauce, optional

1. Whisk together eggs and milk in a medium bowl until well combined. Stir in salt and pepper, and set aside.

2. Set Instant Pot to "Sauté." Add oil, and heat until oil shimmers. Add chorizo, and cook, stirring to crumble, until browned, about 5 minutes. Add onion and poblano; cook, stirring often, until vegetables are tender and onion is translucent, 4 to 5 minutes. Remove sausage mixture from Instant Pot.

3. Line the outside of an 8-inch springform pan with aluminum foil. Add sausage mixture to prepared pan.

4. Place grate insert (or a trivet or steamer basket) inside Instant Pot. Add water to Instant Pot. Place prepared pan on grate insert inside Instant Pot. Pour egg mixture over sausage mixture, and sprinkle evenly with cheese. Cover Instant Pot with lid, and set Instant Pot to 20 minutes on high pressure.

5. Carefully release steam from Instant Pot, and remove lid. Place tortillas on a clean work surface. Spoon about 1 cup egg mixture on bottom third of each tortilla. Top each with 2 tablespoons pico de gallo, 2 tablespoons cilantro, and, if desired, 1 teaspoon hot sauce. Fold in sides of tortillas over filling; roll up tortillas.

Why Diner Toast Is So Damn Good

BY BEN MIMS

The well-publicized backlash to "fancy," pricey toast a couple years ago spoke volumes about the relationship Americans have with cooked bread. Toast is the first thing many of us cook when we're young. It's the last resort meal any self-respecting college student can scrounge up that doesn't involve eating a condiment straight from a jar. And in diners, it is manna: the vehicle for delivering runny egg yolks, grape jellies, and the last remnants of a breakfast plate's grease and gristle to our mouths.

Most everyone I know, even healthy eaters who normally don't consume anything but an avocado and grass puree, will go for toast in a diner. It's the culinary equalizer between the white and blue collars, can be understood by young and old alike, and in our current political and cultural fighting cage climate, it might be the only thing that can truly unite us.

I spoke with J. Kenji López-Alt, author of *The Food Lab*, managing culinary director of *Serious Eats*, and serious toast devotee, to find out why it's so universally satisfying.

He first broke down the chemical changes that happen to bread to make it so tan and delicious. "There are a few things going on when you make toast," López-Alt says. "First is dehydration. High heat will drive off water content, which leaves you with that crunch." Good toast, he believes, should be dry on the outside but still moist and tender on the inside. Then there's the Maillard reaction, which gives toast its brown color and complex flavor.

"As proteins and carbohydrates are exposed to high heat, they break down, triggering a cascade of complex chemical reactions that produce hundreds of new aromatic compounds," López-Alt explains, adding that it's the same reaction that gives flavor to a seared steak, renders crispy brown skin unto a roasted chicken, and creates that heavenly roasted-coffee aroma.

The fact that toast is like the perfectly seared steak of the carb world couldn't be its only charm. In fact, as López-Alt points out, it's the way the flavor of the toast changes what we eat—like fatty or spicy foods change the flavor of wine—that makes it so vital on the breakfast plate.

"Toast can definitely serve simply as a vehicle and a tool, a means for picking up egg

"FOR THE VERY BEST TOAST, DO IT THE WAY THEY DO IT IN THE VERY BEST DINERS: ON A GRIDDLE OR PAN, IN BUTTER."

J. KENJI LÓPEZ-ALT

yolks or delivering jam, but it's also an important flavor and texture element on its own," López-Alt says. "Without toast, jam would be cloyingly sweet and completely soft. Toast adds savory notes as well as crunch and structure."

And at a diner, the same element that balances sweet jam or cuts through rich egg yolk can also act as a safe space for your taste buds, a respite from the onslaught of competing flavors on your plate. It's the same reason pancakes make the ideal canvas for butter, syrup, and herby pork sausage or fatty bacon, stretching out their bold flavors. But toast has the crispness that pancakes lack. Waffles might have the crunch, but they lack the ease and complexity of a well-toasted slice of bread.

"To make great toast you really want to maximize that textural contrast between crunchy exterior and moist center, which means that timing is important," López-Alt says. "Cook too hot and you burn the outside before it dries out enough to give significant crunch. Cook too slowly and you dry out the center by the time the outside is browned."

For everyday toast, he selects freshly thick-sliced bread (all the better to achieve ideal softness inside), pops it in his toaster oven, and spreads it with softened, salted butter. But to take it that extra step further, López-Alt points to the genius of the diner cook's way.

"For the very best toast, do it the way they do it in the very best diners: on a griddle or pan, in butter," López-Alt says. "Slowly frying bread in a buttered skillet will give you deeper, more even browning and less internal moisture loss because conduction (as opposed to dry heat convection, in a toaster) is such an effective means of heat transfer. It also builds that moist, buttery flavor right into the bread—sort of like a grilled cheese but without the cheese."

But breads are a regional pleasure. Many diners in New York City opt for rye, while diners in the South and Midwest might default to a plain white slice. I prefer a whole-wheat slice because it has the bare minimum of flavor competing with my eggs, sausage, and jam.

López-Alt agrees. "In a diner, I do want a soft white, or wheat pullman loaf as opposed to, say, a San Francisco-style sourdough or a French boule, which would be too crusty," he says. "Plain sliced bread, like Wonder Bread, would be okay if it were sliced a little bit thicker. As it is, though, it ends up just kinda too mushy as toast for my taste."

His ideal toasting bread is Japanese-style shokupan, made with milk or cream and possessed of a great buttery flavor and a texture that takes so well to toasting. "It holds up to vigorous post-toast butter-spreading but is still soft and feathery when you bite into it. Try it and you'll never go back to any other toast!" López-Alt claims.

I bought some shokupan and put it to my toast whisperer's taste test. Indeed, it was a superior bread for toasting compared to American white bread. Its extra sugars caramelized better. And richer dairy flavor made it taste like some featherweight pancake/waffle/toast hybrid that I never knew I needed. While I've had few complaints about my diner toast in the past, and would most certainly frequent one that served toasted shokupan, previous toast backlashes have taught me that Americans like our toast unfancy and kind of unremarkable.

There's something to be said for how ordinary bread becomes extraordinary toast. That transformation is why we keep coming back to it day after day and why the ritual of feeling it crunch on first bite will always provide us with enormous satisfaction.

toast slicing
··· TYPOLOGY ···

FOR MINIMALISTS

FOR TRADITIONALISTS

FOR SQUARES

FOR THE FIRST DAY
OF SCHOOL

FOR AFTERNOON TEA

FOR DIPPING

FOR EGGS

FOR THE NEUROTIC

FOR PICKY EATERS

FOR MONDAYS

FOR YOUR
SWEETHEART

FOR THE GLUTEN FREE

HOW TO MAKE PERFECT FRENCH TOAST EVERY TIME

BY PAULA FORBES

French toast is such a treat that they put the word French in the name, so you know it's fancy. The French call it *pain perdu* ("lost bread"), a nod to using stale bread that would otherwise be thrown away. But whatever you call it, it's endlessly customizable and easy to make.

BUILD A BREAD BASE

You want something a little sweet and a little stale, cut a little thicker than a standard bread slice. Challah or brioche are common, and I've used a French or Italian country loaf or even a sourdough upon occasion. Avoid ultrasavory breads like rye or pumpernickel. For something outside the box, try whole croissants or slices of stale cinnamon rolls.

CUSTARD IS A MUST

Traditionally, this consists of an egg beaten with milk and sugar, and possibly some vanilla. The ratio is about 1 egg, a good splash of whole milk, and a pinch of sugar for every couple slices of bread. To make it your own, swap the sugar for maple syrup or honey, try coconut or almond milk, add bourbon or, heck, whisk in creamy peanut butter. Just make sure to soak the bread until it's wet all the way through, but not falling apart. The time depends on the thickness and texture of the bread, so keep a close eye.

STUFF IT

This step is optional, but it can take your French toast to the next level. Take 2 bread slices, spread them with goodies (Nutella, cream cheese, strawberries, caramelized onions, etc.) and make a sandwich. Dip the whole thing in custard and proceed to the next step.

GET YOUR GRIDDLE ON

Heat a skillet. Add oil or butter, brown the toast, 2 to 3 minutes per side until brown. That's it, nothing more to see here. Move on to the fun part.

OR GET BAKED

If you've got time, you can also make French toast as a casserole. The night before, lay the bread in a greased lasagna pan and pour the custard over it. In the morning, bake it in a 375°F oven until the custard is set, about 40 minutes. It should be browned on top and jiggly in the middle.

TRY OUT TOPPINGS

Traditionally, you'd serve with maple syrup, or maybe powdered sugar. Jam and fruit syrups work well, and yogurt can be a refreshing alternative, but why not get crazy? Waffles shouldn't have all the fun: top your French toast with fried chicken. Burrata and chutney. Cheese. *Vive la* French toast!

Homemade Bisquick Is Way Better Than the Boxed Stuff

Bisquick is a breakfast miracle: Recipes that take all morning can come together in minutes. As easy as it is to buy the mix, homemade Bisquick is very simple to prepare. Sure, making a batch of homemade Bisquick requires about 10 minutes of your time, but isn't that less time than it would take you to go to the grocery store? (Unless you live inside a grocery store because, say, your family owns one. And if you do, oh my god what is your life?) Once it's made, homemade Bisquick can be used to make anything the packaged stuff can: biscuits, waffles, pancakes, quick breads, muffins, and oh-so-much more.

5 cups all-purpose flour
2½ teaspoons baking powder
½ tablespoon kosher salt

¾ cup butter or vegetable shortening, cut into
  ½-inch pieces and chilled

1. Sift flour, baking powder, and salt into a large bowl or into the bowl of a food processor. If using a regular bowl, whisk the mixture for at least 15 seconds (whisking aerates the flour in a similar manner to sifting the mixture). If using the food processor, pulse the mixture for a few seconds to fully blend and aerate the mixture.

2. Drop the cubed butter or vegetable shortening into the flour mixture. If not using a machine, use your fingers or a pastry cutter to work the cold fat into the dry ingredients until the mixture is well

blended. If using a food processor, cut the butter into the flour mixture by running the machine for 15 seconds or so.

3. Transfer the DIY Bisquick to an airtight container and store in the fridge for up to 3 months.

NOTE

Technically, if you used vegetable shortening, the mixture should be OK kept out of the fridge (in a sealed container, of course), but as an overeager member of the food-safety police, I like to keep this mixture in the fridge to stay as fresh as possible for as long as possible.

THE ONLY FLUFFY PANCAKE SECRET YOU'LL EVER NEED

You had the dream again last night—endless stacks of buttermilk, blueberry, and chocolate chip banana pancakes so light, fluffy, and piled high to the sky. They're childishly simple to make, so why do the ones you griddled up this morning taste like you're chewing on the edge of your pillow?

To avoid this morning heartbreak, start with the eggs. Instead of incorporating entire eggs into your pancake batter all at once, separate the yolks and the egg whites. Combine the yolks with the wet ingredients while placing the egg whites in the bowl of a stand mixer and whipping them at high speed until soft peaks form. Reserve until you've combined all of the other ingredients and then gently fold the whipped whites into the batter using a spatula.

It is important to know the best way to fold in the egg whites in order to preserve their airy consistency. Add a dollop of the whipped egg whites on top of the batter, then, using the blade of the spatula, cut through the center of the mixture, down to the bottom of the bowl. Scoop up one half of the mixture along the curve of the bowl and fold over into the remaining half. Repeat this process, turning the bowl clockwise every time, until all of the whites have been incorporated. It's slow and tricky, but it's worth it in the end when you finally dig into the pancakes of your dreams.

Brown Sugar Waffles with Orange-Ginger Cranberry Compote

A waffle is the ideal butter and syrup delivery system. It's like a big yellow school bus that takes butter and syrup to school (your mouth) in the morning. In this recipe, orange-ginger cranberry compote is like the cool new kid on the bus who just moved to town from San Diego. He says things like, "Wait, nobody knows how to surf here?" and plays drums. And butter and syrup are completely in love with him.

FOR THE COMPOTE

1 (12-ounce) bag fresh cranberries

Zest and juice of 1 orange

½ cup maple syrup

1 teaspoon ground ginger or to taste

1 cup water

FOR THE WAFFLES

4 tablespoons butter, plus butter for the iron

2 cups all-purpose flour

2 tablespoons brown sugar

1 teaspoon baking powder

1 teaspoon salt

½ teaspoon baking soda

1 cup milk

1 cup buttermilk

4 large eggs

1. Prepare the Compote: In a pan, combine all the compote ingredients and bring to a simmer over medium, stirring occasionally, about 20 minutes. Transfer to a bowl; cover and chill for at least 2 hours. It will keep in the refrigerator up to a week.

2. Prepare the Waffles: Melt the butter in a small saucepan over low heat or in the microwave. Remove from heat.

3. In a large bowl, combine flour, brown sugar, baking powder, salt, and baking soda.

4. In another bowl, whisk milk, buttermilk, and eggs until combined. Add the cooled butter to the milk mixture.

5. Pour wet ingredients into dry ingredients and stir till combined.

6. Heat your waffle iron and lightly coat with butter.

7. Make waffles, about ½ to ¾ cup at a time, adding more butter to the iron as needed. Serve compote with waffles.

NOTE

As you make them, you can keep them warm in a 200°F oven before serving. Pass the waffles around in a towering pile to impress your guests.

THE DUTCH BABY IS THE LITTLE BLACK DRESS OF BREAKFAST

BY DAWN PERRY

Meet the Dutch baby, your new breakfast obsession. It's essentially a big, sharable popover and easily skews sweet or savory. You can eat it for breakfast, at a fancy brunch, or whip one up when you're out of dinner ideas—or groceries. You could even gussy it up for dessert with a scoop of ice cream or a dollop of whipped cream. All you need are a handful of pantry staples and a hot skillet, and in about 30 minutes (for real, no fooling) you'll have one of the easiest and most impressive of all baked items on the table. But be warned: What was intended for four may easily be eaten by two.

THE PREHEAT

Many people are guilty of skirting the preheat and just throwing things in the oven at around 283°F. This is not the time for that. Dutch babies do best in a preheated oven and skillet. Why? Adding butter to an already hot pan creates a nonstick surface so the finished product slides out easily while the batter cooks up fast and even, with dramatic hills and valleys. Get your oven up to temp first, then put the skillet in for about 10 minutes, or 15 if the oven was close but not quite there.

THE PAN

You'll want to use a 10-inch oven-safe skillet. Cast iron is preferable because it gets hot and stays hot, but you can use a durable stainless-steel skillet in its place. Results may vary depending on the shape of your skillet. Straighter-sided cast iron will produce bigger bubbles all the way across the center, while sloping sides encourage a more crater-like appearance. Either

way, the bottom gets golden and crisp while the edges rise around a custardy middle. Don't try a thin-skinned aluminum skillet here; the bottom will get too hot and burn the baby before it cooks through.

THE BLEND

Dutch baby recipes often say to prep the batter in a blender and let it sit overnight. But who has the time? All you really need is a sturdy bowl, a decent whisk, and some focus. Then you just beat the heck out of it until there are no lumps. You'll be done mixing before the cast iron is completely preheated so the batter will have a few minutes to rest. BUT if your blender is on the counter and you'd like to fire it up, by all means, blend to your heart's content. And by that, I mean until smooth and lump-free.

THE HOT TOPIC

The only thing tricky about this recipe is remembering that you're dealing with a screaming-hot pan. Even seasoned chefs will use an oven mitt for this one. Keep the handle(s) covered with a towel (or oven mitt) once it comes out of the oven and warn whoever is around that this is HOT STUFF. Did we mention this is hot?

THE TA-DA

When it's ready, the baby should be puffed and dramatic. Assembled parties may gasp. But once it's out of the oven, it's natural for it to deflate as it cools. So set the table while it bakes and have your cameras at the ready—this baby waits for no one.

Lemon-Butter Dutch Baby

⅔ cup milk (any fat
  percentage will work)

⅔ cup all-purpose flour

3 large eggs

½ teaspoon pure vanilla
  extract

¼ teaspoon kosher salt

2 tablespoons unsalted

butter, plus more
  for serving

1 lemon, optional

Powdered sugar, for serving

1. Preheat oven to 425°F. Place a 10-inch cast-iron skillet inside the oven to preheat, 5 to 10 minutes.

2. Meanwhile, whisk milk, flour, eggs, vanilla, and salt in a medium bowl. Continue whisking vigorously until no lumps remain (this could take about a minute).

3. Remove skillet from oven and add 2 tablespoons butter, swirling until melted.

Pour batter into skillet and return to oven. Bake until golden and puffed up dramatically, 15 to 18 minutes.

4. Dot warm Dutch baby with a little more butter and zest about half of the lemon over top, if using. Halve lemon and squeeze a little juice over top, if desired, then dust with powdered sugar. Cut into wedges and serve.

Ham & Cheese Dutch Baby

⅔ cup milk (any fat percentage will work)

⅔ cup all-purpose flour

3 large eggs

¼ teaspoon kosher salt

2 tablespoons unsalted butter

3 to 4 thin slices Black Forest ham

2 ounces grated Gruyère (about ½ cup)

1. Preheat oven to 425°F. Place a 10-inch cast-iron skillet inside the oven to preheat, 5 to 10 minutes.

2. Meanwhile, whisk milk, flour, eggs, and salt in a medium bowl. Continue whisking vigorously until no lumps remain (this could take about a minute).

3. Remove skillet from oven and add butter, swirling until melted. Pour batter into skillet and return to oven. Bake until light golden and puffed up dramatically, 12 to 15 minutes. Remove skillet from oven and quickly lay ham slices in the center, overlapping slightly, and sprinkle with cheese. Return to oven and bake until deeply golden and cheese is melted, about 5 minutes more. Cut into wedges and serve.

Cinnamon-Sugar Dutch Baby

FOR THE SKILLET

⅔ cup milk (any fat % will work)

⅔ cup all-purpose flour

3 large eggs

1 tablespoon granulated sugar

½ teaspoon pure vanilla extract

¼ teaspoon ground cinnamon

¼ teaspoon kosher salt

2 tablespoons unsalted butter, plus more for serving

FOR THE CINNAMON SUGAR

3 tablespoons granulated sugar

1 teaspoon ground cinnamon

Vanilla ice cream, for serving, optional

1. Prepare the Skillet: Preheat oven to 425°F. Place a 10-inch cast-iron skillet inside the oven to preheat, 5 to 10 minutes.

2. Meanwhile, whisk milk, flour, eggs, sugar, vanilla, cinnamon, and salt in a medium bowl. Continue whisking vigorously until no lumps remain (this could take about a minute).

3. Remove skillet from oven and add 2 tablespoons butter, swirling until melted. Pour batter into skillet and return to oven. Bake until golden and puffed up dramatically, 12 to 15 minutes.

4. Prepare the Cinnamon Sugar: Combine sugar and cinnamon in a small bowl or jar and whisk to combine. Set aside.

5. Dot warm Dutch baby with a little more butter and sprinkle with about a tablespoon (or more) cinnamon sugar. Return to oven and bake until sugar sets, about 5 more minutes. Top with a scoop or two of ice cream, if desired, and eat straight from the skillet.

When You're Broke, Breakfast Is Hot, Buttered Hope

BY JOHN DEVORE

I eat breakfast for dinner. I eat breakfast for lunch. I eat breakfast for breakfast. Sometimes, if I have time to burn between afternoon errands, I will eat breakfast. I eat breakfast when I'm sad. I eat breakfast when I'm triumphant.

I eat breakfast whenever I want. I once ate breakfast because I had no choice. But before I get to that story I need to tell another story because stories are best when they're like pancakes, stacked on top of one another.

My grandfather was a Baptist preacher. I was raised both Baptist and Catholic. I call myself a Batholic, which is like a Catholic who can sing, or a Baptist who loves incense. His name was Jack, and my father was a junior. Jack is a solid name. It's what you call a president, or a famous author, or a world-weary bear fighter. I always wanted to be named Jack. He was a kind and patient man who used to enjoy terrifying me by popping out his dentures. I like to keep a catalog of happy faces in my noggin for overcast days, and his amusement when he'd freak me out is one of those faces.

He raised my father and aunts during the Great Depression. I think we forget that those years were a near post-apocalypse. The system failed. It wasn't hobos eating beans and playing banjos; it was millions of people hungry, lost, and scared. If you want to fast-track systemic social and economic change, a backbreaking 17 percent unemployment is hard to beat.

In addition to the times, of course, was his profession.

THE NEW GENERATION WERE PLUMP, HAPPY WEAKLINGS WHO WOULD NEVER KNOW WHAT IT MEANT TO GO TO BED HUNGRY.

There are plenty of gelled temple merchants on TV who give the appearance of wealth, but for the most part the clergy isn't what you do if you really like money. It's a calling. My granddad made a humble living serving Southern communities.

His generation were not complainers. My generation's current ability to whine about everything is proof our civilization is successful, if overripe. So I never really heard stories about tough times. Maybe once I recall my dad remembering how his family used the last of the flour and milk to make biscuits for dinner, then prayed, and the next day they received a modest sum from a local parish. God's timing is one of His most annoying mysteries.

So my granddad used to tell me a story that I loved. It was a family story. He would tell it to his kids, and then would tell it to the kids of his kids. It's a story born of the Depression. It's been so long since I've heard the story that I don't remember all of the specifics. But it stuck with me.

THE ONLY THING THAT KEPT ME AWAKE DURING SUNDAY MASS WAS THE KNOWLEDGE THAT CANADIAN BACON, GRITS, AND MINI-MUFFINS AWAITED.

Here's the simple version: A farmer had a talking goat. I am not making this up. That talking goat would frequently be kidnapped or get into trouble. The farmer would have to rescue the talking goat, who could bleat the name of the farmer. The climax of the story was the happy reunion between farmer and talking goat and then they'd have a celebratory meal. That meal was breakfast.

At this point, the story became participatory. My granddad would ask us all what were the things they'd eat at this amazing feast and I'd take over. Waffles, sausages, strawberries, eggs, hash browns, I'd list. I was a well-stuffed Little Lord Fauntleroy and I had thoughts about what should be served at The Greatest Breakfast Ever! My grandfather loved all of his grandchildren. But I hope this member of the Greatest Generation looked upon his son's chubby prince and saw that the Depression had been soundly defeated. The new generation were plump, happy weaklings who would never know what it meant to go to bed hungry.

Samuel Taylor Coleridge's famous line "Water, water, every where / Nor any drop to drink" from "The Rime of the Ancient Mariner" applies to America and food. We've got food everywhere. Piles of it. Our supermarkets are ziggurats of plenty. The freedom to waste isn't exactly enshrined in the Constitution but it's a lovely little by-product. And, yet, almost 49 million of our citizens don't know where their next meal will come from.

Here's the other story I warned you about, and thanks for reading this far. At the turn of the century I was

hungry. This was before the country truly lost its mind. Like so many, I sought my fortune in New York City. I had just graduated from college with a BFA, and no practical skills. But I had dreams—vague dreams, but still—and New York City was where dreams flowed like concrete.

My plan was simple: Move to Manhattan, get a high-paying job in either art or literature, live a comfortable life of moderate wealth. A month later I had moved deep into the heart of Queens, I was nigh-unemployable and living a life of desperate hustle. This was not the plan. The plan was the American Dream: Whatever you want, cheap and easy.

But this isn't a story about a young, dumb, broke bro living off knishes. Oh, wait a minute. Sorry. It is. One way to have your privilege checked is to have that privilege reduced, even minutely. There's no pain like your own pain.

Still, I knew no one in New York. But that's what a state school gets you. I had no money. I was losing weight the old-fashioned way. I knew nothing except what TV had taught me, which was to grow a shitty goatee. Every young man in history is a stumbling foal. It's almost funny, in retrospect, but most things can be funny if you pretend they didn't happen to you but to some other dope with your name.

I was raised in a middle-class family but my parents were both frugal from habit. They were raised humbly and so was I. I went to school in secondhand clothes. Meals were gravies, sauces, salsas. Every penny was counted. The 1930s taught a lesson that has been forgotten: Things can change for the worse very quickly. So my folks had tried their damndest not to raise a spoiled little snot. They were almost successful. Despite their efforts, I was still a coddled suburban ponce. I craved snacks and pillows and comfort. I wanted success delivered to my door in thirty minutes or less. Pride not only goeth before the fall, it also goeth before calling your parents for money.

But what they tried to teach me came in handy. You can't roast ego and eat it. So I learned how to shop for groceries at the dollar store and cultivated a taste for tinned mussels. There was a local bakery in Queens that would thoughtfully bag day-old bread before dumping it in a dumpster from which one could conveniently pilfer, far from judging eyes. A kingly meal was a two-hot dogs-for-a-buck deal at a nearby cart. This story has a happy, if predictable, ending. I am a biracial man who looks white with a college degree. Statistically speaking, things work out for us. Many years later I gained back all the weight—and more! I always knew I could charge a plane ticket and fly home to the Lone Star State to eat a pickup truck full of my mother's enchiladas. It was never really, truly touch-and-go but it was a lesson I do not take lightly. There are few things more terrifying than not knowing if you're going to eat that day, or the next.

There was a week, however, when I did come into a little cash. Enough for the essentials: electricity, wart remover, beer. There was some left over and I decided to splurge on a filling repast. It's important to feel "full." A national ideal. Sorrow is an empty tank of gas or an empty wallet. The glass is always half-empty. Always.

I'd say it's more important than having a head full of information or a heart full of love. Mostly because you can't inhale information and self-sacrifice at a buffet, and then drive home to nap. I didn't want to waste my funds at a diner or fast-food restaurant because I felt I wouldn't get the maximum carbohydrate tonnage I required. So I would buy food and cook it at my kitchenette stove that rattled when the upstairs neighbor slammed the door.

I needed a meal that would satisfy for very little money. A meal that was not rice and beans with Spam cubes. Then I remembered my grandfather's story, you know, the one that delighted me. That would make me clap my hush-puppy hands together in excitement when we got to the part when I could shout out the foods that were near and dear to my heart.

It helped that we were a breakfast family. Eggos, Egg McMuffins, huevos rancheros, biscuits and gravy or Karo syrup. The only thing that kept me awake during Sunday mass was the knowledge that Canadian bacon, grits, and mini-muffins awaited.

But it wasn't until that moment that I realized who that story had to be for, and it wasn't weeble-wobble me. You invent a story that concludes with heaps of food when you don't have heaps of food. Once upon a time, during many lean years, a struggling preacher told his hungry children a tale with a happy ending: Everybody gets to eat the delicious treats they dream about. There are desperate times when the only thing you can feed a grumbling stomach is hot, buttered hope.

I would eat breakfast for dinner. The groceries were relatively inexpensive; it's not like I was buying steaks and fresh vegetables. Breakfast foods, for their cost, deliver what your taste buds crave: sweet and savory, crunchy and creamy, carbs and protein.

I had a cheap metal skillet and mostly spoons. I didn't have a toaster so the Eggos slowly browned in an oven that clicked like a bomb. The bacon was too cold and the skillet too hot so I got fatty wrinkles of chewy pink pig flesh. I scrambled eggs with too much milk. The frozen orange juice was sugar slurry. But I had syrup and hot sauce and those two things fix most things. I scrambled more eggs with less milk. I burnt an Eggo but I am a clever scraper. What I wanted was fresh strawberries and runny fried eggs and juicy sausages and cantaloupes and chocolate croissants and both hash browns and potatoes fried up with onions and peppers and spicy chorizo with eggs wrapped in warm tortillas. But after my sad little evening breakfast, I slept with a full belly and did not worry about anything until morning, when I would have breakfast for breakfast.

I dreamt of goats. I called his name. I was rescued.

HOW TO MAKE CRISPY POTATOES EVERY TIME

BY ALLISON ROBICELLI

I don't think I need to convince you that breakfast potatoes need to be extra crispy.

Breakfast potatoes are a firm base upon which a fluffy scramble can luxuriously perch. They're a field of crunchy bits that readily welcomes runny yolks. Soggy breakfast potatoes are a waste of everyone's time. Who knows how many days have been wasted, all because of subpar breakfast potatoes. Today, we fight back.

Hash browns are easy enough to get crispy thanks to the fact they're shredded into tiny bits with lots of surface area. I didn't know much about them until adulthood, because I grew up in New York City where hash browns weren't a thing and I had never heard of a Waffle House. The only breakfast potatoes I knew were home fries: preboiled slices of potatoes mixed with sautéed onions, smashed and fried on the griddle next to your eggs. And yes, they were sliced. Every recipe I've seen on the internet says to use cubed potatoes, and I have no idea what they're talking about. Slices are the best for home fries because, like I mentioned with hash browns, they have lots of surface area, and you can smash the hell out of them with the back of a spatula. Surly Greek diner cooks in tank tops have no time to be gentle with your dainty potatoes. GREEK HULK SMASH.

Here are the hard-and-fast rules of ultracrispy home fries.

1. USE RUSSETS

These are nice and starchy, and extra starch means extra crispy. They're also quite fluffy and break down easily— which is why we use them for things like mashed potatoes.

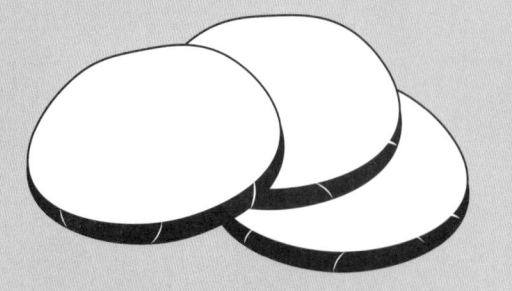

2. SLICE RIGHT

You don't want paper-thin pieces, because that's Pommes Anna (a recipe for another day), and you want potato fluff between the crunchy layers. About ⅛-inch wide is perfect.

3. PARBOIL THE SLICES

There are two reasons for this. One, you don't want to end up with raw insides. Two, parboiling helps that starch swell up, meaning that when it hits the hot pan those surface granules will explode into a crunchy exterior. Don't boil your slices to death, just until you can barely pierce with a fork, like how it feels when you are picking up a cucumber slice in a salad.

4. DRY WELL

Wet potatoes in a pan = steamed potatoes. After you parboil, drain them into a colander, give them a good shake, then lay them out on a tray lined with paper towels. Water will drip off, and the steam will disperse into the air. (If you want to add onions or peppers to your home fries, now is a good time to sauté them.)

5. ROCKET-HOT SKILLET

Your best bet is cast iron. You want to get the temperature of the flattop grill at a diner, which is hot enough to make you a full breakfast in less than 90 seconds. Next, coat the bottom with oil. You're not deep-frying, but you don't want to chintz, either. Make sure you've got an even coat in there, around ⅛ inch.

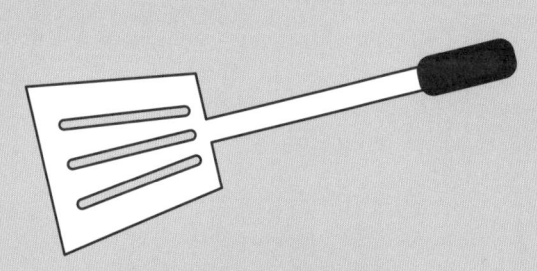

6. SMASHY SMASHY

Put your dried potatoes in a small bowl, toss with some salt and pepper and the onions/peppers if you went that way. Carefully tip the whole mess into the rocket-hot skillet, spread out a bit with a flat-bottomed spatula, then smash those suckers down and make them sizzle. Give them a bit of time to brown up, then flip. It's fine to be sloppy.

Once they're done, lift them out and spread onto your plate to let them cool a bit. And look at them. Take a few seconds to really appreciate those textured niblets of crispity crunchity starch. You put the effort in, and you deserve to enjoy your handiwork on all the levels.

How to Make the Best Biscuits and Sausage Gravy of Your Life

We don't take the term "best" lightly in this book. When we say best, we mean it, and in the case of Kelly Fields's biscuits and sausage gravy, which you can find at her restaurant Willa Jean in New Orleans, we say it with our mouths full and our hearts full of joy. Her biscuit technique is unorthodox: She folds and re-folds the dough into a book shape to create plenty of layers, then cuts them into squares. The result is a tall, crunchy exterior that gives way to a fluffy, flavorful center. Eat them straight from the pan, bake and freeze them, or save the dough in the fridge for a few days.

FOR THE BUTTERMILK BISCUITS

2 cups Caputo flour (cake flour works, too)

2 tablespoons baking powder

2 teaspoons sugar

1 teaspoon salt

5 tablespoons butter, grated through a cheese grater and chilled

1 cup buttermilk, plus more for brushing

FOR THE SAUSAGE GRAVY

32 ounces pork sausage

1 cup all-purpose flour

9 cups milk

2 tablespoons salt

1 tablespoon pepper

1 tablespoon crushed red pepper

1 tablespoon Tabasco sauce

1. Preheat oven to 365°F.

2. Prepare the Buttermilk Biscuits: Add all dry ingredients to a large bowl and mix by hand until combined. Grate cold butter and add to dry mixture. Add buttermilk to mixture and combine until all of the dry ingredients are hydrated.

3. Put the dough onto a floured surface and roll into a rectangle measuring 12 inches by 8 inches.

4. Fold the top of the rectangle halfway toward the middle; fold the bottom of the rectangle on top. Flour the top and invert.

5. Roll out into a rectangle approximately 12 inches by 8 inches. With seams down, roll into a square. Cut into squares of desired size. Brush with buttermilk.

6. Bake until tops and bottoms are golden brown, and the middle has set—about 30 minutes.

7. Prepare the Sausage Gravy: Cook sausage in a large skillet over medium, stirring until pork is no longer pink.

8. Once meat is cooked, sprinkle the flour over it until all meat is coated and a light fond is created (do not let it get dark).

9. Turn heat to high, gradually whisk in milk, whisking constantly, 7 to 10 minutes or until gravy is thickened. Add in salt, pepper, crushed red pepper, and Tabasco. Cook for another 5 minutes. Taste to make sure flour has cooked out; if not, cook for another 5 minutes. Adjust seasoning as needed.

HELPFUL TIPS

If the gravy is too thick, thin it out with milk. Make sure milk and gravy are both hot. If gravy is too thin, melt 4 ounces of butter, stir in 4 ounces of flour, and cook for 5 minutes (until flour taste is gone). Slowly add into hot gravy. Cook for 5 minutes or until gravy thickens (you may or may not use all of the roux).

A DRAWN OUT AND USEFUL HOLLANDAISE-MIDDLE SCHOOL DANCE METAPHOR

BY CAROLINE LANGE I know you came to this story thinking we were going to talk about eggs Benedict— aka everyone's favorite brunch. We are, but first we're going to talk about dancing. Bear with me.

Think for a moment about the last middle school dance you went to. The event is a crazy anthropological experiment, but the essence of it is overwhelming awkwardness. Initially, the groups won't and don't mix at all, preferring to stay utterly separated (while, ahem, checking out the other groups). For everyone to warm up, there needs to be some personal fortitude and some asking of permission. It always begins extremely slowly—and has to—or it will break apart and everyone will return uncomfortably to their initial groups.

Hollandaise sauce and other emulsions like mayonnaise and vinaigrettes start out like this, with oil and water steering clear of each other, refusing to mix. To achieve an emulsion is to get fat and water to dance with each other. And like encouraging 13-year-olds to dance with each other, this is no small feat. The result is something both sturdy and precarious. And delicious. And great on eggs.

It all starts with egg yolks whisked together with a little water in a bowl set over a pot of water set over a very low flame. A tiny bit of salt and lemon juice go into the mixture, too. All of this is whisked together vigorously until the eggs have lightened in color and appear to have thickened slightly.

The butter needs to go in sloooowly, not only because it's warm but also because of that whole water-oil thing. As you add the butter drop by drop, whisking

all the while, you'll notice the mixture starting to come together. It will be pale yellow, very creamy, and thickening slightly. Add butter and whisk, whisk, whisk until the mixture is thick but still pourable, almost like a very thick heavy cream (another emulsion).

If the sauce breaks—maybe you added a bit too much butter at once—you can save it. Ladle a bit of the broken mixture into a fresh bowl with a new yolk and whisk until they come together and look creamy, then very slowly add the broken mixture into the new bowl, whisking all the while. If this doesn't work, simply start again. It's a delicate dance.

Hollandaise Sauce

10 tablespoons unsalted
    butter

2 egg yolks

Pinch kosher salt

2 teaspoons lemon juice

2 teaspoons water

Freshly ground black pepper
    and smoked paprika to
    taste

1. Melt the butter in a saucepan with a bit of a lip, swirling the butter in the pan regularly. Meanwhile, put an inch or two of water in another saucepan, and set a heatproof bowl over the top. (Ideally, use a stainless steel or glass bowl—an aluminum one can discolor your sauce.) Set this double boiler over a medium-low flame.

2. Crack 2 egg yolks into the bowl, add the salt, lemon juice, and water, and whisk well, until the yolks have slightly lightened in color. Remove the double boiler from the heat while you very slowly add the melted butter—1 tablespoon at a time at first, then more quickly, whisking enthusiastically all the while. Return to the heat and continue whisking until the mixture has fully come together. It should be a pale buttery yellow, thick enough to coat a spoon, and completely smooth. Taste for seasoning; add a little black pepper and/or smoked paprika, and a squeeze of fresh lemon juice if you like. Whisk together well.

3. At this point, the sauce is ready. Remove the double boiler from the heat and spoon the sauce over steamed asparagus, dip artichoke leaves into it, or use it as an egg Benny's crowning glory.

4. For eggs Benedict for 4 people, fry or bake bacon (classically, Canadian bacon) if you're serving meat eaters; slice up some avocado or sauté some spinach with a bit of garlic. Lightly toast 4 English muffins—too crispy and they're hard to cut. Meanwhile, poach 4 to 8 eggs (up to 2 per person). See pages 24–25 for a refresher. To assemble, lay the bacon or avocado or what have you onto the toasted muffin, carefully set a patted-dry poached egg onto each muffin half, and carefully spoon sauce over each egg.

DON'T WHISK YOURSELF INTO AN EARLY GRAVE

Instead of whisking hollandaise ingredients all day, dust off your blender and swirl them together for a couple of minutes. It's totally foolproof and won't leave you with jelly-arm (a real affliction) from all that whisking. The sauce won't break because, well, science.

HOMEMADE JAM PRESERVES SUMMER FOREVER

BY BEN MIMS

My love affair with making jam and jelly started with a dollop and swirl. When I was growing up in Mississippi, my family always had jars of local muscadine jelly in the pantry for scooping onto steaming hot biscuits, toast, or into a bowl of plain, instant grits. The deep-purple jelly bled light pink into the white porridge, masking its often bitter flavor with fruity sweetness. Learning how to make fruit jam meant introducing a hint of the lavish life in a very thrifty home. Its delicate grape jelly taste was all I knew until I tried commercial strawberry and blueberry offerings from the likes of Welch's and Smucker's—made with fruit juice, plenty of corn syrup, and pectin.

I began squirting grape jelly from plastic packets onto my Egg McMuffins with glee. I relished opening those cubes of diner jelly, peeling back the golden cellophane to reveal the jiggler ("mixed fruit" was my favorite) and spreading it over my cheese-stuffed omelet at Waffle House. And I, like every red-blooded American child before and after me, used it as a foil to the not-unpleasant dryness of a peanut butter sandwich. My sweet tooth was born from this love of jelly, and that love was deep and gloppy.

This affinity for bad fruit spreads may have started me on my course as a lover of all sweets, but real fruit jams—made simply and with the best fruit I could find—kept me there. Real jam is fruit's highest calling, especially in summertime, when it's made in massive batches to preserve the glut of produce before it spoils.

In the cold, less generous months, those summer-made jams are the lighthouse that gets me through the winter until spring's first strawberries arrive. The bright, sweet jolt of jam cuts through the richness in roasted game meats. It adds elegance and a perceived healthy-ish-ness when spread over morning toast, scones, and biscuits. And slathered between tiers with whipped cream, it gives layer cakes a reason to exist.

A few years ago, while working as a pastry chef in San Francisco, I developed my own easy formula for how to make jam because I loved eating it and wanted to make my own from the gallons and gallons of seasonal fresh fruit the restaurant got and couldn't possibly use up. Like many people starting a new project, I was intimidated by the use of store-bought pectin and craved a more relaxed, romantic way to get my jam fix. Through years of experience of candy making, I knew that sugar, when proportioned just right with water, has enough ability to thicken as pectin does—but you'll never get that same hard-set, shearing effect. I wanted a product thin enough to spread easily over toast but thick enough to not flow over the sides. What I came up with was an all-in-one jam-preserve-fruit butter hybrid that only has four simple ingredients.

The formula I developed for my jam goes a little something like this:

First, weigh your fresh, cut-up fruit and place it in a large, heavy-bottomed pot. I like apples, pears, plums, or peaches in wedges, figs quartered, and berries left whole. No need to be fussy about it; you want everything in bite-size pieces, which will hold up to long cooking but also fall apart just enough to thicken the jam naturally.

Second, take one-third the weight of the fruit and add that amount of granulated sugar. Then, take one-third the weight of the sugar and add that amount of fresh lemon juice to brighten the fruit through all that sugar.

Next, lightly season the jam with salt, as if you were seasoning onions in a pot at the beginning of making soup: sufficiently but not overwhelmingly. (For about three pounds of fruit, I use about one teaspoon

kosher salt.) Stir the fruit, sugar, juice, and salt together and let it sit for as long as you can possibly stand it, so that most of the water in the fruit can be drawn out and act as the conduit for the sugar to dissolve. I often let mine sit overnight in the refrigerator, but if you're in a rush, one to two hours is fine.

Then, place the pot over medium heat and stir and cook and stir and cook until the fruit begins sticking to the bottom of the pot. This is when you'll know that most of the moisture in the fruit is evaporated and only fruit matter and sugar remain. Some pieces will still be whole, but a lot will have fallen apart in a beautiful sludge bubbling under their own weight. Let the fruit cool completely, pack it in jars (for canning or not), then refrigerate the jam until set. Like most foods, this cooling and setting phase is crucial so as to give the jam time to set up chemically but also gives flavors time to mingle a little more and get to know who they'll be sharing a jar with for the next two weeks.

Once you've mastered this formula, begin playing around with different sugars and acids to better suit the fruit you're using. I love honey and orange juice with figs, while brown sugar and grapefruit juice make an astounding strawberry jam. As any good Southern jam maker would, I also developed a pepper jelly using a mix of tomatoes and strawberries with sugar, orange juice, and a couple of chopped serrano chiles.

Fruits that don't fit our modern, harsh beauty standards, and those that are about to go too soft or overripe, are perfect for jam since shape is not important here. I'll often pick around the last bits of fruit at a farmers' market before it closes, and take home all the busted and bruised babies I can carry for a fraction of what the whole beauties were selling for that morning.

Once the jam is made, I can it all, keep one jar for myself and give away the rest. After all, once you've fallen in love with jams—the secret to happiness, the distillation of summer feels, and the balm to life's ails, boiled down into one glorious glop—you'll want to spark the sweet tooth in everyone you meet.

MAKE GRANOLA, SAVE MONEY, BE HAPPY

BY DAWN PERRY

One of the easiest things you'll ever make is granola. You dump a bunch of stuff in a bowl, stir it, and about 30 minutes later you have one of the most compulsively edible snacks and/or breakfast cereals known to (this) woman. It's sweet, but not so sweet that you can't call it breakfast. It's predominantly oats, as granola should be, but offers enough by way of nuts, seeds, and coconut to keep things interesting. That's not to say it's the end-all-be-all of granolas. That's the thing about granola: each batch can and should be as unique as its maker. This recipe is a reliable place to start figuring out how you like it. Make the base recipe first and see what you think. Then start playing. Tinker with the ratios until you find your own ideal blend.

THE DRY

Old. Fashioned. Rolled. Oats. That's all you need to know. But a quick word on the wheat germ. One of my favorite granolas turned out to be made largely of all-purpose flour, which felt like cheating, because then it's basically broken-up cookies. A bit of nutrient-dense wheat germ offers the same binding power with a more righteous message. Be careful about adding too much because in larger proportion it can make the granola chewy.

THE FAT

Fat is your friend. It helps toast the oats and nuts and binds everything together. Melted butter, olive oil, vegetable oil, or coconut oil (heated until liquid) are all great options. Each adds a subtle flavor to the mix so if you're adding anything additional like spice, or taking things in a savory direction, go with a neutral oil like safflower, grapeseed, or canola.

THE SWEET

I like two sweeteners: one liquid and then brown sugar (light or dark brown) in a ratio of one part sweet to six parts oats/nuts. Unlike maple or honey, agave syrup lends a neutral sweetness that won't distract from other flavors. A little brown sugar offers a caramely base note but also helps to bind the mix together in the oven. Don't skip it.

THE FILLER

Granola, in my opinion, should be mostly oats, but NOT all oats. I like nuts and I always include coconut. If coconut is not your thing leave it out and add more oats. Use whatever nuts you like: almonds, walnuts, pecans (my favorite), and cashews are good choices. Sunflower, sesame, poppy, or hemp seeds are also welcome. For nuts and seeds, pick one big and one small: almond/sunflower or walnut/pepita, unless you're making a seed-heavy batch in which case use two egg whites.

ON NUGGETS

The brown sugar and liquid sweetener will offer some clumping, but just one egg white transforms a batch of granola from healthy cereal to snackable goodness. If you do use an egg white, watch the time. Batches with egg tend to brown faster, so set your timer to the low end of the range.

VARIATIONS

Once you figure out your favorite combos, play around with other flavor profiles. Be brave and get creative. For savory granola (great for yogurt bowls or salads), turn to the spice rack for inspiration. Try coriander seed/garam masala; dried thyme/sumac; oregano and—Parmesan cheese! We could add some tomato paste in the wet mix. Do you see where I'm going with this? Pizza granola! See? Endless opportunities for experimentation. Now get in the kitchen and start experimenting!

BREAKFAST COOKIES

Bonus round: granola cookies (page 67), I promise they count as a decent breakfast— whole grains, healthy fats, fiber, and no refined sugar. They're excellent if you are a breakfast-skipper (but don't want to be).

MAKES **ABOUT 4 CUPS**

Maple-Nut Granola

2 cups oats

½ cup pecans, walnuts, almonds, cashews, or pistachios

½ cup pepitas or sunflower, sesame, flax, or hemp seeds

½ cup unsweetened flaked coconut

¼ cup maple syrup

¼ cup vegetable oil

2 tablespoons light or dark brown sugar

1 tablespoon wheat germ

½ teaspoon kosher salt

1 large egg white, optional

1. Preheat oven to 300°F with rack in the center. Combine oats, pecans, pepitas, coconut, maple syrup, vegetable oil, brown sugar, wheat germ, salt, and, if desired, egg in a large bowl and toss until evenly coated.

2. Transfer to a rimmed baking sheet and bake, tossing gently with a metal spatula and rotating sheet halfway through, until golden brown, 25 to 30 minutes.

3. Let cool completely on sheet (granola will crisp as it cools) then transfer to an airtight container. Granola will keep, tightly covered at room temperature, for about a month (if it lasts that long).

MAKE GRANOLA BARS AND BECOME THE MASTER OF YOUR OWN DESTINY

BY ALLISON ROBICELLI

Granola bars are so shockingly easy to make that you'll wonder why you didn't attempt them sooner. Seriously, search for a random recipe for granola bars right now and read it. Odds are that it's going to look something like this: Step one: Put a whole bunch of stuff in a bowl. Stir. Step two: Put the stuff in a pan and press it down, then bake it. Step three: Cut into bars and boom. Now don't you feel stupid for wasting ten grand on Luna bars?

You can dress up your granola bars with whatever fruits or nuts you fancy, sneak in a bit of whatever superfood-of-the-month you bought at Costco. The only thing that has the chance of being intimidating is the ingredient list, which on the low-end contains things you find in the supermarket, and on the high-end ticks off items that can only be found on the organic black market. So let's break down this DIY granola bar method:

SECTION 1 BULK

In a classic granola, this is plain rolled oats. You may be tempted to use steel-cut oats, but do not do this if you want to keep your teeth. Same goes for any raw supergrain, such as quinoa. A small amount can be used to add some crunch, but in bulk, they need to be cooked. Just because we're baking the granola bars doesn't really mean we're "cooking" them. The oven is used to get the granola to set into a solid bar and to add flavor by lightly toasting. If you've got a no-bake granola recipe, you may want to toast your oats and nuts ahead of time, solely for flavor.

SECTION 2 OTHER STUFF

Recipes for granola are highly flexible (remember page 63). Swap out ingredients as you like, just keep your volume ratios the same: for example, one cup of walnuts can be replaced by ¾ cup of cashews and ¼ cup of dried blueberries. You never need to be stressing out over finding niche items like "golden flaxseeds" or "coconut nectar." Use what you have.

SECTION 3 BINDERS

Your nut butters, honeys, and syrups need only be warm enough so they are loose and pourable, allowing them to seamlessly blend with the rest of the ingredients. The safest, most foolproof way to do this is to microwave them in 30-second spurts.

SECTION 4 MOLDING

Lining the pan with a foil or parchment sling is a must if you want to be able to unmold your bars easily. Spread the granola mix using your hands. Once spread, cover it with a sheet of plastic wrap, and roll over the surface with a small can or a flat-bottomed glass to smooth the top and ensure evenness.

SECTION 5 CUTTING

After the bars come out of the oven, use a long knife or pastry scraper to score the top into sections. Once cooled completely, use a serrated knife to cut along those lines.

TURN YOUR HOUSE INTO A WACKY NUT BUTTER FACTORY

BY CAROLINE LANGE

If you have a food processor and any kind of nut, you can make your own nut butter. This is a process that takes all of five minutes and makes you feel powerful. It's a truly open door: Roast the nuts, keep them raw, or sprout them. Add salt or don't, sweeten with sugar or maple syrup or honey or don't. Keep it classic or turn to your pantry for inspiration and add shredded coconut, chocolate chips, cocoa powder, matcha, and spices of all types and intensities, from sweet (cinnamon, ginger, cardamom) to savory (cayenne, curry powder, turmeric).

ONE FINAL NOTE BEFORE YOU BEGIN

You may find that with some firmer, less buttery nuts (for example, almonds as opposed to cashews) you can't get beyond a gravelly paste. If that's the case, add a bit of neutral oil, a teaspoon at a time, and blend until you get the texture you want. You can also use oil to add flavor to your butter. If you're making peanut butter with dried ginger and cayenne, you might try adding, sparingly, a little sesame oil. Coconut oil is another good add-in. Do not add water to nut butter. Oil and water are not pals and they don't mix well in nut butter.

TO MAKE THE BUTTER

In a clean, dry food processor, add however many nuts you want. Keep in mind that two pounds of almonds will yield about four cups of almond butter.

Add a little sweetener if desired, or some spice, or a pinch of salt, or just leave as is. Start with less of any additional flavoring than you think you'll need. You'll be surprised at how well the flavor is distributed.

Turn your food processor on and wander off. Play some Tetris on your phone or check your email. Listen for the noise to change: At first, the nuts will skitter and clunk noisily, but after a couple of minutes the sound will change to a swish. When it does, turn off the processor and check it. Has it started to become a spreadable butter, or is it still sandy? If it's not the texture you're looking for, add a little oil, turn the machine back on, and process a few more minutes. A long blend will get you creamy, smooth butter. When you've arrived at the proper texture, taste and adjust. Now you're ready to store. Scoop the butter into a jar and stash it in the fridge.

A FEW FLAVOR IDEAS

For maple-walnut butter, add a little maple syrup and a small pinch of salt.

For homemade Nutella, toast hazelnuts and let cool completely before adding them to the food processor with a handful of semisweet chocolate chips.

For cardamom-pistachio butter, add a pinch of salt, less cardamom than you think you need, and honey to taste.

Breakfast Cookies

We're not talking about waking up, farting around the house, feeling too lethargic to make eggs so you suck down a half-sleeve of Oreos. These are nutritious breakfast cookies with oats and dried cranberries. But the star of the show is the sunflower seed butter. The cookies will also work with almond or cashew butter, if that's what you happen to have, but seriously, if you've never tried sunflower butter before, the time is now.

½ cup unsweetened sunflower seed butter

¼ cup olive oil

1 large egg

5 tablespoons maple syrup

1 teaspoon pure vanilla extract

¾ cup whole wheat pastry flour

1 cup rolled oats

⅓ cup unsweetened shredded coconut

½ teaspoon fine sea salt

4 tablespoons chocolate chips or chopped chocolate

2 tablespoons dried cranberries

Toasted sunflower seeds and/or chopped toasted almonds to taste

1. Preheat your oven to 350°F. Line a baking sheet with parchment paper while you're at it.

2. In a medium bowl, whisk together unsweetened sunflower seed butter, olive oil, egg, maple syrup, and vanilla extract.

3. In a small bowl, whisk together whole wheat pastry flour, rolled oats, unsweetened shredded coconut, and sea salt.

4. Dump the flour mixture into the sunflower seed butter mixture, then add chocolate chips or chopped chocolate and dried cranberries. Add a handful of toasted sunflower seeds and/or chopped toasted almonds.

5. Use a 2 tablespoon cookie scoop to scoop mounds of dough onto the baking sheet, then flatten each cookie slightly. Bake cookies for 12 to 14 minutes, then store in an airtight container in the fridge for 1 week, and in the freezer for months.

6
7

NOTE

While many brands of sunflower seed butter exist, and you can even make your own if you want, SunButter Organic works very well.

CHAPTER TWO

COFFEE, BOOZE &

OTHER LIFE-ENHANCING DRINKS

10 COFFEE FACTS YOU DIDN'T KNOW
(BUT DEFINITELY SHOULD)

Does the thought of having to face the morning without coffee make you want to dig a deep hole and live in it forever? Justify your obsession by learning these facts.

1 COFFEE BEANS?
Not so much. Coffee beans aren't actually beans. They're seeds from the fruit of a coffee plant, often called a coffee cherry.

2 THANK GOATS FOR COFFEE
The actual origins of coffee are unknown, but one common legend says that an Ethiopian shepherd discovered it when he noticed his goats couldn't fall asleep at night after eating coffee cherries off the plant.

3 ONLY TWO TYPES OF COFFEE
Though there are dozens of varieties and hundreds of different roasts of coffee beans, there are only two main coffee types: arabica and robusta. Chances are you're drinking arabica, since that bean comprises 75 to 80 percent of global coffee production.

4 STRAIGHT FROM THE BEAN BELT
All coffee is grown in the Bean Belt, which lies around the equator, so the only American-grown coffee is from Hawaii. Otherwise, the cup you're drinking is made from foreign beans.

5 THE RIGHT SIZE IS SMALL
The U.S. Food and Drug Administration has rules for how big a serving of coffee should be. It's eight ounces (four ounces less than a tall at Starbucks).

6 COFFEE VS. ENERGY DRINKS
Energy drinks are often called out for being overcaffeinated, but coffee actually has a higher concentration of caffeine.

7 DECAF ISN'T 100% CAFFEINE-FREE
Decaf coffee isn't free of caffeine, though a serving usually contains less than 10 milligrams of caffeine.

8 IT'S NOT THE BEST PART OF WAKING UP
The best time to have a cup is the late morning, ideally between 9:30 a.m. and 11:30 a.m., to take advantage of your body's natural hormone-production cycles.

9 ANOTHER REASON TO LOVE THE SMELL OF COFFEE
There's some research indicating simply smelling coffee in the morning can be enough to help wake you up.

10 YOU'RE NOT ALONE
According to a 2015 Gallup poll, about two-thirds of Americans drink more than one cup of coffee per day.

KNOW YOUR COFFEE

AN ESPRESSO FIELD GUIDE

BLACK COFFEE
- drip coffee

CAPPUCCINO
- foam
- steamed milk
- espresso

LATTE
- foam
- steamed milk
- espresso

MACCHIATO
- foam
- espresso

MOCHA
- steamed milk
- chocolate
- espresso

ESPRESSO
- espresso

CAFÉ AU LAIT
- steamed milk
- coffee

AMERICANO
- hot water
- espresso

RED EYE
- drip coffee
- espresso

IRISH COFFEE
- whipped cream
- whiskey
- drip coffee
- brown sugar

FLAT WHITE
- steamed milk
- espresso

AFFOGATO
- ice cream
- espresso

THE GOLDEN RATIO OF GROUNDS TO WATER

BY TIM NELSON

Most coffee lovers have their own tried-and-true preparation methods developed through trial and error over the years. But for those open to some advice, the National Coffee Association USA in 2017 revealed the "golden ratio" for making a damn fine cup of coffee.

According to them, the ideal pot of coffee uses one or two tablespoons of freshly ground coffee per six ounces of water. One tablespoon makes for a tamer brew, while two is perfect for people who prefer bolder flavors and an extra caffeine jolt.

These experts also had some specific advice that can help you elevate your grounds game. It turns out that over-extracted coffee grounds (jargon for too fine of a grind) can leave a bitter taste in your mouth. Conversely, coarse, under-extracted grounds mean your brew may taste flat and lack flavor. And maybe it's because it's their job to get people to buy more coffee, but the NCA also strongly advises against using coffee grounds a second time.

They also mention that the optimal water temperature for brewing coffee is between 195°F and 205°F. Bring cold tap or filtered water to a boil, and then let it rest away from a heat source for a minute first. Finally, the amount of time your coffee brews is crucial. They recommend a contact time of five minutes for drip coffee and two to four for a French press. It's unclear what this means for those who use automatic coffee makers other than that you're probably being judged for taking the easy way out.

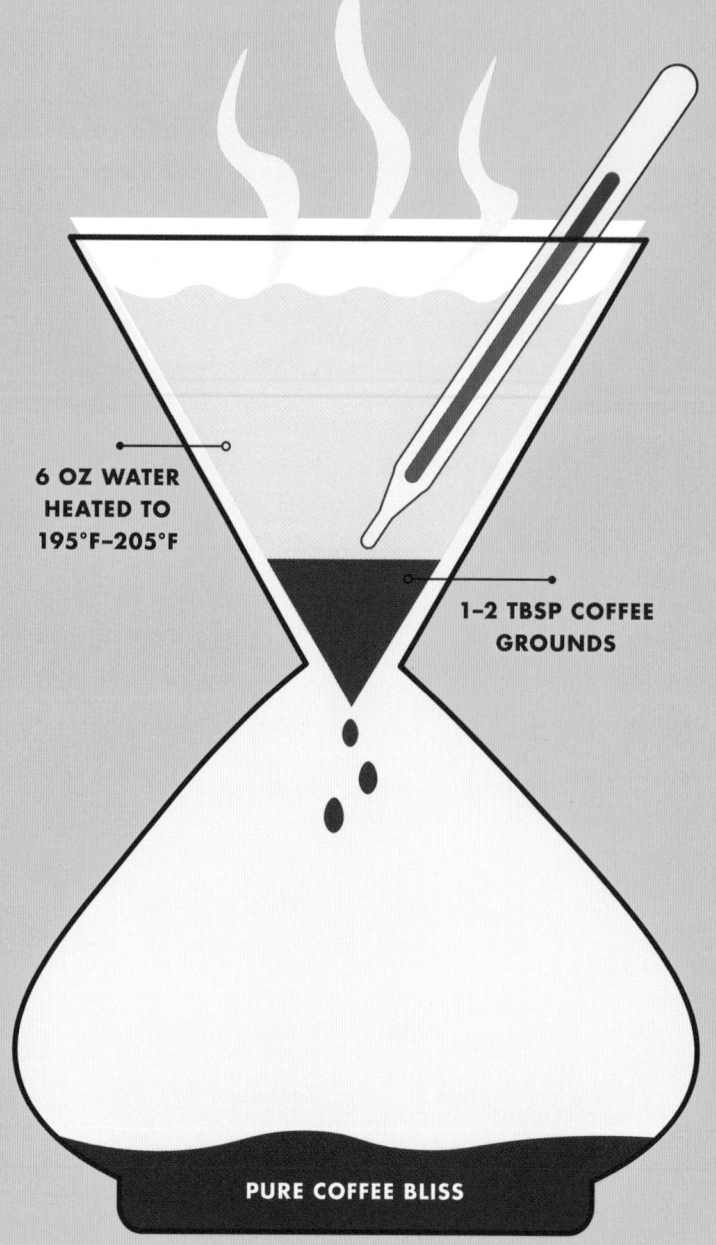

6 OZ WATER
HEATED TO
195°F–205°F

1–2 TBSP COFFEE
GROUNDS

PURE COFFEE BLISS

How to Make Cold Brew Concentrate at Home

Those little bottles of cold brew concentrate are awfully cute, but once you learn how ridiculously easy it is to DIY, you'll definitely want to save that cash for something else—like those single-origin Honduras beans you've had your eye on.

2 cups coarsely ground coffee beans

4 cups cold filtered water

Simple syrup, optional

1. Place coffee in a large glass measuring cup or bowl. Slowly add water, stirring to moisten all coffee grounds. Let stand 8 hours at room temperature.

2. Place a coffee filter in a funnel or fine wire-mesh strainer over a bowl. Pour coffee through funnel. Repeat with additional coffee filters until coffee runs clear, 2 or 3 times.

3. Serve cold-brew coffee over ice with cream or milk, or simply dilute coffee with water at a 2:1 water-to-coffee ratio. Sweeten with simple syrup, if desired.

GROCERY STORE COFFEE BATTLE ROYALE

BY JOHN SHERMAN

THE METHODOLOGY

Over two days, I prepared an eight-ounce mug of coffee from each of these widely available coffee brands. I selected the most basic variety of each brand—i.e., blends labeled as "house," "original," or "breakfast." Each mug was brewed using a ceramic pour-over cone with an unbleached paper filter and consumed black. I assessed the flavor at brew and room temperatures, and after microwaving to warm it back up. Microwaveability is essential to any home coffee and can indicate whether coffee left on the burner will deteriorate or stay more or less stable.

THE CANS

	**FOLGER'S HOUSE BLEND**	Folger's is dark enough to mask distracting flavors, thin enough not to coat the esophagus with silty grounds, and so, so cheap. Its flavor depends greatly on proper drinking temperature—it is punishing when tepid. A microwave brings it almost back to where it needs to be.
 BEST IN SHOW / BEST IN CATEGORY	**MAXWELL HOUSE ORIGINAL**	Maxwell House tasted the best of all the canned coffees. It is a perfectly reasonable coffee to start the day with, and one that doesn't sacrifice flavor for affordability. It turns a bit as it cools, taking on a bitter aftertaste, but a quick drinker with a small mug should get by OK. Don't microwave Maxwell House and expect to enjoy what comes out; it tastes like airplane coffee, which in the grand hierarchy of complimentary coffee ranks just below single-serving hotel room coffee.
	**CHOCK FULL O'NUTS NEW YORK ROAST**	This is the only brand I know of to offer three varieties of half-caf, but its per-pound cost approaches bagged coffee, making it a questionable deal. Chock full o'Nuts' flavor has a tinge of burnt bread and an aftertaste that causes the corners of my mouth to turn down involuntarily. It is undrinkable cold, but worse when reheated.
	CAFÉ DU MONDE COFFEE AND CHICORY	Café du Monde may be the best-known domestic producer of chicory coffee, if not the only one. The flavor of chicory is initially enjoyable, but the romance was gone for me after about two minutes. Cold black chicory coffee is nothing compared to microwaved chicory coffee. After a single sip I poured it out.
 RUNNER-UP	**CAFÉ BUSTELO**	Unlike the other coffees under consideration, Café Bustelo is espresso ground, which is much finer than drip ground. This, in addition to the dark roast of the coffee beans, makes it a robust sipping coffee. Café Bustelo is cheap and not for the faint of heart (seriously, I'm having palpitations as I type this) but ultimately is quite drinkable.

THE BAGS

RUNNER-UP		**GREEN MOUNTAIN BREAKFAST BLEND**	Green Mountain is an impressively good coffee for the price. It is thoroughly pleasant, light-roasted, and gentle on an empty stomach. It also has a nice thermal shift, remaining drinkable even as it cools and microwaves decently, too.
BEST OVERALL VALUE		**EIGHT O'CLOCK COFFEE THE ORIGINAL**	Eight O'Clock Coffee is a sleeper in this set, brand-wise. It's the only brand here about which I had no preconceptions, and it turned out to be one of my favorites. It's dark without being bitter, and is solidly microwaveable. It costs less than $8 per bag, but tastes more expensive.
		GEVALIA HOUSE BLEND	Gevalia may have the prettiest packaging and is widely available and usually fairly cheap. It is the rare coffee that microwaves well and tastes as good reheated as it does freshly brewed.
BEST IN CATEGORY		**NEW ENGLAND COFFEE BREAKFAST BLEND**	Like inexpensive wine, inexpensive coffee is best when its flavor is innocuous, and New England Coffee is a safe and delightful option. It reheats well, tastes good, and costs less than $10 a pound.
		NEWMAN'S OWN ORGANICS BREAKFAST BLEND	This is a feel-good coffee—it's organic, profits go to charity, and Paul Newman's face on the bag grins approvingly at your choices. It tastes like the last coffee of the day should taste—a 3 p.m. pick-me-up that tows you calmly to the end of the workday rather than punching you in the eye-bags like a morning coffee needs to. It falls short in thermal shift and microwaveability, though.
		365 EVERYDAY VALUE PLEASANT MORNING BUZZ	Pleasant Morning Buzz is a Vienna roast-style coffee, a dark roast just shy of a French roast-style, which gives the coffee a heavy, bittersweet flavor that's easy to sip on for a black coffee drinker. As a rule, darker roasts do not microwave as well as lighter roasts, and this coffee is no exception.
		DUNKIN' DONUTS ORIGINAL BLEND	This at-home iteration of Dunkin' coffee is roasty without being burnt and easy on an empty stomach. It is nearly indistinguishable from takeout Dunkin' and has a gentler thermal shift than most coffees in its price range. It continues to be enjoyable all the way down to room temperature and is admirably microwaveable.
		STARBUCKS HOUSE BLEND	Starbucks coffee black tastes like drip coffee made with day-old coffee instead of water, and the headache it produces is textbook coffee-ache—right behind the eyes, accompanied by an involuntary grimace. Only drink it if you must.

HOW FAR CAN YOU RUN IF YOU RUN ON DUNKIN'?

BY ALANA MASSEY

Most of the doughnuts I've had in my life were eaten on a boardwalk at sunrise. This would make sense if there were an especially delightful doughnut shop on the beach near my house, but there isn't. I also don't live by the beach, and I don't especially like doughnuts. Yet I often find myself walking the stretch of Coney Island Boardwalk, just as dawn hesitates to peak over the North Atlantic, eating a doughnut and drinking a medium coffee with skim milk and one Equal from the Dunkin' Donuts below the last subway stop in Brooklyn at Coney Island. Despite my general ambivalence toward doughnuts, I have found these sugar-soaked, calorie-dense snacks that masquerade as a legitimate morning meal to be among the most satisfying breakfasts of my life. It is not the particular quality of the doughnuts that have sated me but the circumstances under which I eat them: moderately starved and fresh off of four-and-a-half-mile runs to Coney Island in the dark.

To understand how I came to this peculiar breakfast ritual, I should start by saying that I believe selectively in junk science and firmly in the placebo effect. I practice lifestyle habits that appear reasonable even if they have been repeatedly debunked by evidence-based research. I spend an embarrassing amount of time browsing fitness websites full of unhealthy or suspicious advice for achieving extreme leanness. Articles on these sites use terms like "the fed state" and "blunted lipolysis" without explaining what they are and take as a given that their readers are juicing and supplementing and own a full rack of weights. I have nearly cracked my supraorbital arch raising my eyebrows so hard at some of the claims on these sites but every once in a while I think, "Eh, makes sense. I'll try that one." This is how I became a practitioner of an exercise method called fasting cardio.

The idea behind fasting cardio is that over the course of a night's sleep, the body stops using recently consumed food for fuel and starts breaking down and burning the body's fat stores. By performing cardio exercise on an empty stomach, the body should ostensibly continue converting fat during the workout until something is eaten, maximizing fat burned during a routine and delivering a leaner body in less time. Despite the dubious evidence about the true efficacy and safety of fasting cardio, I was a true believer from the get-go.

The term "stubborn fat" appears often in fitness articles. It conjures an image of sentient slabs of vermin fat living under your skin, invoking squatters' rights to your body and requiring drastic measures to evict. The idea of starving them and then burning them for fuel was perversely thrilling. And so one day, when I rose for the four-mile run I take five times a week, I eschewed my usual breakfast of bananas or almond butter on toast. I was determined to feast on my own endurance for the duration of the run.

I should note that when it comes to popular bits of wisdom relating to mind and body, I either adore them and deploy them often or deplore them and go to great lengths to disprove them. "Today is the first day of the rest of your life!" is vacant of any moral values by being devoid of any qualitative element. "Nothing tastes as good as skinny feels!" is a category error. "An apple a day keeps the doctor away" is the misguided single-issue voter of clichés. And "Breakfast is the most important meal of the day" is only true if you submit to society's conception of time and its suggestions of when one ought to rise, eat, and sleep. I have pushed back the hardest on this last one, neglecting breakfast often and trying to game the system so that I might avoid the meal without diminishing my overall health. It is a mostly symbolic rebellion against the strictures of linear time, but it is the best I can do.

I run before sunrise, when the tree-lined boulevard that leads to the beach is mostly desolate and the air is as cool as it will be all day. My initial hunger generally wears off within the first mile, when an influx of endorphins soothes my exhausted body into the elusive state of "runner's high." There are six Dunkin' Donuts locations within a mile radius of my apartment in South Brooklyn, but I am tempted by none of them during this stage of my run. I listen to upbeat music and keep pace with it. For the first few weeks of attempting fasting cardio, bass lines and endorphins made it possible to arrive at the very edge of Coney Island and return on the subway triumphantly to my home to eat bananas and almond-butter toast without ever feeling hungry. But deprivation has a way of accumulating in

I STUMBLED IN AS IF I WAS WOUNDED AND ORDERED A COFFEE AND A GLAZED DOUGHNUT FROM THE CASHIER WITH THE DRAMA ONE MIGHT EXPLAIN THEIR SYMPTOMS IN AN EMERGENCY ROOM.

secret and coming to collect its debts unexpectedly.

The first hunger pang on one of these fasting cardio runs came like a punch to the right side of my abdomen that caused me momentary terror that my appendix was rupturing. It subsided into mild nausea in a few minutes only to return again as I approached the last stretch of Ocean Parkway before landing on the boardwalk at Brighton Beach. There was an urgency to the pain, more like the need to use the bathroom than the discomfort of hunger. Though I had been running to Coney Island for years, the only establishment I knew to be open 24 hours a day was the Dunkin' Donuts on Surf Avenue. I stumbled in as if I was wounded and ordered a coffee and a glazed doughnut from the cashier with the drama one might explain their symptoms in an emergency room.

You would think realizing that fasting cardio is not a good fit for my disposition would stop me from trying it again. But I am not a reasonable person. I am a person who is defiant of harmless clichés and who trusts junk-science websites when the mood strikes. And so I often find myself breaking down at the end of a two-week fasting cardio regimen, famished and panicked. And though it hits most often near the beach at dawn, when the sky and ocean prepare to meet in brilliant colors, I find more solace in a wholly different glow: the bright pink-and-orange sign of the sugar and caffeine merchant situated at the last subway stop in Brooklyn and the first step on my way back home.

Vietnamese Coffee Is a Sweet Present You Give Yourself

Vietnamese coffee is a strong brew walloped into submission by a generous dose of sweetened condensed milk and drunk as the antidote to something spicy or at the end of a meal. Or just because. Where Vietnamese tea is as sweet as a bell is clear, its coffee counterpart is a bit more subtle—a little sultry, more velvet than silk. Because of this, Vietnamese coffee is much more suited to breakfast, just the thing to accompany a piece of toast. Sweetened condensed milk is a goopy superhero and does a heck of a lot of work for something that was scooped out of a can.

2 tablespoons freshly ground coffee (something dark, ideally French roast)

6 ounces very hot water (bring to a boil, let sit a minute)

2 teaspoons sweetened condensed milk, or more to taste

Ice, optional

1. Brew the coffee using whatever method you like. I use a pour-over filter, which I really love and which will most mirror a Vietnamese coffee you'd buy. Add the coffee to the filter (set over a mug) and pour a small amount of the water in a circular motion over the grounds, just enough to wet them. When you stop hearing it drip into the mug, pour the remaining water in a circular motion over the grounds.

2. Stir in the sweetened condensed milk, taste, and add more if you like. Drink hot and as is, or pour it into a tall glass filled with ice. Straw optional, but not really optional.

NOTE

If you are using a Vietnamese metal coffee filter, add the sweetened condensed milk to the mug first. Place the metal coffee filter on top of the mug, fill with coffee, pour in the hot water, and cover with the lid, allowing the coffee to slowly drip through the filter into the mug.

London Fog Is a Drinkable Blanket

The London Fog creeps into a room (on little cat feet, you might say, if you were Carl Sandburg) and curls itself around you like a thick blanket. Like an actual fog, it's soft and full without being dense, and there's a sort of cozy-grey insulation effect to it. There's a debate about which city's fog it's supposed to have been born of—London or Vancouver. Some say it's the Seattle fog, although this might be due to the popularity the drink gained at Seattle-based Starbucks. Call it whatever you like, but do make it, especially on a day, foggy or otherwise, when you feel like you might enjoy being nuzzled by a warm drink.

The London Fog is simple to make, and even though it's often called a "tea latte," it doesn't require any special equipment like a milk steamer, nor any hard-to-find ingredients like flavored sweeteners or syrups. As long as you've got Earl Grey tea, vanilla extract, a milk of your choice, and a big mug to put it all in, you have everything you need.

1 Earl Grey tea bag (or 1 heaping teaspoon of loose Earl Grey tea)

½ cup boiling water

½ cup whole milk (This is not the time for skim—we're going for creamy-dreamy here. But almond, soy, or oat milks are all lovely substitutes.)

¼ teaspoon pure vanilla extract

Honey to taste, optional

1. Brew a strong half-cup of tea with the tea and the boiling water while you heat the milk in a smallish saucepan over medium heat until small bubbles begin to form around the pot's edges.

2. Whisk in the vanilla and, if you like, honey, then whisk aggressively, until the milk is very frothy. (If you have a frothing wand or fancy milk-steaming machine, you could use that instead, but a whisk gets the job done admirably.)

3. Remove the tea bag from your mug and pour in the milk, holding back the foam with a spoon until all the liquid is in the mug, then spooning it over the top.

The Time I Thought I Invented Smoothies

BY CHRIS OFFUTT

Every few years I make a personal pledge to maintain better health. In the old days this usually followed a week-long bender of mammoth proportions. Now, it comes after a 10-minute walk that leaves me gasping by the side of the road. First on my list of big changes is always breakfast, aka the Most Important Meal of the Day, except if you're a chicken intent on protecting your eggs. (I believe that all meals are created equal, and the breakfast myth is perpetuated by Big Egg.)

For decades I ate the true Breakfast of Champions—a cigarette and coffee—but have recently acknowledged the error of my ways. Medical investigation is an extensive undertaking with tons of fancy words and phrases such as "nutrient timing" and "hunger hormones." Exercise is alleged to be beneficial, but I'm not convinced that the physical act of eating counts. (My idea of exercise is playing a video game in a strenuous fashion, battling pixilated opponents for hours on end.) After extensive research, my layman's understanding of health is that smoking is bad and fruit is good!

Consuming fruit feels like a necessary task, a resentful chore, a dutiful burden like gathering sticks from the yard. To begin with, eating an apple is not only time-consuming but very loud. There's simply no way to take a bite in a gentlemanly fashion. Juice squirts in long arcs. The biting sound amplifies in one's mouth like the hole in a guitar, and the skin of an apple can wedge itself between your teeth and stay there for hours. The only cure is digging it out with a toothpick, which prolongs the entire fiasco. Worse, the toothpick can splinter, and you wind up swallowing pieces of birch. (No doctor recommends eating tree.)

Pears are pretty but way too soft to fool with. The innards will flow down your chin, plus the skin can be gritty and bitter. To top it off, both apples and pears carry stickers that must be peeled off, furthering the time involved in preparation. (Although I hear that the stickers are actually edible.) A peach is a cunning little traitor—lurking inside is a stone hard enough to chip teeth. The soft banana offers an illusion of simplicity until the crucial decision: method of peeling. Humans typically break the tapered end off a banana, then peel the first section midway down, a process that mashes the interior fruit and makes your hands sticky. Online videos depict the monkey style of peeling, which is the opposite: They gently compress the blunt end of a banana, and the peel practically falls away. Although I possess great admiration for the intelligence of our simian cousins, I refuse to take culinary lessons from a monkey.

Citrus fruit is out of the question. Not only do they squirt like the dickens, but the tart juice unerringly targets the eyes. Grapefruit is too heavy to handle easily except as a weapon. Many people add sugar to grapefruit, defeating the purpose of a healthy meal. The orange, though quite lovely in appearance, is an unpredictable rascal. Its skin might be very thin and full of mush, like sheetrock damaged by water. Or the skin might be three-quarters of an inch thick, requiring supreme effort for a highly disappointing amount of inner meat. Each individual orange has white thready stuff in the middle, which, though edible, is likely to get caught halfway down your throat. I find the name off-putting as well. Surely it should be called something other than its color! Don't even get me started on the tangelo, the Prius of the citrus family.

I THREW EVERYTHING IN A LARGE, LIDDED CONTAINER, ADDED A COMBINATION OF RED AND GREEN FOOD COLORING TO MAKE THE CONTENTS BROWN, AND AFFIXED A LABEL TO THE SIDE SAYING BRAIN SOUP.

This leaves berries, which have their own inherent perils: seeds. Grapes are the worst of the lot. Some have seeds and some don't, and the only way to learn is by nibbling delicately, using your tongue to root around in the tiny oval. Not worth the trouble. Strawberries and raspberries are adorned with exterior seeds, a desperate act of procreation, which invariably lodge between my molars and gumline. An extra complicating step is the rigorous cleaning procedure beforehand. If you wash the berries with sufficient force to eradicate the herbicides, there's nothing left but stained hands and a sink full of mush.

In my headlong pursuit of a healthy breakfast I latched onto the idea of making a week's worth of Fruit Formula. My technique is to throw everything in a colander, then rinse the contents while I play video games. I then dump the "clean" fruit into a standard blender. A banana adds a certain froth to the mix, and I developed a method of removing the recalcitrant skin with two hands, a technique I call "squeeze-and-squirt" (patent pending). Then I simply place a lid on the blender and let it run while I finish a few quests in my video game. Afterward, I pour the liquified mess into a large container in the refrigerator. Every morning I drank a glass full. Voilà! All that fruit enters my system with no mess or wasted effort.

I was intensely proud of my creation until my sons pointed out that a product idiotically called a fruit smoothie has been on the market for years. They implied that if I ever left the house, I'd know about this.

My family actually liked my Fruit Formula and began eating it on the sly, which I didn't notice until measuring the contents at night and comparing the figures at midday when I rose from bed. My sons vehemently claimed that the loss was due to natural evaporation. My wife implied that I stayed in bed too long to fully understand the process. According to her, all the water in the world just runs around in a big circle of evaporation and return. That makes no sense to me. What happens to the salt in seawater? You never hear of salty rain! Science aside, my family ate my breakfast, but I couldn't prove they did. The prospect of rising early enough to guard my breakfast was pretty much off the table. I needed another plan to foil their greediness.

As a young man I lived in a rooming house and shared a refrigerator with three other guys. I worked in a restaurant that offset my lousy pay by giving me food to take home. Unfortunately, the other boarders had the habit of eating everything available. My solution was pragmatic: I threw everything in a large, lidded container, added a combination of red and green food coloring to make the contents brown, and affixed a label to the side saying BRAIN SOUP. No one ate my food. In fact, my roomies treated me with a certain respect and trepidation, undoubtedly believing that my diet made me smarter than them. Unfortunately my family already knows I'm a buckethead so I had to actually be smart, not merely create the illusion.

I made a rare trip out of the house and purchased several packets of unsweetened black cherry Kool-Aid. I added it to the blender. The result was a very dark, nearly black mess. I labeled the Tupperware container PLATYPUS OIL and told my family it was for high blood pressure. They were extremely grateful that I was trying to take care of myself, thinking maybe I'd live long enough to provide an inheritance. At this point my will consists of a short list that includes books, taxidermy, video games, and recipes.

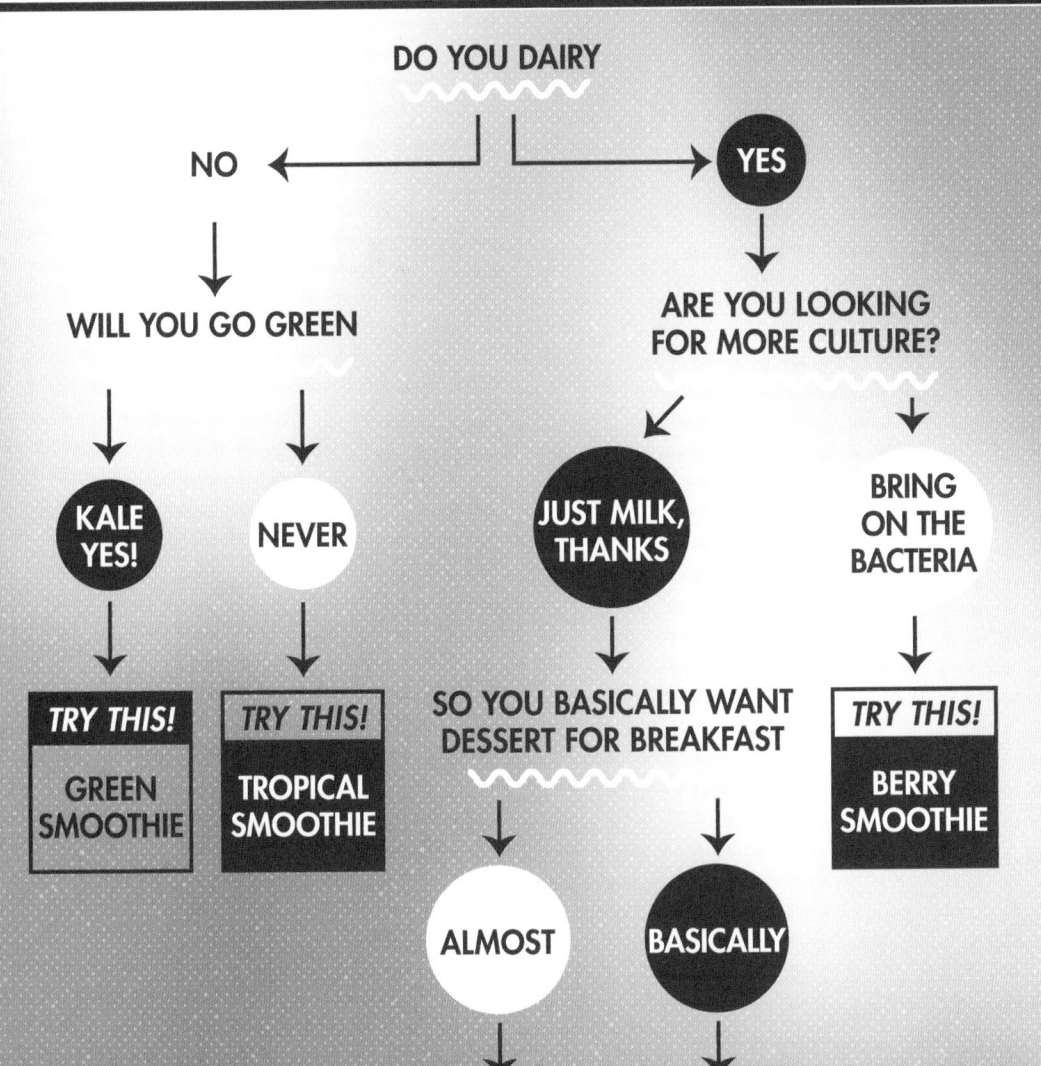

THE ONLY 5 SMOOTHIES YOU'LL EVER NEED

FOLLOW THIS FLOWCHART AND SEE WHICH ONE IS FOR YOU

DO YOU DAIRY

NO ← → YES

WILL YOU GO GREEN

ARE YOU LOOKING FOR MORE CULTURE?

KALE YES!

NEVER

JUST MILK, THANKS

BRING ON THE BACTERIA

TRY THIS!
GREEN SMOOTHIE

TRY THIS!
TROPICAL SMOOTHIE

SO YOU BASICALLY WANT DESSERT FOR BREAKFAST

TRY THIS!
BERRY SMOOTHIE

ALMOST

BASICALLY

TRY THIS!
PROTEIN SMOOTHIE

TRY THIS!
CHOCOLATE SMOOTHIE

RECIPES →

5 EASY SMOOTHIE RECIPES WITH ONLY 5 INGREDIENTS

There's no special technique involved when it comes to making basic smoothies. Buy or pick fruits you like. Cut off the inedible parts. Throw them in a blender. Press the button. That will give you a serviceable drink that you could call a smoothie. But you're not reading this book to merely keep things serviceable.

Even for the most experienced smoothie aficionados, it can be intimidating to nail that magic combination of ingredients that'll produce a superior smoothie. After all, there are so many different smoothie recipes out there, from sweet chocolate smoothies to almost-savory green smoothies. So how do you know what combination of ingredients is actually going to taste good?

We streamlined the whole process for you and put together five easy smoothie recipes with just five ingredients each. All of these ingredients are things you've heard of—like bananas and dates and kale—that are readily available at your local grocery store.

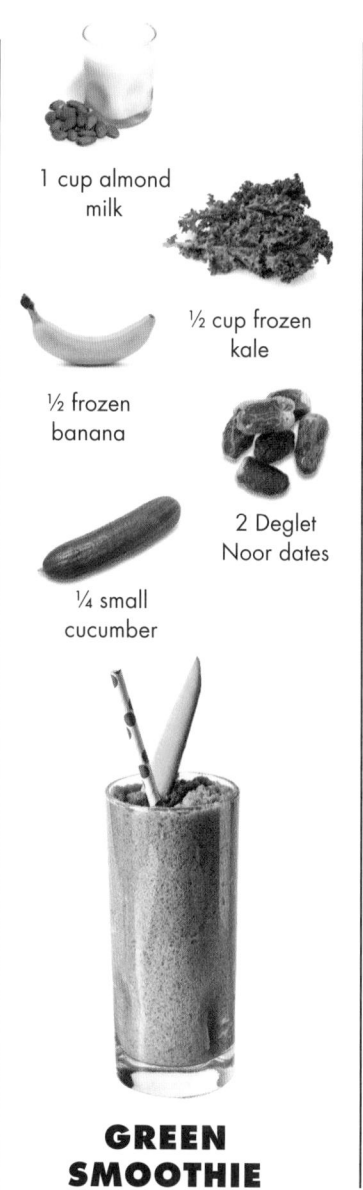

1 cup almond milk

½ frozen banana

¼ small cucumber

½ cup frozen kale

2 Deglet Noor dates

GREEN SMOOTHIE

1 cup coconut water

¼ cup frozen cubed mango

2 teaspoons chia seeds

½ cup fresh cubed pineapple

½ frozen banana

TROPICAL SMOOTHIE

1 cup milk

2 tablespoons peanut butter

½ frozen banana

2 tablespoons protein powder

1 tablespoon ground flaxseed

PROTEIN SMOOTHIE

1 cup milk

½ frozen avocado

2 Deglet Noor dates

3 tablespoons cocoa powder

1 teaspoon honey

CHOCOLATE SMOOTHIE

½ cup Greek yogurt

¼ cup frozen blueberries

¼ cup frozen strawberries

¾ cup pomegranate juice

2 teaspoons honey

BERRY SMOOTHIE

DIY Italian Soda

Imagine it's 90 degrees out and you're walking around a city you don't know very well. You simultaneously need a drink and to use the bathroom. You spy a café, which could provide you with both, so you go in. Ordering a free tap water won't land you the bathroom key (the barista is a stickler), so you fork over four bucks for the coldest, sweetest drink they sell: a can of blood orange San Pellegrino soda. It's so good and does the trick and grants you access to a toilet, but it's only a treat, a brief dalliance. It will never be a regular part of your life because those cans aren't cheap. Or could it be? Here's how to make your own Italian soda.

1 cup water

1 cup granulated sugar

1 cup washed fruit (if using stone fruit, peeled and sliced; if using citrus, use only the peel)

Ice

Seltzer

1. Mix the water, sugar, and fruit together in a medium saucepan. Bring the mixture to a boil, stirring to ensure the sugar dissolves.

2. After the syrup boils, reduce the heat to low and simmer for 5 to 10 minutes, or until slightly thickened.

3. Pour the syrup over a fine wire-mesh sieve balanced over a bowl and let the syrup strain on its own. You're going to want to press down on the fruit to drain out every last drop of moisture (and I know, mushing things is just plain fun) but resist the urge. Larger bits of fruit pulp will make

the syrup cloudy, which isn't what we're going for here. Instead, save that mushy fruit for spooning over yogurt or blending into a smoothie.

4. After the strained simple syrup has cooled a bit, fill a glass halfway with ice. Spoon in syrup until it just barely covers the ice. Fill the glass with very fizzy seltzer and swirl just a bit with a spoon. If you'd like to turn the Italian soda into a French soda (also known as an Italian cream soda), pour a bit less seltzer into the glass and top the drink with a splash of heavy cream.

EASY AGUA FRESCA

BY STEPHANIE BURT

I love some agua fresca served fresh with a salted rim right after I've spent the morning Instagramming artfully arranged piles of fruit in a foreign market ("wish that you could SMELL these mangos!"). I also enjoy a glass of agua fresca spiked with tequila while sunning by the pool or during a Sunday funday with my friends eating $7 tacos and day drinking.

But what about those times when you're keeping one eye on the time? Are we to be denied agua fresca? And should we even bother?

Everyone deserves the refreshment that is agua fresca at breakfast, brunch, or beyond and we don't need anyone to make it for us. A beginner batch is easy. For summer's sake, "agua fresca" means "fresh water." How hard can it be? Not very. Just do this:

STEP 1. Buy a watermelon. Not one of those fancy, personal watermelons that cost twice as much for half the fruit. Look for a good, old-fashioned watermelon with a flat yellow bottom (so you know it ripened in a field). You can move on to other fruit once you master the method, but watermelon is the easiest.

STEP 2. Get in there with a knife of some sort and start separating rind from fruit. It doesn't need to be pretty, but you'll need about **2 cups of fruit** for a blender batch. You can always make more than one batch.

STEP 3. Halve a lime. Even that withered one from the bottom drawer will do as long as it doesn't have powdery white spots.

STEP 4. Filch some herbs from your neighbor or friend who is growing **basil, rosemary, mint, or even cilantro.** I'm assuming you don't, well, because we are being honest here. You'll need a handful of leaves, or around ¼ cup, to give you a good herbal kick. Give those leaves a rinse.

STEP 5. Put the watermelon in the blender. Yep, seeds and all. Add **2 cups water**. Squeeze in lime juice. Bruise, rip, or smack herb leaves and throw in.

STEP 6. Pulse lightly. Seriously. Otherwise it becomes a middle school volcano project. You just want to break up the fruit but not pulverize the seeds. A Vitamix blender will definitely decimate the seeds, but then again, if you had one, you wouldn't be making this. You'd be on vacation hashtagging wildly.

STEP 7. I usually skip this step, but you can add **a sprinkle of sugar.** That doesn't mean Splenda or Stevia, which will give it a weird non-refreshing aftertaste.

STEP 8. Using a fine wire-mesh strainer or cheesecloth, strain the contents of the blender over a bowl. The liquid in the bowl will be relatively chunk-, leaf-, and seed-free, depending on your method.

STEP 9. Transfer the strained liquid to a pitcher and chill at least 30 minutes in the fridge. Serve over ice.

STEP 10. Instagram if desired, or just drink it and feel refreshed. Repeat.

HOW TO CUT
WATERMELON CUBES

1 cut your melon in half lengthwise

2 cut each half in half again so you have quarters

3 cut a wedge into the melon, just to the rind

4 continue to make slices 1- to 1½-inch wide across the rest of the melon

5 slice 2 lengthwise cuts along one side of the melon (3 for a large melon

6 repeat the lengthwise cuts on other side of the melon

slice between the flesh and rind

7

8

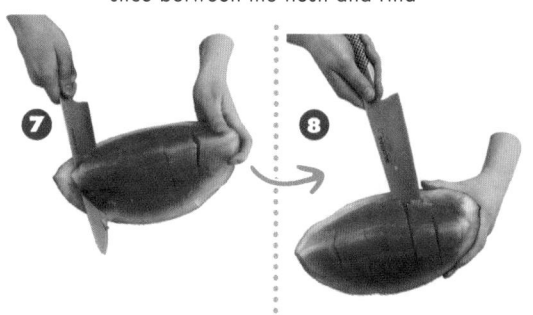

9 enjoy

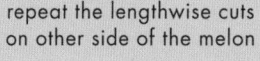

Watermelon Rum Punch

This is the best way to kill an afternoon like you're an old guy on vacation with nothing to do but hang. St-Germain sounds fancy but it's easy to get.

1 (2½- to 3-pound)
watermelon

1 cup rum

6 tablespoons fresh lime
juice (from about 3 limes)

¼ cup simple syrup

¼ cup elderflower liqueur
(such as St-Germain)

Ice

1. Using a small paring knife, cut 1 end off watermelon in a zigzag pattern. Discard end. Using a spoon, remove watermelon flesh, and place watermelon flesh in a blender. Process until smooth. Pour through a fine wire-mesh sieve, and discard solids.

2. Return 1 cup of the watermelon juice to watermelon rind; reserve remaining watermelon juice for another use. Add rum, lime juice, simple syrup, and elderflower liqueur to watermelon; stir to combine. Top with ice, and share with 3 friends.

8 MIMOSAS FOR SUMMER DAY-DRINKING

Mimosas are a good choice no matter who and where you are. Are you a 21-year-old marketing intern at a boozy brunch where your buds are oversharing about awful internet dates and weird bodily abnormalities? Order a mimosa. Are you a mom locked in your room with an issue of *Redbook* avoiding your terrible kids who have just formed a pots-and-pans band? Make yourself a mimosa.

A classic mimosa, with fresh orange juice and Champagne, is a perfectly fine drink—but we're not always into perfectly fine. These eight twists on the OG mimosa will turn your predictable summer day-drinking session into one of those blissful fabric softener commercials with flowing bedsheets, Caribbean music, and well-coiffed golden retrievers.

THE CLASSIC MIMOSA

½ cup Champagne
½ cup orange juice

LOOKING TO SWITCH IT UP? SWAP YOUR ORANGE JUICE FOR:

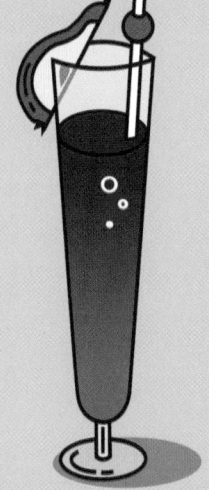

PEAR-BERRY MIMOSA

½ cup pear juice
Splash of berry nectar

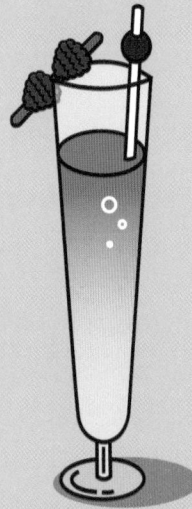

RASPBERRY-LEMON MIMOSA

¼ cup raspberry lemonade
Muddled raspberries

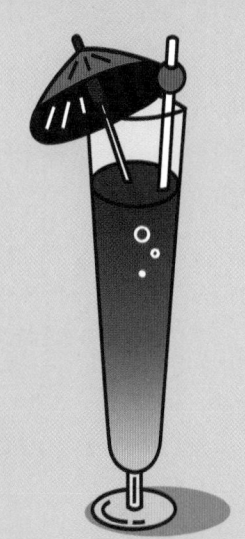

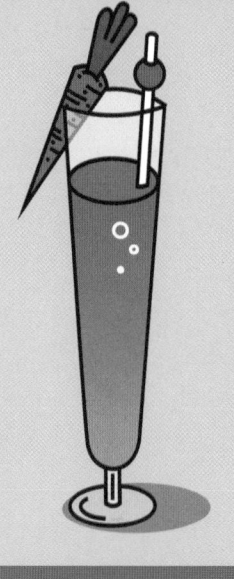

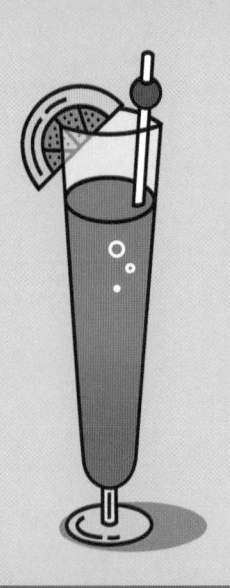

SWEET TEA MIMOSA

½ cup black tea
¼ cup pear nectar
¼ cup simple syrup

CARROT-GINGER MIMOSA

½ cup carrot juice
¼ cup ginger beer

GRAPEFRUIT MIMOSA

½ cup pink grapefruit juice
Rosemary sprigs

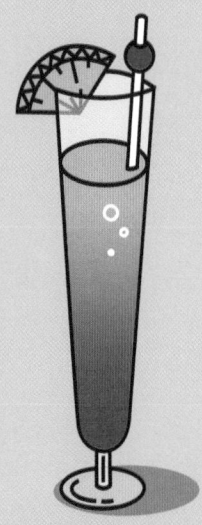

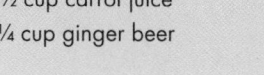

TEQUILA SUNRISE MIMOSA

½ cup pineapple juice
Splash of grenadine

GUAVA-MINT MIMOSA

½ cup guava juice
Julienned mint leaves

TANGERINE-THYME MIMOSA

½ cup tangerine lemonade
Thyme sprigs

Beer Can Brunch Cocktails

Brunch cocktails tend to fill a very particular purpose: Make everything hurt a little less, without being at all challenging. You've got your mimosas, bloody marys, and bellinis, but ugh—so much glassware to contend with. Embrace the beer can cocktail, where the most challenging step is chugging half the contents to make way for the rest of the ingredients. Just go into it with a can-do attitude, and you're golden.

BEER CAN BELLINI

1 (12-ounce) can cold Hefeweizen beer

½ cup cold peach nectar or juice

1 peach slice

Pour off or drink ½ cup of the beer from can. Pour peach nectar into can. Serve cold out of the can, or pour into a glass and garnish with peach slice.

BEER CAN MIMOSA

1 (12-ounce) can cold, citrusy
    pale ale beer

½ cup cold fresh orange juice
    (from about 2 oranges)

1 orange slice

Pour off or drink ½ cup of the beer
from can. Pour orange juice into can.
Serve cold out of the can, or pour into
a glass. Garnish with orange slice.

BEER CAN
BLOODY MARY

1 (12-ounce) can cold lager beer

½ cup cold tomato juice

1 teaspoon prepared horseradish

1 teaspoon Worcestershire sauce

½ teaspoon black pepper

3 to 4 dashes of hot sauce

1 celery stalk

1. Pour off or drink ½ cup of the
beer from can. Set aside.

2. Stir together tomato juice,
horseradish, Worcestershire sauce,
pepper, and hot sauce until well
combined. Pour mixture into beer
can. Serve cold out of the can, or
pour into an ice-filled glass and
garnish with celery stalk.

Jungle Juice Mimosas

BY MARGARET EBY AND KAT KINSMAN You might know Jungle Juice by one of its many other colorful aliases—Trash Can Punch, Hairy Buffalo, Hunch Punch—but you get the gist. It's usually made in large batches in either a cooler or a (hopefully clean) trash can, involves the cheapest available booze, and is most commonly found at college parties. It's basically a method to get a large crowd of people quite drunk very quickly, one that might not hold as much of an appeal once you don't go for the sugariest or cheapest drink on the menu. Indeed the very smell of Everclear mixed with fruit-punchy Kool-Aid powder might send you right back to your freshman year. But here is something you may not have considered: Jungle Juice makes a great mimosa.

Our recipe here is an amalgam of our pieced-together college memories, but this would probably work with any kind of frat elixir that you could come up with. We opted for a mix of peach schnapps, Everclear, Budweiser, and both Tang and Kool-Aid mix, plus a smattering of fresh-cut fruit soaked overnight in true college dirtbag style. Then you take your Solo cup, or stemware, or mason jar, or coffee mug, fill it about a third full of Jungle Juice and top with cheap sparkling wine so it's suddenly transmogrified into a semi-respectable brunch beverage.

It's way better than it deserves to be, but beware: It's also pretty lethal. You can always dilute it somewhat by actually making Kool-Aid rather than adding the mix directly to the alcohol. But where's the fun in that?

Everclear (in an 18-ounce square Solo cup, measured to the top of the "S")

Peach schnapps (same, but to the top of the "L")

1 to 2 Budweiser tallboys

¼ cup Kool-Aid powdered drink mix (we used Tropical Punch flavor)

¼ cup Tang powdered drink mix

Fresh cut fruit (we used strawberries, pineapples, and grapefruit)

Cheap sparkling wine (we used Korbel)

1. Mix together the Everclear, schnapps, 1 can Budweiser, and ¼ cup each Kool-Aid and Tang powders. Stir thoroughly, making sure that the drink mixes are thoroughly dissolved and that you are spiritually onboard with your impending fate.

2. Add fruit, making sure that fruit is coated with liquid, and allow to soak for several hours,

ideally overnight. There's still time to abandon mission and/or get your affairs in order.

3. Add more beer, schnapps, or Everclear to taste. Pour into drinking vessel, making sure to include some of the alcohol-soaked fruit. Top with sparkling wine. Accept your fate.

Slurpee Brunch Cocktails

BY MARGARET EBY Nothing against December, but we all know that July is actually the most wonderful time of the year. Popsicles can be eaten as meals, and your winter coat is somewhere under the bed gathering dust. Of all the unofficial holidays of summer—Shark Week, The First Day Fireflies Come Out—my favorite has to be July 11, or, as 7-Eleven recognizes it: Free Slurpee Day.

A Slurpee is the ideal mixture of ice and sugar to get you through the sticky mid-summer days. It also makes a damn fine base for a brunch cocktail. You could, as high school students have since the dawn of convenience stores, simply mix your Cherry Coke-Piña Colada-Fanta-Lime mixture with whatever alcohol you have on hand. But with a little pre-planning (a cooler bag isn't the worst idea) you can make something truly glorious.

SLURPIMOTXO

The recipe for this one is simple: fill up your chalice with a **healthy amount of Coca-Cola Slurpee** (or Diet Coke Cherry, if that's your speed.) Top that off with **cheap red wine**. Done and done: a kalimotxo but with Slurpee. We used burgundy Franzia, but basically anything works. Sorry, not sorry.

GIN FIZZURP

For this number, you're going to want to put down a base layer of **⅓ of a container of Blue Raspberry Slurpee**, and top it with about **⅔ a container of Mountain Dew**, then pour in your **gin** and stir. Seltzer would not go awry in this, nor would a little bit of citrus if you have it. Or a **dollop of the Peach Lemonade**, now that you mention it.

SLURPMOSA (PEACH LEMONADE SLURPEE + CHEAP SPARKLING WINE = SLURPMOSA)

For our purposes, we used Korbel, but the truth is that the **Peach Lemonade** is an excellent base for **any bubbly**. André? OK! Cook's? Sure! The leftover dregs of that nice bottle you had over the weekend? I can't see why not. If you want to go for the gusto, you might even want to pair it with peach André. Garnish it with a tiny umbrella and your morning is off to an excellent start.

TEQUILA SLURPRISE

Fill your Slurpee vessel of choice with ½ **Cherry Slurpee** and ½ **Piña Colada Slurpee**, and finish with a **touch of Mountain Dew** flavor for a tiny zing of citrus. Add a **shot of tequila** (or two, or three, if it's that kind of day). Mix, garnish, and watch your friends be super jealous. If your local 7-Eleven happens to have the coveted Orange Creme flavor, throw a dab of that in there, too.

BREAKFAST OF CHAMPIONS

As any Slurpee mixologist knows, adding alcohol to the mixture hastens the melting process, therefore leading to strangely-mingled flavors, sometimes in a good way. The Breakfast of Champions starts out red, white, and blue, and then gently melts into a rich purple. America! To whip this one up, put down a **layer of Blue Raspberry**, followed by **equal layers of Piña Colada and Cherry**. Top with the rest of that **cheap sparkling wine**, or the **clear liquor of your choice**. Rum would probably be good. Vodka could work. Bud Light might be pushing it, but I believe in you. Drink. Feel patriotic.

THE BRUNCH DRINK ORDER OF OPERATIONS IS MATH YOU NEED

BY MARGARET EBY

Hangovers are monsters or, at best, extremely rude. They upset your regular bodily operations with gleeful bursts of disorder. They run through the peaceful streets of your brain like so many aggro soccer hooligans after a victorious match, making the things that normally sustain you—sounds! light! friends!—seem like treacherous infiltrators bent on your destruction. Some bar veterans would tell you that hangovers are chaos, and to fight them requires still more chaos, an action painting of grease to quell your morning or early afternoon plight. But they are wrong.

Hangovers have a grammar to them. They are logical. To fight them, you need math. Specifically, the Brunch Drink Order of Operations.

The Brunch Drink Order of Operations has a simple premise: Brunch is a meal that is secretly all about liquids. It is a time you can sit at a restaurant with up to seven beverages without anyone really looking askance. Your mug of coffee seems a natural fit next to your frosty bloody mary, as would a thermos of tea nestled next to several exotic juices.

For purposes of the BDOO there are five main categories of beverages: alcoholic, caffeinated, sugary, hydrating, and nutritious. Yes, some things can be both caffeinated and alcoholic (rest in pain, Four Loko) or sugary and hydrating (I see you Gatorade). Plain seltzer is just hydrating, but add lemon juice and it could be considered nutritious, if your nutrient of choice is vitamin C.

To neutralize the hangover brutes, make sure to have a beverage from at least three of those categories. Hydrating first, then two other candidates, depending

on your need. Seltzer, coffee, and a bloody mary is my personal trinity, though you could also have an iced tea, a Perrier, and a mimosa, or a Gatorade, Red Bull, and coconut water. A kombucha, a Mountain Dew, and a shot of Jager also qualifies. (And if that is your choice, where are you going and can I come?) If you opt for a frozen Irish coffee and a side glass of water, that's all your categories right there.

Hydration is always step one, but the second and third categories vary according to what kind of day it will be. At the lake on vacation, leaning into the alcoholic makes sense, with a little back note of instant iced coffee. If this is a day that you've decided to start living a healthier lifestyle, then pull from the nutritious zone with caffeine for motivation. Make math work for you.

DIY Baileys Irish Cream

Not to bum you out too much, but in your lifetime or your kids' lifetime there is bound to be a disastrous, irreversible event that will forever affect life on earth. Could be nuclear war. Could be aliens. Whatever the cause, in 50 or 100 years we could be living in a dusty hellscape straight out of *Mad Max*. It won't matter how much money or power you have. All your fancy book learning and whatever job you thought was so important won't help you in the new world order. Everyone will be roaming around aimlessly, clinging to people with ancient, tangible skills like metallurgy and farming. Start asking yourself now, What will my apocalypse skill be? What could I trade for food to stay alive? Here's an idea: Baileys. You could be the person who makes the Baileys.

1 (14-ounce) can sweetened, condensed milk

1 cup cream, nondairy creamer, or half-and-half

1 tablespoon vanilla extract

2 packets hot cocoa mix

1 cup Irish whiskey

1 tablespoon instant coffee crystals

Put everything in a blender and blend for 30 seconds to one minute, until well combined.

THE BOOZY DRINK THAT KEEPS YOU AWAKE

BY KYLE CHAYKA The problem with drinking in the morning is that it tends to ruin, or at least put a depressive damper on, the rest of your day. It doesn't matter if it's orange juice and Champagne; whiskey in your drip coffee; or a shot of vodka in your green juice—booze makes it hard to soldier on into the afternoon, which will probably end in a nap far from wherever you were planning on going. Thankfully, I've discovered a solution: a breakfast cocktail so potent that it will keep you effervescently awake as long as you keep drinking it. It's not an illegal substance; it's the coffee Negroni. This drink is nothing but caffeine and alcohol, and maybe a bit of orange peel, which you could also eat if you're feeling a touch of scurvy. There's nothing in it to drag you down.

Late one weekend morning I was drinking espresso from a stovetop moka pot, and the bitter, citrus-y taste of the coffee reminded me of something. I thought of fernet, the herbal liqueur, but that was too extreme. What the espresso brought to mind was Campari, the orange-red aperitif that's core in a Negroni. The Negroni is simple: Just combine equal parts Campari, gin, and sweet vermouth, stir with ice, and strain into a glass. Slice a thin twirl of orange peel, twist in the direction of the glass for a spray of essential oils, and then wipe the peel around the rim.

Pairing the Negroni with espresso was surprisingly perfect. The brightness of the espresso highlighted the fruitiness of the Campari and the coffee's oily texture melded with the liquor and

THIS DRINK IS NOTHING BUT CAFFEINE AND ALCOHOL, AND MAYBE A BIT OF ORANGE PEEL, WHICH YOU COULD ALSO EAT IF YOU'RE FEELING A TOUCH OF SCURVY. THERE'S NOTHING IN IT TO DRAG YOU DOWN.

liqueurs. As with all great cocktails, the different components became something more than the sum of their parts. The only thing I changed was to add a splash more of sweet vermouth to balance out the funkier flavors of the coffee—perfect Nordic light roast beans might make that addition unnecessary, but the final proportion is up to you.

This cocktail is perfect either for brunch or an afternoon outdoor party where staying active is paramount. The first one will wake you up, but the next few—and you can't drink just one—will make you feel like a kindergartener right after naptime. From personal experience, I will say that it is inadvisable to continue this process for more than a few hours. By then you should switch to beer or wine. Or, you can move on to the kalimotxo, the Spanish red wine-and-Coke combination, to stay even more caffeinated. Who needs to sleep?

The Coffee Negroni

1 part gin
1 part sweet vermouth

1 part Campari
½ part espresso

Orange peel

1. Fill two glasses with ice. In one glass, mix equal parts gin, sweet vermouth, and Campari; stir to chill. Pour one stovetop pot or one shot of espresso into the other glass; stir to chill.

2. Strain liquor into a third, empty glass. Add strained, chilled, espresso, ½ part or to taste.

3. Squeeze orange peel over the glass, wipe it around the rim, and add to the cocktail.

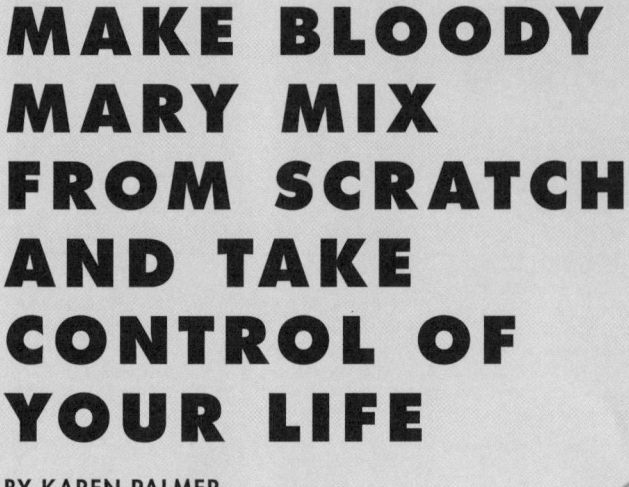

MAKE BLOODY MARY MIX FROM SCRATCH AND TAKE CONTROL OF YOUR LIFE

BY KAREN PALMER

Hydrating tomato juice. Nose-clearing horseradish that wakes you out of your booze-breath stupor. A hefty dose of black pepper so you can at least start to sweat out some of last night's booze. And, of course, vodka to get the sweet, sweet alcohol flowing through your veins again. Those are a few of the reasons why the bloody mary is the ultimate hair of the dog. It's somewhat perplexing, though, why most people choose to buy pre-made bloody mary mix when they're serving the drink at home. Sure, there are some decent bottled bloody mary mixes out there, but as with any balanced cocktail, you want to maintain as much control over the ingredients as you can to make sure they all line up. IT'S ALL ABOUT CONTROL, PEOPLE. (Takes breath, goes back to organizing books on bookshelf by spine color.)

So the next time you're about to make a bloody mary (or my personal favorite, create a bloody mary bar with mix-and-match spirits and garnishes), it doesn't hurt to whip up a base of your own.

HERE'S WHAT YOU'LL NEED FOR A STANDARD BLOODY MARY MIX

Tomato juice

Worcestershire sauce

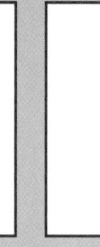
Fresh lemon juice

Salt

Grated horseradish
(not the creamed
stuff—gross)

Tabasco

Black pepper

Celery salt*

Once you've got all your ingredients, the best part about making bloodies is that it's all to taste: Use whatever tomato juice you'd like (canned is totally A-OK). Add a couple of tablespoons of horseradish, a few dashes of Worcestershire and Tabasco, a squeeze of lemon juice, a LOT of cracked black pepper, a pinch of salt. and a pinch of celery salt, taste, and add more of whatever's missing. Like it extra-nostril clearing? Dollop in some more horseradish. Just make sure you mix it together the night before you're planning to serve it, so that you can chill it overnight and let all those flavors meld together.

Then, once you've got your basic mix down, you can really start to play: If you like briny stuff, glug in some olive or pickle juice. Add fresh lime juice if you've got it handy. Swap out the Tabasco for other hot sauces, like Sriracha or Cholula. And if you want to be Instaclam famous (and aren't planning on serving the drink to vegetarians), use crisp, ocean-y Clamato instead of tomato juice. It's my secret weapon at the bloody mary bar I set up every year at my holiday brunch. Guests can't place their fingers on why the bloodies are so good, but they can't put 'em down.

"There's something about those Marys," they say. (That's never happened—but that's what they should be saying.) Happy mixing.

*This oft-overlooked ingredient is non-negotiable. It's what gives the bloody that vegetal nose and a depth of flavor that you just won't get without it. Go directly to the spice aisle in your local supermarket, suck it up, and shell out the $5 for a plastic container.

Flamin' Hot Cheetos Bloody Mary

There are a lot of things to do with Cheetos: bake them into bread and make Cheetoast; use them as the topping for a seriously orange breakfast casserole; or even steep them in milk to get a less wellness-oriented version of golden milk. One of our favorite ways to use Cheetos (especially ones of the Flamin' Hot variety) is to blend them into a bloody mary.

¼ cup Cheetos Crunchy Flamin' Hot Cheese Flavored Snacks, finely crushed

1 lime wedge, plus more for garnish

1 cup tomato-clam juice (such as Clamato), chilled

¼ cup vodka

3 tablespoons lime juice (from 2 limes)

¾ teaspoon Worcestershire sauce

½ teaspoon prepared horseradish

¼ teaspoon celery salt

Ice

Celery stalk, for garnish

Cheetos Crunchy Flamin' Hot Cheese Flavored Snacks, for garnish

1. Place crushed Cheetos in a small bowl. Rub lime wedge around the rim of a pint glass. Dip glass rim in Cheetos, turning to coat rim. Set aside crushed Cheetos and glass.

2. Stir together tomato-clam juice, vodka, lime juice, Worcestershire, horseradish, celery salt, and reserved crushed Cheetos in a glass measuring cup.

3. Fill prepared pint glass with ice. Pour tomato-clam juice mixture into glass. Garnish with celery stalk, lime wedge, and whole Cheetos. Serve immediately.

THE BEST LACROIX
HANGOVER CURES

BY MAXINE BUILDER

Some of the best hangover cures are born of necessity, in a dash to the fridge the morning after to find something that will hydrate you, keep you awake, and prevent you from yacking. That's how I came to know LaCroix as a hangover cure.

You can't really go wrong with any flavor, but there are some that will cure a hangover more effectively than others. I'm partial to lemon LaCroix for mornings when I'm looking to take a cold can of sparkling water straight to the face, maybe because I don't have the wherewithal to do more than pop a tab on a can. The strong citrus scent perks me up, the bubbles settle my stomach, and the water makes me start to feel human, and hydrated, again. Peach-pear LaCroix is a divisive flavor, but I also find it's a reliable hangover cure on

its own. It might have something to do with the fact that pear juice is a scientifically-supported hangover cure (Australian researchers found consuming pear juice before alcohol will lessen hangover symptoms the next day), but since peach-pear LaCroix only includes natural flavors of pear, not the juice itself, I doubt it.

Sparkling waters like LaCroix are pretty effective at getting you hydrated, but to make the most of it as a cure, mix it with other brunch beverages—because sometimes you still need a little hair of the dog with your seltzer. Try one out the next time you wake up with that cottonmouth and a pounding headache in the middle of a spinning room, and you'll believe me when I say that LaCroix makes everything better, even hangovers.

COFFEE AND LACROIX

Coffee is not generally recommended as a hangover cure because it is a diuretic that will dehydrate you more. Sometimes, when I'm hungover, the thought of the taste of coffee makes my stomach turn, but I know that I need something caffeinated in order to make it through the day, which is how I came up with this coffee and LaCroix combo. The mix of sparkling water and coffee is a one-two punch—with the sparkling water offsetting the negative, dehydrating effects of coffee. Plus, fizzy coffee is totally a thing right now, so you'd be so on trend. You've got two options here, depending on what's readily available to you. ½ **glass cold brew + coconut LaCroix** or **ice + espresso shot + orange LaCroix**

CHAMPAGNE AND LACROIX

Sometimes you need a little bit of alcohol to help take the edge off your hangover. Replace the orange juice in your mimosa with tangerine LaCroix. This works best if you have a leftover bottle of sparkling wine from the night before. Pour that into a glass and top with either pamplemousse or tangerine LaCroix. Again, using chilled sparkling water is going to get you the best results.

CIDER VINEGAR AND LACROIX

People who love apple cider vinegar really love apple cider vinegar and tend to claim it's a cure-all for everything that might ail you. But ACV, as it's known among health food aficionados, can actually be a great hangover cure. It's something about enzymes or balancing your pH? I've never been too clear on the science, but I do know that drinking a tablespoon of apple cider vinegar that's been diluted with a full can of apricot LaCroix and a lot of ice cubes will put your stomach at ease and make your head feel less cloudy.

BITTERS AND (BERRY) LACROIX

Seltzer and bitters is one of those strange hangover cures that you don't think is going to work, but then you drink it, and you're like, "Oh." Bitters are a traditional cure for an upset stomach, and though they're generally paired with citrus-y drinks, try them with berry LaCroix.

The Orange Juice Boycott That Changed America

BY JOHN BIRDSALL

As she heeded the call to come on down, descending *The Price Is Right* audience riser wearing a headscarf with juicy swirls of lemon, tangerine, and lime, Yolanda Bowsley's breasts jiggled out of her tube top. Producers flashed a thick blue bar over the contestant's naked bits, people in the studio howled, but Bowsley looked neither freaked nor ashamed. Meanwhile, on ABC's new sitcom *Three's Company*—a show with double entendres about three-ways and casual lust—a pair of tangy orange throw pillows on the set's central couch visually throbbed, the implied accoutrements of seduction. Sexual freedom in 1977 tended to express itself in fearless, provocative hues of citrus.

But not for the queen of orange juice herself. Not for Anita Bryant, who wore shirtdresses the color of lemon meringue pie filling and tangerine cap-sleeve bodices as if they were the armor of the righteous in battle. Bryant saw sexual openness as a challenge to God's order, a threat to what she liked to call "straight and normal America." It lacked decency. It corrupted children. It had to be stopped.

Bryant had been Miss Oklahoma once, beautiful, with pale skin and dark eyes. She was Jackie Kennedy with a hard-spray flip and a soft country twang, raised on church suppers and sticky flour gravy. As a tightly poised pop singer in the early '60s, she'd built a shortstack of hits, earning three gold records. She married her manager, Bob Green, a hunk with a handsome mess of sandy hair who knew how to pair a blazer with a turtleneck. They were a dream couple, country stylish like Elvis and Priscilla but without the obvious diet pills and demons. They lived in a six-bedroom mansion on Miami Beach's North Bay Road, where palms rustled and clouds billowed like rococo scrollwork framing a crystal blue sky.

In 1969 Bryant began her second and most lucrative career—the Florida Citrus Commission, a politically powerful consortium of the state's largest growers, crowned Bryant the Sunshine State's official OJ Sweetheart. She became the star of TV spots and magazine ads, a lifestyle ambassador for frozen concentrated orange juice.

In an early commercial, Bryant strolls a sunny citrus grove, stabs a spigot in a dangling orange and sings a loping jingle, "Come to the Florida Sunshine Tree," as a five-foot glass fills with juice. She tugs the spigot out and collects the last golden sluice in a tumbler of normal size. She sips. And in an Oklahoma drawl that's genuine, gentle, and perfect, with just enough post-production echo to make it sound infallible, Bryant drops the tagline: "Breakfast without orange juice is like a day without sunshine."

Per capita American OJ consumption would end up just about filling the Citrus Commission's mighty sloshing prop glass. Houseware manufacturers like Libbey included pony-size juice tumblers in starter sets. Bars invited in a back squad of OJ party cocktails—Screwdrivers and Tequila Sunrises—to soak up the glut of concentrated juice. They invented the Alabama Slammer and the Harvey Wallbanger to keep things percolating in fern bars and fairway lounges.

There was something else bending in OJ's favor: a cultural tilt South. Starting in 1969, the collapse of the Rust Belt—factories in the Northeast and Upper Midwest closing, towns boarding up, labor unions shrinking—became an unavoidable narrative for papers and the evening news. The Sun Belt, a made-up political projection encompassing a westward sweep of the map from Jacksonville to San Diego, was where a new conservatism was spreading like the creep of subdivisions in the desert near Phoenix. Orange juice was, in a way, the Sun Belt's symbol: healthy, wholesome, and optimistic, like…well, sunshine. Anita was its avatar. Then she became its avenging angel.

The year Bryant stabbed that orange with a spigot, 1969, was a year of events more tumultuous billowing up North. At New York City's Stonewall Inn, demonstrations smoldered for days following a routine bust of queers, trans women, and drag queens that set off a riot, the official start of the gay liberation movement. In spite of an ambient distaste for homosexuals and the lack of even one openly gay or lesbian elected official anywhere in the nation, by the end of 1976, legislative bodies in 40 cities and counties and one state (Pennsylvania) had passed LGBT nondiscrimination laws in some form. An enlightened consensus was jelling. It said citizens shouldn't be fired, or evicted, or denied service because they were gay, all standard under the old rules when America discriminated righteously to thwart sodomy and other acts of moral degeneracy. But righteousness didn't evaporate in the heat of Stonewall. Righteousness festered, biding its time.

As 1977 dawned in South Florida, liberals on the Miami-Dade County Commission passed a pretty standard homosexual nondiscrimination ordinance. Religious conservatives, including Bryant, representing her church, drew a line in the pale, sugar-fine sand. She spoke against the ordinance at a Commission hearing, arguing that the ordinance violated her rights as a person of faith. When it passed anyway, Bryant promised retribution, spinning a metaphor that, consciously or not, conjured a vision of Florida orange groves choked by a homosexual radicalism inching its sinister tendrils toward Washington and the Constitution. "The seed of sexual sickness," Bryant said, "that germinated in Dade County has already been transplanted by misguided liberals in the U.S. Congress."

Bryant's retribution came weeks later, when she and her allies delivered, in an enormous bulging old

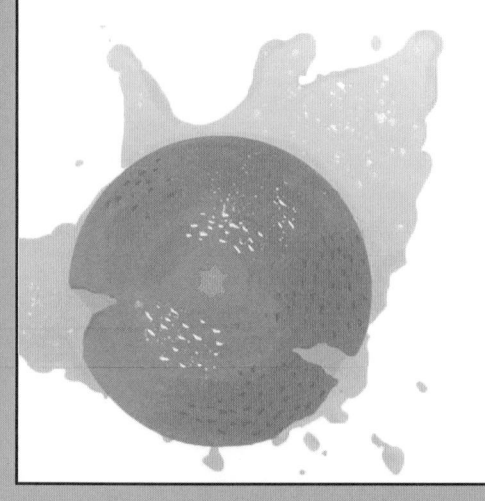

suitcase wheeled into the county registrar's office on a dolly, signatures in favor of calling a special referendum on the Miami-Dade ordinance. Bryant and her allies launched Save Our Children, to urge voters to bury the homosexual nondiscrimination ordinance with a special referendum in June. Children were the true victims of the ordinance, which enabled homosexuals (and especially gay teachers) to bend the innocents to a menacing evil. "Gays can't reproduce," Bryant would say—often—in variations on the line, "so they have to recruit."

Gay and lesbian political groups nationally saw what was happening: Suddenly, Miami was America's test case for the strength of the nascent homosexual civil rights movement. And they were going up against a star, a woman with a national profile, with the strength of one of Florida's major industries tacitly, at least, behind her. They were up against the queen of frozen concentrated orange juice herself.

Some raised money to send to activists in Miami defending the ordinance. Jim Toy, an LGBT-rights pioneer in Michigan, remembers driving from Ann Arbor to Detroit to make the round of gay bars with a donation jar. Others tried to hurt Bryant at the source of her fame. "We didn't know any way to get back at her," says Wayne Friday, who in 1977 was president of San Francisco's Tavern Guild, a powerful association of gay bar owners and employees. "So we just targeted orange juice."

Weeks after the Miami-Dade special referendum was called, gay bars across the U.S. were boycotting orange juice from the Sunshine State, and activists including Harvey Milk, a vocal organizer in the new queer scene in San Francisco's Castro neighborhood, were urging people to drop it at breakfast. Consumer boycotts were a persuasive tactic of the left, starting with farm labor organizer Cesar Chavez's call in 1966 for shoppers to shun California grapes and lettuce. In 1977, organized labor called for a boycott of Coors beer to protest the company's labor practices, its union-busting and alleged racism and homophobia. But the Florida orange juice boycott was the first organized by gay and lesbian activists. They called it a gaycott. And it

ORANGE JUICE WAS, IN A WAY, THE SUN BELT'S SYMBOL: HEALTHY, WHOLESOME, AND OPTIMISTIC, LIKE…WELL, SUNSHINE. ANITA WAS ITS AVATAR. THEN SHE BECAME ITS AVENGING ANGEL.

was strongest in what was, in 1977, the gayest city in America.

In April, San Francisco's Tavern Guild printed up notices on orange construction paper for its member bars to post. The signs didn't state so much as throw down: "TO PROMOTE HUMAN RIGHTS this establishment DOES NOT SERVE FLORIDA ORANGE JUICE or orange juice from CONCENTRATE."

Wayne Friday says the public boycott started at a Polk Street bar, the N'Touch. Friday tended bar there. "Bars up and down Polk Street," Friday says, "they'd have a thing where they'd say, 'Okay, at 11 in the morning everybody pour out your orange juice in the street.' We even got some non-gay bars to do it. The police would get a little mad but the city would just wash down the street."

In some bars you could get a Screwdriver for half price if you brought in your own sack of oranges and squeezed them yourself, on little hand squeezers set out on the bar. You could bring in your own juice, but you had to know what you were carrying. "God help you if you brought a bottle of orange juice that was from Florida," Friday says. "I've seen a bartender take it off the bar, look at the label, and pour it right down the drain." Other bars pushed Greyhounds (vodka and grapefruit juice). Dan Perlman, a member of Ann Arbor's Gay Student Union during the boycott, remembers a horrible grapefruit Tequila Sunrise, though a grapefruit Alabama Slammer tasted better (and still tastes better, he says) than the OJ original.

In his April 14 column for the Bay Area Reporter, a weekly gay newspaper, Harvey Milk urged readers to switch to pineapple juice for breakfast. "Some say that ONE can of OJ won't make any difference," he wrote. "Before Bryant becomes more powerful, remember that your ONE can adds up to millions of ONE cans throughout the nation. The only way to stop this bigot is to have a fully effective economic boycott."

A queer cottage industry of anti-Anita protest gear popped up, with oranges as symbols of active (and sometimes passive) defiance: "Anita, Dear... Cram It"; "Stop V.D. Fuck Oranges." People wore orange buttons that said "Squeeze Anita!" "A Day Without Human Rights Is Like a Day Without Sunshine" read a popular T-shirt in all-caps bold, under a rough-skinned orange lurking like the Death Star.

Bryant spent the five months of the Miami-Dade campaign defiant, showing up at her church school to sing "Glory, Glory Hallelujah" with kindergartners as props. "Anita Bryant was once known as an orange juice saleswoman," the local Miami NBC affiliate reported. "Not anymore. With a religious fervor that has made her the nation's most controversial woman overnight, she has been selling her Save Our Children group."

Bryant portrayed her own martyrdom at the hand of the gaycott. "They're coming, attacking my livelihood," Bryant told a TV reporter, "and it has undermined a 10-year relationship with Florida citrus of goodwill. But I feel strongly, and I have great faith in God, that he's going to take care of me. I'm not afraid. I have not been moved in that respect. And I do not believe that the product and the people I represent will be intimidated by that kind of a force." She vowed to fight on, even if what she called her livelihood (in 1977 the Florida Citrus Commission paid her $100,000; adjusted for inflation that's a little over $400,000 today) was stripped from her.

SUDDENLY, MIAMI WAS AMERICA'S TEST CASE FOR THE STRENGTH OF THE NASCENT HOMOSEXUAL CIVIL RIGHTS MOVEMENT. AND THEY WERE GOING UP AGAINST A STAR, A WOMAN WITH A NATIONAL PROFILE, WITH THE STRENGTH OF ONE OF FLORIDA'S MAJOR INDUSTRIES TACITLY, AT LEAST, BEHIND HER. THEY WERE UP AGAINST THE QUEEN OF FROZEN CONCENTRATED ORANGE JUICE HERSELF.

"We're dealing with a vile and a vicious and a vulgar gang," a young Jerry Falwell, Bryant's supporter, said of Save Our Children's foes.

The gays and their allies were simply outplayed. Save Our Children hired a Republican political consultant to produce a devastating ad, contrasting Miami's annual Orange Bowl Parade with the San Francisco Pride march. The image of a baton twirler at the Orange Bowl, a girl with rosy cheeks, in a white, stylized military uniform, gives way to washed-out footage from San Francisco of a shirtless man in worn jeans and feathered hair, pelvic-thrusting on a float with a sad-looking palm tree, then cuts to another man in a black jockstrap and studded leather halter.

"The Orange Bowl Parade," you hear a man say in voiceover, "Miami's gift to the nation, wholesome entertainment. But in San Francisco, when they take to the streets, it's a parade of homosexuals, men hugging other men, cavorting with little boys. The same people who turned San Francisco into a hotbed of homosexuality want to do the same thing to Dade County." The dystopian gay metropolis appears furtive and frantic, fueled by speed and menace.

They never really had a chance, the gays and lesbians on OJ pickets at supermarkets or arguing their case at grocery co-op meetings, squeezing oranges or passing donation jars in gay bars. They thought the cause of civil rights, pretty much alone, would rally voters of conscience. They expected easier grounds for common cause with other minorities who'd suffered oppression.

As election news from 3,000 miles away seeped in through TVs, bars bumping Thelma Houston and Donna Summer emptied onto the streets of San Francisco's burgeoning gay neighborhood that chilly night in June. By a two-to-one margin, voters in Dade County had killed the nondiscrimination ordinance. At an event she called the Lord's victory supper, Anita Bryant was gleamingly triumphant. She vowed to take the fight to every city, county seat, and state capitol in the nation with laws protecting gay people.

The crowd in San Francisco marched from the Castro to Polk Street, chanting, carrying candles in Dixie cups. They milled around City Hall, returned to the Castro, and sat down in a busy intersection. Harvey Milk marched at the head of the crowd; later he spoke. Nobody had seen such a large and spontaneous takeover of the streets by so many calling themselves "faggots" and "dykes." "I feel like the bill of rights has been wadded up on a cheap piece of paper and thrown in the wastebasket," a woman told a radio reporter that night. You could hear her anger.

Others glimpsed a measure of victory in defeat. Bob Kunst, Bryant's opponent on the ground in Miami, said the ordinance fight had galvanized world opinion. "She gave us every access to world media," Kunst said from the post-referendum party in a quietly reflective mood

"A DAY WITHOUT HUMAN RIGHTS IS LIKE A DAY WITHOUT SUNSHINE" READ A POPULAR T-SHIRT IN ALL-CAPS BOLD, UNDER A ROUGH-SKINNED ORANGE LURKING LIKE THE DEATH STAR.

at the Fontainebleau in Miami Beach. "We had over 50,000 news clippings, this was the turning point where 'gay' became a household word, and we opened up the entire debate on human sexuality."

For Milk, defeat was a reckoning, a reminder that gays and lesbians had to unify, to organize, and most of all to come out. Later that year, Milk would become the first openly gay person to be elected to public office in America. Just 17 months later he'd be assassinated, shot by a former cop, but not before he'd inspired a more active national LGBT movement and urged every one of the estimated 15 million queer Americans to come out to President Jimmy Carter, by letter. It wasn't until 1998, 20 years later, that Dade County passed a new gay and lesbian rights ordinance. It's still in effect, though conservative groups tried to repeal it in 2002.

The orange juice gaycott went on after the referendum, petering out gradually. Bryant continued the work of Save Our Children; she was met with picket lines and protests everywhere she went. In Iowa, a protester nailed her with a cream pie. It is, perhaps, the enduring image of Anita, flicking pie crust out of one eye, praying for the man who threw it.

"At first the Florida Citrus Commission was bombarded," Bryant told the Miami Herald after the referendum. "I guess people had nothing better to do than to write and to boycott. Then the mothers of America retaliated, I think. Sales are up 15 percent over last year. The citrus people say I'm a private citizen, that I can express my views." It was an exaggeration, or wishful thinking. Two weeks after the referendum the public relations spokesman for Florida citrus said he wished Bryant would resign. At the end of 1978, in the same month Milk was assassinated, Bryant was fired. In 1980 she and Bob Green divorced. She experienced bankruptcy and decline. In 1990, trying to make a comeback with a new album, Bryant told *Inside Story* she had no regrets about what she did in Dade County in 1977. "I don't regret it because I did the right thing." She now lives quietly in Oklahoma.

On the night of the referendum, people called in to Fruit Punch, a gay radio show broadcast across the bay from San Francisco in Berkeley, to express their anger, fear, or despair. "I just about broke down in tears, something like this happening in our country," a woman said in a weary tone. Another seemed almost chipper in her resolve. "I'm not gay myself," she explained. "I just want to say that Anita Bryant has made me really mad because she's wasting her time on negative things."

She said she had a solution, said it with the optimism of the perpetually just. "We are giving up orange juice."

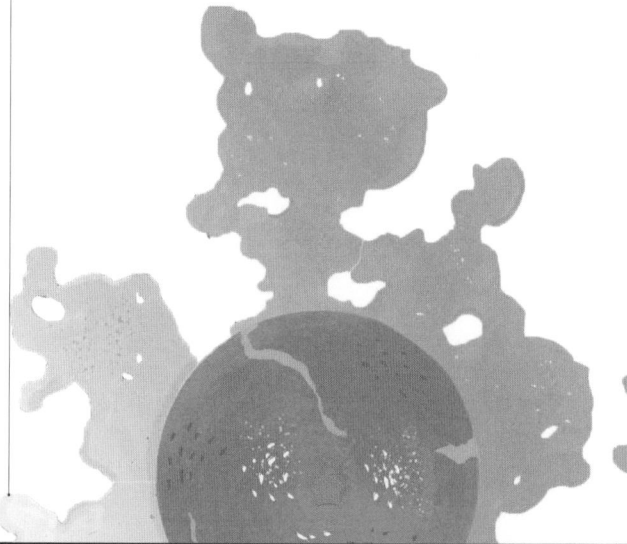

CHAPTER THREE

REGIONAL

MEATS

Goetta - ('get-a): the "O" is silent, until you try it.

Come To
GLIER'S
GOETTAFEST
Newport at
the Levee
August 6,7,8 & 9

GLIER'S
GOETTA

ORIGINAL

ORIGINAL

ORIGINAL

ORIGINAL

Goetta Is Crispy, Mushy, and Perfect in Every Way

BY KEITH PANDOLFI

Cleaning out my freezer on a recent Sunday morning, I pulled out an assortment of oddities: a two-year-old pork chop from the grocery store down the street; a three-year-old package of biscuit mix from Tupelo Honey, in Knoxville; a Krackel bar from this past Halloween. But as I dug deeper into the frozen abyss, I felt something unexpected that sent a wave of excitement through my Cincinnati-raised soul: It was solid and slick and cylindrical, wrapped tightly in plastic and twisted shut on each end by two metal clamps. *No effing way,* I thought. But, yes, pulling it from the depths, I read the words I hoped to see: Glier's Goetta. My God. Glier's Goetta.

To a homesick Cincinnatian, those words are as comforting as a bowl of Skyline Chili or walking into a bar and unexpectedly catching a Reds game on TV. Goetta—pronounced "get-uh"—is the city's signature contribution to the world of breakfast meats, and something that, despite the food media's obsession with regional cuisines, has remained largely confined to southern Ohio and northern Kentucky.

For the uninitiated, goetta is usually a mixture of pork shoulder and sometimes beef, which is ground together with onions, spices, and, most notably, pinhead oats. It is formed into a loaf, chilled, sliced, and fried in a skillet. It is to Cincinnati breakfast joints what scrapple is to Philadelphia, and grits are to Charleston. But let my highly biased opinion be clear: It's better. It's so much better. Even so, while I love goetta more than any other breakfast side, it took me a while to come around to it.

Growing up, we didn't eat goetta all that much in my family. As transplants from Massachusetts, it simply wasn't on our radar. I wasn't all that into sausage that much either. Aside from a bite or two off my parents' plates at Bob Evans or Bill Knapp's, I didn't eat it. It was far too greasy, too salty, too porky. I felt the same way each time Dad ordered sausage on our LaRosa's pizza, or served Italian sausage at home, tucked into a plateful of ziti.

A dislike of sausage is a shameful thing in Cincinnati. After all, our economy was practically built on the backs of our sows and stags. In the mid-1800s, the city was known as Porkopolis—it packed, shipped, and slaughtered more pigs than any other place in the world. From late fall through deep winter, the streets of Cincinnati ran wild with swine, so much so that nineteenth-century residents often tossed their garbage into the streets at night, knowing it'd be devoured by packs of hungry piglets by morning. Cincinnati was also home to an enormous German population, which settled in a neighborhood just across a canal from downtown that was dubbed, none too kindly, Over-the-Rhine. There, German butchers made and sold

BUT THEN I KEPT ON EATING IT. AND THEN I STARTED CRAVING IT. LIKE A MILKY CUP OF DINER COFFEE OR A LETHAL DRUG, EVENTUALLY I COULDN'T IMAGINE LIFE WITHOUT IT.

a cornucopia of bratwursts and mettwurst, blood sausage, and other German specialties, including, of course, goetta.

Goetta is what's known as *grützwurst*, a sausage made from ground pork and grain. Most people place it in the scrapple family, even though it's stretched out with steel-cut oats instead of cornbread. To me, it's less mushy, more porky, and generally more flavorful. Instead of the offal found in scrapple, it's often made with braised pork shoulder, and sometimes beef. Throughout most of the twentieth century, it remained a little-known holdover from the old days, something the city's German grandmas would whip up for Sunday breakfast, or something you might find at a good German butcher shop or an old German restaurant.

As I grew older, I noticed goetta gaining traction on restaurant menus, as well as in people's homes. I'm not sure why, exactly. Maybe it was something everyone was ashamed of for a time but eventually admitted they couldn't live without. As a teenager I never had a burning desire to try it, despite the encouragement of a friend's German-American parents, or a waitress at the local diner, where I sat in a booth drunk on Miller Genuine Draft at 2 a.m.

"It's like sausage," old people would tell me. "Just try it." Eventually, and very reluctantly, I did. And while it wasn't a revelation per se, I thought it was just fine.

But then I kept on eating it. And then I started craving it. Like a milky cup of diner coffee or a lethal drug, eventually I couldn't imagine life without it. I fell hard for how the outsides got all caramelized and crispy and how the insides were mouthwateringly mushy. I loved how it broke up so easily, making it perfect for mashing into a hash with my eggs-over-easy. It's salty as any breakfast sausage, but the oats make goetta seem lighter somehow, less cloying, and they even give it a bit of a chew. It changed my attitude toward sausage, serving as a gateway to the boudin, andouille, braunschweiger, and even scrapple I came to love later in life while living in the South.

Sure, you can order goetta from Glier's—they make it with offal, including hearts and, well, minds (brains). I also love the beefier version of goetta that comes from Eckerlin Meats, a beloved butcher shop in Cincinnati's Findlay Market that's been making goetta for more than a century. Still, I'm pretty steadfast in my belief that regional foods should always be experienced in their native lands. So yes—YES, you have to go to Cincinnati to truly experience goetta. Because eating goetta requires feeling goetta. And feeling goetta requires a trip to Cincinnati, or maybe a trip just across the Ohio River in Covington, Kentucky, when Glier's hosts Goettafest.

There are a lot of restaurants that serve goetta in Greater Cincinnati, some simply, some fancily. Among the best are The Echo in Hyde Park, where it's served as part of the Glier's German Greats breakfast, alongside two eggs, potato cakes, baked apples, and toast. The best late-night goetta can be found in Covington, at the Anchor Grill, where you can wolf it down with a few cups of black coffee and pray that it'll suck up all the beer in your stomach.

Long under the radar of more highfalutin chefs, goetta is also finding its way into our more lauded establishments. At Senate, chef Daniel Wright often serves his Goetta Superstar Hot Dog, which features fried goetta with pickled ramps, lettuce, and foie gras. At Yat Ka Mein in the city's Oakley neighborhood, it's

a component of their Goetta Fried Rice. There's goetta quiche and goetta omelets and goetta nachos. When I visit the city next time, I'm going to try goetta pizza. I dream of that friggin' pizza. God willing, it'll be as good as it sounds.

Still, there's one place I like to eat goetta more than any other. It's a diner in Over-the-Rhine called Tucker's, owned by Joe Tucker and his wife, Carla. Tucker fries his up (he gets it from Eckerlin; his dad did, too) on a flattop like nobody's business. As the meat sizzles and the oats pop, he'll talk to whoever's listening about the Bengals maybe winning a playoff game one of these days, or the Reds getting their pitching game together. He might even talk about the old days at that punk rock club in Clifton, where he met Carla way back when. She was a manager at a Gap outlet in Kenwood, and he was determined to never, ever work for the family diner his mom and dad opened in the 1950s. But once that goetta arrives on your plate, you'll be happy he did, and that Carla quit working at the Gap to join him. That goetta is something worth devoting your life to; that goetta is something worth learning to love.

HEADCHEESE, SOUSE, AND YOUR PATH TO ENLIGHTENMENT

When life hands you a pig's head, make headcheese or souse—two closely related, rustic meat loaves made by boiling down a pig's head, tucking the scraps into a mold, chilling, slicing, and serving. How this pig's head happens to trot into your life, that's your business. Pig heads happen. They're not an anomaly. There's pretty much one per every four legs and splendid belly, and it would be a terrible shame to waste one—especially when there's so much rich, succulent meat in there, plus the bones. My god. The bones.

A head is chockablock with bones, and simmering them down for a few hours brings out the rich gelatin that binds the meat together. That's plenty of people's nexus of yuck when it comes to headcheese (which BTW, involves no dairy) and souse (which is pretty much just headcheese with extra vinegar), but if you're down with bone broth, you're halfway there. It's all just meat water at various levels of gelatinousness, but then again, so are we, man. So are we.

Basic Headcheese

1 pig's head, split

2 pig's feet

2 bay leaves

2 tablespoons allspice

Salt

Hot sauce or chile flakes

1. Place the head and feet and bay leaves in a large stockpot with enough water to cover them. Boil until the meat falls off the bones. Remove meat and bones from the water.

2. Mince the meat finely, picking out any small bones or excess fat. Strain the liquid. Refrigerate the liquid and the meat overnight, then skim off the grease.

3. Boil the liquid down until there is just enough to cover the meat. Add the meat and seasonings, to taste. It should be slightly thick after the meat is added.

4. Pour into molds and chill until jelly forms and it is firm enough to slice.

(continued)

Basic Souse

1 pig's head

6 pig's feet

6 pork hocks

2 teaspoons salt

¼ teaspoon pepper

1 bay leaf

2 onions, sliced

3 peppercorns

1 blade mace

¼ cup cider vinegar

1. Split the head in half, and place all of the pig parts in a large pot with enough water to cover them. Add the salt, pepper, and bay leaf; bring the water to a boil, and cook the meat until tender.

2. Remove the meat from the water and cool. When the meat has cooled, pick it off the bones and chop it into small pieces. Add the onions and spices to the liquid and boil until it's reduced by half. Remove bay leaf. Strain, cool, and skim the fat.

3. Put the meat, fat, and vinegar in a pot and bring to a boil. Remove from the heat, pour it into a mold and add as much of the spiced liquid as the container can hold.

4. Chill until firm; slice, and serve.

Souse

Headcheese

How to Make Scrapple, the Hearty Pennsylvania Breakfast Meat

Say you find yourself in possession of a pig's heart and liver, ground buckwheat and cornmeal, and about an hour and a half to kill. There's only one thing you should absolutely do: make scrapple. Some uninformed people like to make fun of the Pennsylvania breakfast dish because they think it's weird, but they haven't tried Patti Jackson's. The chef at Delaware and Hudson in Brooklyn makes a rich and creamy scrapple loaf that you'll scarf down like iron-rich candy. So swing by your butcher shop to buy the necessary offal and make scrapple. Don't fear things you don't understand!

- 1 celery stalk, coarsely chopped
- ½ medium onion, coarsely chopped
- 1 thyme sprig
- 1 sage sprig
- 1 tablespoon salt
- 1 medium-size pork heart (8 to 10 ounces)
- 1 medium-size pork liver (14 to 18 ounces)
- 3 cups coarse cornmeal
- 1 cup ground buckwheat
- 2 tablespoons of very finely chopped sage
- 2 teaspoons salt
- 1 teaspoon ground black pepper

1. Bring 2 quarts of water to a boil with the celery, onion, thyme, sage sprig, and 1 tablespoon of salt. Add pork heart and simmer for 1 hour (until tender enough to pierce with a fork; replenish water if needed). Add the liver and continue cooking for 15 minutes, or until liver is cooked through. Remove the heart and liver and cool; discard the water and vegetables. Finely chop the heart and liver.

2. Meanwhile, bring 1 gallon of water to a rapid boil and slowly whisk in cornmeal and buckwheat. Reduce temperature and cook until thick, stirring often with a wooden spoon.

3. Add the heart, liver, chopped sage, salt, and pepper. Stir constantly for 5 to 10 minutes until quite thick and well blended.

4. Pour into 2 greased loaf pans and press oiled or wax paper on top to prevent a crust. Cool thoroughly, for about 1 hour.

5. Turn solid scrapple out of pan onto a cutting board. Slice.

6. Heat a large sauté pan, add a neutral oil, like vegetable or canola oil, and a small knob of butter. Add scrapple slices when butter is foamy, and cook over medium heat until nicely crisp and golden. Scrapple will keep well in the refrigerator for 4 to 5 days or can be frozen.

NOTE

You can use stone-ground buckwheat flour, but I prefer to use whole buckwheat ground in a coffee grinder.

The Case for Taylor Ham, New Jersey's Beloved Mystery Meat

BY JIM BEHRLE

The perfect breakfast sandwich looks pretty similar throughout our great land. Some combination of eggs, cheese, bread, and bacon is required. Bacon has been passed down to us directly from heaven to reward us for being Americans. But I'm not here to praise bacon. Bacon needs no praise. Many religions forbid bacon—that is how good it is and how little new praise it needs. I have come to praise—wait for it—New Jersey.

Ben and I were younger men when we decided to move to New Jersey. Ben in his late 60s, I just nibbling into my 40s. We had come from Williamsburg, Brooklyn, land of artisanal sausage and fancy brunches, looking for a simpler way of life. We had heard tales of a magical PATH train that ushered people into New York with stops in places like Grove St. and Exchange Place. They sounded like parts of Narnia to me, a Brooklyn-wearied soul. My ten-plus years in Brooklyn had been a never-ending journey of being priced out of neighborhoods. As a gentrifier, I had never anticipated the green wave. All the empty storefronts on my block became wine bars overnight, and I was quietly shown the door. We decided, being broke, we would look for lodging where even the brave dared not follow. I said, "Staten Island!" Ben said, "Jersey City!"

No one names their son or daughter Jersey City. Unlike the word Brooklyn it does not adorn the signs of Parisian skateshops as a conch call to the young and cool. Jersey City was named Jersey City because people here were working too hard to even come up with a cool name for it. It was called Bergen back when Peter Stuyvesant roamed the fair shores of the Hackensack, peg-legging up and down its greenish sloping fields. Near our house in the currently gentrifying Journal Square area, Lafayette once ate breakfast beneath an apple tree on Stuyvesant land with George Washington himself. They chatted wildly, arms waving about. They spoke of revolution and the Revolutionary War. They spoke of the desires of all people to live free. And they ate Taylor Ham sandwiches.

There is no proof that Taylor Ham sandwiches were eaten at this historical encounter. But there is no proof they weren't. Taylor Ham sandwiches are the preferred breakfast sandwich of all self-respecting New Jerseyans— and of interlopers like me who are trying hard to fit in. Most New Jerseyans are not filled with self-respect. I take it you have heard of Chris Christie. We've elected him governor twice. We're a rage-fueled people. We rage through traffic. We rage as we pay our taxes. And what fuels this rage? A strange, round mystery meat.

If an invisible line separates New York and New Jersey, a real-estate line that only the most foolish and fearless ever bravely cross, then let's imagine a line separates the top of New Jersey from the bottom. Cut it down the middle and you'll have a rough estimate of the demarcation line between "Taylor Ham" and "Pork Roll." In the Northern parts of New Jersey we proudly celebrate the expansive vision of our dear John Taylor, popularizer of the brand that has captured the popular imagination of New Jersey breakfasts for generations. Below, in the darker reaches of the bowels of South Jersey and further into Philadelphia, Delaware, Maryland, and other netherlands, they call this majestic creature a "Pork Roll," a tip of the cap to the fact that it does not technically fit the legal definition of pork as laid down in the Pure Food and Drug Act of 1906. When the government starts passing laws against your breakfast choices, you know you must be on the right path. Legislation is pending before the New Jersey Legislature to decide the "Taylor Ham"/"Pork Roll" divide that has split this great land. Governor Christie, on his radio program, decreed that the sandwich was officially "Taylor Ham, egg, and cheese" but then added "on a hard roll," which opened bread-related controversy.

Here are some lyrics from the Ween song "Pork Roll Egg and Cheese":

So dynamic is life, staring into the sight's
Not right, but wrong in a good way
So momma, if you please, pass me the pork roll egg
*   and cheese*
If you please, on a kaiser bun.

"Wrong in a good way" is the best explanation of a Taylor Ham sandwich. (If you can believe that there is a rivalry in New Jersey as to which part of New Jersey is the best part of New Jersey I have decided to ally myself with the North, naturally. North Jersey rules!) A soft bologna-hued disc with white spots vigorously sprinkled throughout, a slice of Taylor Ham may look unremarkable upon first inspection. Is this a slice of bologna? No, if it were bologna it would say "bologna" on the box. And it does come in a box, further deepening its allure. Just as we are told not to ask what is in a delicious sausage, we should not wonder what is the difference between this pale, speckled meat and other meats. Suffice it to say, the people who know meats best know there is a difference. Let us trust their judgment and think not of it. It is a pale, speckled wheel of drab nothingness. That is, until it is fried.

Taylor Ham sandwich recipes call for one to cut the circle of meat in four places at compass headings. Are we calling upon the Father, Son, and Holy Ghost to forgive our bodies of the damage we are about to do? Possibly, but that's just the Catholic altar boy in me talking.

TAYLOR HAM SANDWICHES ARE THE PREFERRED BREAKFAST SANDWICH OF ALL SELF-RESPECTING NEW JERSEYANS— AND OF INTERLOPERS LIKE ME WHO ARE TRYING HARD TO FIT IN. MOST NEW JERSEYANS ARE NOT FILLED WITH SELF-RESPECT. I TAKE IT YOU HAVE HEARD OF CHRIS CHRISTIE.

He must be muted by delicious breakfast meats with great regularity. I assume there is a reason. Along the lines of the reasons we don't feed mogwai after midnight. No matter how small or how random the rules are, they have been crafted by people who have made mistakes and tried to correct them. We tip our caps to all their efforts.

As the Taylor Ham cooks, its center begins to rise up from the pan dramatically. This is where the magic begins. There must be some magic to it. It is the kind of sandwich that one might say "will put hair on your chest." I want hair on my chest. Although I have lived many places in search of belonging, I find that I want to belong here in New Jersey most of all. Because others dismiss New Jersey as an armpit of a state, I believe that these hills must be filled with gold. Secret gold only the most careful of poet's eyes can see. There's also chromium. Lots of chromium, just covered over with asphalt. That you can certainly count on.

So after cutting this meat disc with scissors (I'm not exactly the Cake Boss) and watching it bubble at its core, I flip it over to see that it has been transformed beneath. And by transformed I mean browned pleasantly. The slice is a darker shade now, and it curls upward like a plunger top. The Taylor Ham slice does not require much cooking, but I trust cooking is a must. Bologna may be eaten cold; it is by nature a cold-cut. Taylor ham, with its red box and intricate plastic wrapping inside, yearns to be browned. Once brown it raises its sides and shouts "hooray!" at the fan above your stove.

Taylor Ham goes best with the yellowest of cheeses and the eggiest of eggs. I have tried a number of cheeses. Ben likes a horseradish cheddar that simply is not melty enough for a Taylor Ham sandwich as I understand them. Cabot cheddar is tastier but not sufficiently gooey. One does not put Cheez-Its in New England clam chowder. They make tasteless oyster crackers for that. For Taylor Ham sandwiches, one should find a cheese that lacks in taste but makes up for it in gooeyness and yellowhood. Just as the pork roll is not sufficiently ham to be ham, one must hunt out a cheese food that is not sufficiently cheese to be cheese.

Taylor Ham sandwiches have filled a hole inside me I didn't even know was there. The quickest way to belong to a place is to eat there. Home is where you don't shit where you eat, if I'm remembering that correctly. If I can become a New Jerseyan, a true New Jerseyan, simply by eating and being angry all the time, I believe I am on the right track. If Schlitz is the beer that made Milwaukee famous, the Taylor Ham sandwich is the thing New Jerseyans own. Like Snooki or toxic waste, it is ours and we ought to love it.

Even if I have enjoyed Taylor Ham sandwiches far and wide, my favorite is still the first one I ever had, from a food truck called Bill's Lunch. I don't think his real name is Bill, but his Taylor Ham sandwiches are really tasty and much neater looking than the ones I make myself. Bill's are the most perfect combination of toasted, gooey, and yellow, with cheese-like substance dripping down the side and a cut down the middle as if you were looking at the slice in a cadaver, up and down, open wide to see all the strange wonders inside. I recently asked him how many he sells. "A few a week," he said with a shrug, adding, "it's a New Jersey thing." Yes, yes. Yes, I desperately hope it is.

THE UNITED STATES OF GRAVY

SALT PORK & MILK GRAVY

HAMBURGER GRAVY

CHOCOLATE GRAVY

SAWMILL GRAVY

CORNMEAL GRAVY

SHRIMP GRAVY

CREAM GRAVY

RED EYE ROAST BEEF GRAVY

CHICKEN GRAVY

REDEYE HAM GRAVY

RED GRAVY

CHILI GRAVY

Squash and Spam Hash

Spam is often a punch line of a meat, but the canned mystery mush is almost comically good when it's hashed together with potatoes, fresh summer squash and zucchini, and powdered ranch dressing. Yup—ranch. The beloved blend of buttermilk, onion, garlic, herbs, and spices isn't just a savory foil for the salt-and-sugar-spiked pork, it also technically makes this dish a salad. Hey, we don't write the breakfast rules; we just enforce them.

¼ cup extra virgin olive oil, divided

1 can Spam, chopped

1 cup chopped onion

1 cup chopped potato

½ teaspoon kosher salt

1 cup corn kernels (fresh or frozen)

1 cup chopped yellow squash

1 cup chopped zucchini squash

3 tablespoons ranch seasoning mix

2 large eggs, fried

1. Add 1 tablespoon of the oil and Spam to a cast-iron skillet. Cook for 2 to 3 minutes over high heat or until Spam is golden brown. Remove from skillet and reserve.

2. Add 1 tablespoon of the oil and chopped onions to the skillet. Sauté onions for 3 minutes over medium heat until soft and translucent. Add potatoes and ½ teaspoon salt. Cook potatoes for 5 minutes or until a fork goes through the potatoes easily. Add remaining 1 to 2 tablespoons of oil, corn, squash, and zucchini. Cook for 3 to 4 minutes or until the vegetables are golden.

3. Ranch-ify the hash. Add reserved Spam and ranch seasoning mix to the skillet. Mix everything together and continue cooking for a few minutes. Slide onto a plate for serving.

4. Put an egg on it. Fry an egg in the same skillet, so it'll pick up more flavor. We suggest sunny-side up so it's easy to mix the runny yolk in with the hash, but you do you.

Why Livermush Matters to North Carolina

BY SHERI CASTLE

Even the most precocious child knows only what she knows. The term "square meal" baffled me as I sat at my grandmother's table and ate from round plates and bowls, except for the weekly livermush sandwiches she served between sunrise and the noon news. Anybody paying the least bit of attention could see that was a square meal: four-cornered slabs of crisply fried breakfast meat aligned between two slices of store-bought gauzy white bread of equal dimensions, edges as straight as if they'd been planed. People act like there's mystery about livermush, but the name (sometimes written as "liver mush") offers blatant clues to the main ingredients. There's pork liver and cornmeal mush. No one is selling a pig in a poke here.

On the other hand, such candid words are what make some people blanch and back up. Many people who enjoy charcuterie in which pig livers and lesser parts are pureed and molded find meats with tonier pseudonyms, such as pâté and terrine, more in their verbal comfort zone. As with many regional foodstuffs with a small footprint, at the mention of livermush, people either get a faraway look of reminiscence or take on an expression that says they'd rather stay far away.

Livermush is working-class and blue-collar. It hails from North Carolina hilltops and foothills that once hummed with tractors, textile mills, and furniture factories, manned by the foot soldiers of industry. For the most part, families that ate livermush lived frugally and made do with

FOOD THAT'S WEIRD TO PEOPLE WHO'VE NEVER HEARD OF IT ISN'T WEIRD TO THOSE WHO GREW UP EATING IT.

homemade. But most of them started buying commercially made livermush instead once it became available in country and company stores. The livermush business was born during the Depression, an unlikely time to launch a successful enterprise, unless you sold a product that hungry people could recognize, afford, and enjoy.

Unlike bacon and country ham (or, for that matter, chitlins), livermush never took off and captured a wider palate and audience. To this day, the epicenter of livermush is a handful of counties in western North Carolina that run partway up the sides of the Blue Ridge Mountains. In those loyal counties, where the five commercial producers—Mack's, Neese's, Jenkins, Hunter's, and Corriher's—remain, livermush is loved and feted. Wherever two or more are gathered in its name, a festival breaks out. Consider Mush, Music and Mutts in Shelby, North Carolina—the official but not only livermush festival, where, for one weekend in October, the downtown squirms with 10,000 people seeking a big time and a little livermush.

The angel is in the details when it comes to livermush. It shares lineage with scrapple, souse, headcheese, liver pudding, and other scrape-together pork products that utilize the slim pickings left from a fat pig, but it's not the same. Livermush is finely ground, fully cooked (but not smoked), and includes enough cornmeal binder to make it sliceable. It's smooth, but not slick. Rich, but not greasy. Seasoned, but not spicy.

Livermush comes in one-pound blocks the size and shape of a brick. The blocks were once sold neatly wrapped in butcher paper with perfectly creased, gift-wrap corners, but these days it comes sheathed in plastic. For serving, slabs sliced about a half-inch thick are seared in a greased cast-iron skillet, which works wonders, browning and crisping the outside while gently warming the inside. Cooked livermush fills the air with eau de innards, like giblets on Thanksgiving Day.

People eat livermush for breakfast meat alongside eggs, or on a sandwich made with sliced bread, toast, or maybe a biscuit (though that kind of square-peg-in-a-round-hole incongruity bugs me). Unlike sausage or bacon, livermush is never the base of gravy because it renders almost no grease. The simple sandwiches remain undressed other than a big squirt of yellow mustard. Not even Duke's mayonnaise or Miracle Whip.

I was served plenty of livermush when I was a little kid, mostly because my granddaddy loved it and my grandmother fixed what he loved, and in those days kids were fed as though they were family instead of a subspecies that requires pelleted food. I tapered off livermush as I grew up, learned to drive, and headed farther out into the world, where more meals were drive-through with friends instead of sit-down with family.

For about 30 years, there was one annual exception at the North Carolina State Fair. Neese's and/or Jenkins always had a booth in the Jim Graham Building in the heart of the fairgrounds. All day, workers cut bricks of livermush into bites the size of sugar cubes, fried them up, and stabbed them onto frill picks. Fairgoers would queue patiently, awaiting their turn to lift a pick from the tray, and pop that free bite into their mouths as though it were a communion wafer. The liver of our pigs, given for you. Even during the years I was staunchly, even insolently, vegetarian, I had my annual bite of livermush.

These days I don't eat livermush as often as I could, but I defend it as often as I can. Food that's weird to people who've never heard of it isn't weird to those who grew up eating it. Livermush matters to people who matter to me. I am from western North Carolina, and I know my place.

Merguez M'hancha Hits All Your Sweet and Savory Spots

M'hancha is a delicate pastry shaped like a snake—the word even translates to "snake pie" in Arabic. Traditionally stuffed with nuts and soaked in orange water and honey, the Moroccan dessert can go savory with the addition of merguez sausage. Don't let the tricky coiling technique deter you, and don't sweat it if you can't shape m'hancha like a pro. Phyllo dough is perfect for stitching together tears. Just patch and move on until your snake pie looks sufficiently snake-like.

1 pound merguez sausage, casing removed

3 tablespoons harissa

¼ cup pitted green olives, halved

¼ cup raisins

1 (16-ounce) box phyllo dough sheets

1 stick butter, melted

1. Preheat the oven to 350°F.

2. Heat a large nonstick skillet over medium-high. Add sausage and cook for 3 minutes, crumbling with a wooden spoon. Add harissa, olives, and raisins and continue cooking until sausage is browned.

3. Lay one sheet of phyllo flat and brush with melted butter, followed by another sheet of phyllo and more butter. Continue this until you've stacked 4 sheets of phyllo. Place about ¼ cup of the cooled merguez mixture across the edge closest to you. Carefully wrap the phyllo around the merguez and away from you. Brush the stuffed, rolled phyllo with butter and starting from one edge, carefully roll the phyllo like a snake coil.

4. Continue this process until all of the merguez filling is used, connecting each stuffed phyllo roll to the last as you coil. Don't worry if the phyllo rips. Just use some of the extra phyllo dough and melted butter to patch the holes.

5. Place the m'hancha in the oven and bake for 20 minutes or until golden brown. Let cool for a couple of minutes before slicing it.

Boudin Is a Sausage for All Seasons and All People

BY SARAH BAIRD

It's rare to encounter anyone who would admit to eating morning meat all by its lonesome. Bacon needs, at the very least, a side of toast. Ham's partnership with the almighty biscuit is accepted as gospel. Even lox doesn't really fly without the help of a bagel. But when it comes to boudin—the beloved, signature sausage of the Acadiana region in South Louisiana—most eaters lose the biscuit and forget the eggs. Boudin is a strong, independent sausage that doesn't need any propping up. It's a breakfast meat that stands out and stands alone.

It's convenient that there's practically a square meal contained within each casing. Made of ground pork, rice, green peppers, onion, and a blend of seasonings unique to the boudin-maker, the final product is surprisingly soft, often spice heavy, and—if executed properly—will have a texture that will make you learn to love the word "moist."

More often than not, boudin is simply cooked in hot water, but it can also be grilled, smoked, or sculpted into boudin balls and fried. (A particularly popular type of ball comes stuffed with molten pepper jack cheese. It's as swoon-worthy as it sounds.) Seafood boudin also makes frequent appearances, especially during Lent, when pork is a no-no on Fridays but your boudin cravings didn't get the memo. It's a morning food, to be sure, but it's also a midnight treat, afternoon snack, and hell—a dessert if you want it to be. Boudin is a sausage for all seasons and all people.

Throughout Acadiana, rice cookers filled with warm boudin links are about as omnipresent at gas stations as pots of burnt coffee, hinting at the sausage's best avenue of consumption: being eaten on the go. There's nothing more auspicious than smearing a little bit of boudin grease across your steering wheel at the start of the day as an edible sun salutation.

And while a person grabbing hold of a standard-issue link of Jimmy Dean and biting off a hunk seems like the alpha-dog move of a comically swole cartoon character, boudin really shouldn't be eaten any other way. Boudin offers a more tactile experience than other sausages, and to eat it with utensils is akin to knife-and-forking a piece of pizza. Cajun country doesn't generally allow a lot of room for shyness, and when it comes to their darling sausage, you're expected to get very intimate, very quickly. Most meat markets will hand over a link swaddled in a paper towel, but my preferred wrap-job method is tin foil, which more effectively keeps the boudin warm and can—with a little finagling—become a kind of porky push pop that's ideal for parking lot snacking.

Since boudin is a food in motion, it's also one that's tightly tethered to the highways and byways of the region. Get just a ways past Beaumont, Texas, coming east or Baton Rouge going west and you'll start to see billboard after billboard—Billy's! Best Stop! Don's!—calling out like porcine siren songs to hungry travelers. The billboards feature everything from an anthropomorphized boudin link with a goofy smile just asking to be eaten, to a cheery pig who's found itself in some hot water. An Acadiana-born friend recently reported that on Highway 90 there's a new sign reading, "Don't boo-day! Eat boudin!" (Boo-day, cheekily, being the Cajun French word for "pout.") Without fail, all claim that their boudin is the best.

"If you ask a dozen people in Lafayette who makes their favorite boudin, you will get a dozen answers—with a strong opinion," says Lafayette native and sausage expert Simone Reggie, owner of New Orleans-based, Simone's Market.

"My personal favorite is Chops in Broussard, and I love their boudin over all the other boudin in the land. There's a good meat-to-rice ratio, good spice, and the meat is slightly chunky—but not too much so. When I go there, I usually get a few links for the moment, and they offer to cut them in half so it's easier to eat on the road," Reggie says.

There are a blue million boudin options out there, and allegiances run deep. It's difficult to imagine another sausage inspiring such ardor, and the range of grand gestures that have gone down in the name of boudin love are a little mind-boggling. Scott, Louisiana, proudly bills itself as the Boudin Capital of the World, hosting an annual festival and crowning a boudin queen. There's the painstakingly mapped out Cajun Boudin Trail, and an entire website devoted to grading the various boudin links of the region. I know more than a few expat Cajuns who have boudin shipped cross-country on a regular basis just to have that hot and juicy taste of home at the ready.

MOST MEAT MARKETS WILL HAND OVER A LINK SWADDLED IN A PAPER TOWEL, BUT MY PREFERRED WRAP-JOB METHOD IS TIN FOIL, WHICH MORE EFFECTIVELY KEEPS THE BOUDIN WARM AND CAN—WITH A LITTLE FINAGLING—BECOME A KIND OF PORKY PUSH POP THAT'S IDEAL FOR PARKING LOT SNACKING.

"People in South Louisiana recognize that boudin is a cultural and regional point of distinction. This awareness makes them loyal to it in a way not manifested with any other culinary item besides, maybe, crawfish," says Bob Carriker, founder of Boudin Link. Since 2004, Carriker posted reviews of over 180 different boudins, complete with tasting notes, on the website.

"Every place that sells boudin has a slightly—and sometimes not so slightly—different recipe, so it is easy to see why people become partial to, and even defensive of, the link they identify as their favorite," Carriker says.

Despite its inherent mobility, boudin has been surprisingly slow to trickle into the nearby New Orleans area or, really, anywhere else. Maybe, though, this limited reach is for the best. The Bermuda Triangle-like draw of boudin can continue to lure in those in the know, and then—poof!—disappear, leaving travelers to wonder whether the sausage was real, or just a delicious fever dream.

How Peameal Bacon Became Toronto's Signature Sandwich Meat

BY ANDREA YU

Not too long ago, Toronto mayor John Tory stood on a stage facing a small crowd of food festival-goers. At his side, an assistant held a museum-like bell jar displaying a flour-dusted white bun stuffed with slices of lean and salty pork and a ruffle of lettuce. A tiny Canadian flag on a toothpick pierced the pillowy bun's top. Lifting off the glass top with a flourish, Mayor Tory unveiled the sandwich and announced it as Toronto's official signature dish. "It's very Canadian," said Mayor Tory, continuing in the polite honesty stereotypical of the nation, "[it's] not necessarily absolutely everybody's taste but something that's very Toronto." After a weeklong public online vote, the peameal bacon sandwich had beat out a curious list of contenders—the Jamaican patty, street hot dog, and burrito—and was crowned the winner.

The story of how the peameal bacon sandwich became so iconically Torontonian dates back centuries. One of the forefathers of pork processing was William Davies, who in 1854 founded the William Davies Company in Toronto "for the purpose of exporting Hams and Bacon to England." By 1907, Ontario farms bred 75 to 85 percent of the country's hog stock. Farms would send their pigs to packing houses in Toronto for processing, making the city a hub for pork processing and earning it the nickname Hogtown, which is still used today.

In order to compete with fresher cuts of bacon from Ireland and Denmark, bacon from Toronto was cured to survive the longer shipping journey. The story goes that Davies salted lean cuts of pork loin and, for a preservative effect, rolled them in dried, crushed yellow peas—the same peas fed to his pigs—giving the iconic cuts of meat the name peameal bacon.

Today, cornmeal is used in place of crushed peas but the salty slices are still known and loved as peameal bacon. It's a popular breakfast staple appearing on brunch menus across the city, whether as part of a classic breakfast or in place of Canadian bacon (which is actually an American creation that has more in common with deli ham than traditional bacon) in eggs Benedict.

However, unlike other signature city foods like Chicago's deep-dish pizza or Philadelphia's cheesesteak sandwich, Toronto isn't rife with peameal bacon sandwiches. You're unlikely to spot a Torontonian walking down the street eating one or to find the sandwich on the menu of your average breakfast joint. "If you go outside the downtown core, a lot of people will probably not ever have had a peameal sandwich in their lifetime," says *Toronto Star* food writer Karon Liu.

For Torontonians that are familiar with the peameal bacon sandwich, if you ask them where to grab one, the location that typically comes to mind is St. Lawrence Market, a sprawling indoor food fair that's been around longer than the William Davies Company. One stall in the market—Carousel Bakery— has been touting the peameal bacon sandwich as Toronto's signature food long before Mayor Tory's official announcement. Carousel's sandwich might be the city's most famous, but it's the simplest option—a pre-made, foil-wrapped sandwich with an inch-thick stack of peameal bacon slices in a white bun. It's a satisfying hit of meat and carbs but could sing so much more with thoughtful additions, which modern Toronto eateries are experimenting with. One local purveyor topped their peameal bacon sandwich with cheddar cheese, onions, lettuce, and barbecue sauce, while the Hogtown Sandwich from Rashers is dressed up with a simple smear of grainy ale mustard.

But, like John Tory said, the peameal bacon sandwich isn't for everybody. There's still a significant chunk of the city that's being excluded by naming a non-Halal, non-Kosher, and non-vegetarian/ vegan-friendly item as its signature dish. "In my near decade of living in TO I have never had one and probably never will, as a Jewish vegetarian," wrote Rachel Lissner in a Facebook comment discussing the sandwich's recent crowning in a group she admins— the Young Urbanists League.

It isn't easy to pick a wholly representative food for a place that has half of its population born outside of Canada. "I don't even know if there is one dish that can encapsulate a city like Toronto because it's so diverse," says *Toronto Star*'s Liu, who argues that West Indian rotis or bowls of Vietnamese pho might be the 'iconic dish' to a certain neighborhood or demographic.

Toronto prides itself on its multicultural community with the palate to match. Within this landscape of global offerings, the peameal bacon sandwich stands as a relic of the past—a nod to Toronto's legacy as Hogtown. So, enjoy our peameal bacon sandwiches. But we hope that you won't stop there. "Don't limit yourself to this one sandwich," says Liu. "There are so many different things that Toronto has to offer."

CHAPTER FOUR

BAKING FOR THE

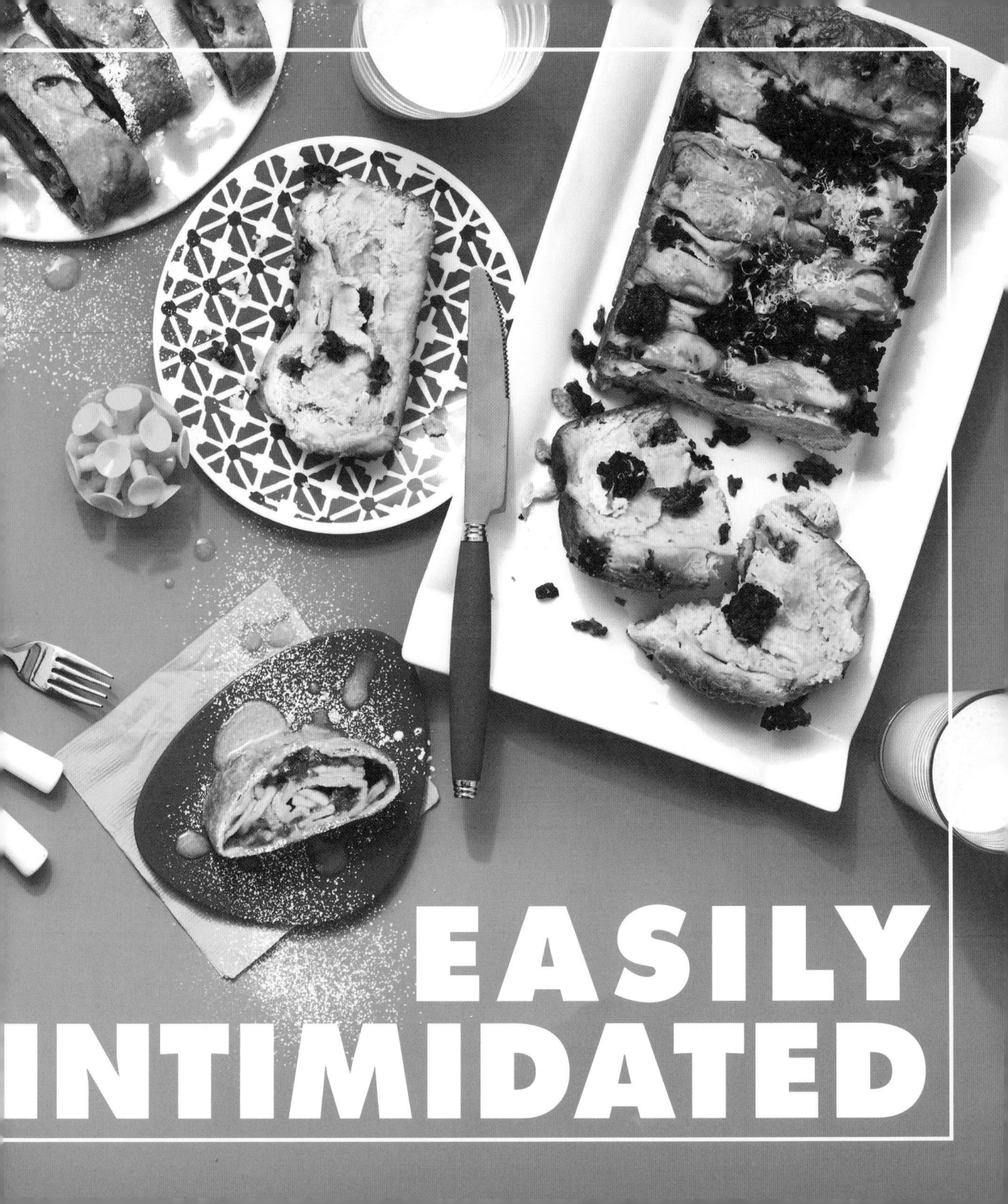

EASILY
INTIMIDATED

MUFFINS ARE CAKE FOR BREAKFAST

BY DAWN PERRY It's been asked of me before, and I have no doubt it will be again: What's the difference between a muffin and a cupcake? I'll give you the same answer I always give: frosting. And that's about it. The ingredients are almost identical—butter, flour, eggs, sugar, etc.—they come in a familiar one-size-fits-most shape and size, and minus that mop of frosting, could easily be mistaken for one another in a police lineup. All that to say, muffins are really just a good excuse to eat cake for breakfast which, if you know me, you know I am all for.

Muffins are humble. They don't need to put on a show to get your attention in the pastry case and they know how hard it is to turn it on first thing in the morning. But what they lack in flash, they make up for in low-key satisfaction. They don't need fondant or sprinkles to get the job done. In fact, we've done everything we can think of to dress them down in order to sell them as a morning meal. They're cake dressed in business casual. We've substituted some of the fat in muffins for banana or mashed avocado. We've added shredded veggies (carrots, zucchini) in an effort to pack in a "whole serving of fruits and/or vegetables!" We've swapped in as much whole-grain flour as we could without just selling paper liners full of Metamucil. We've bulked up muffins with as much bran as the eggs could bind.

It's a noble pursuit this healthy muffin-making, but it's not worth it. Let's just admit that we like cake for breakfast and enjoy it. I'm not proposing we do anything insane like put Nutella on top of a blueberry muffin. (Nutella is not a breakfast food, but that's another opinion piece.) I'm just saying let's be honest and keep it simple.

With that I present you with a pretty great basic muffin. Nothing fancy here: butter, flour, an egg, some fruit. I did cut the white sugar with a little brown sugar. You know why? Because that's what I had in the cupboard, but you can use all white sugar if you have it. I folded in some frozen blueberries, but you can use any frozen or fresh berry that you have on hand or you can fold in chopped firm bananas or apples, pears or walnuts or raisins. You get the idea.

Pretty Basic Muffins

2 teaspoons baking powder

½ teaspoon kosher salt

2 cups plus 2 teaspoons all-purpose flour

1 stick unsalted butter, room temperature

⅓ cup granulated sugar

⅓ cup brown sugar

1 large egg

½ teaspoon pure vanilla extract

¾ cup whole milk

1½ cups frozen blueberries, raspberries, or blackberries

1. Preheat oven to 350°F. Line a 12-cup standard muffin tin with paper liners (or coat with nonstick spray and dust with flour).

2. Whisk baking powder, salt, and 2 cups flour together in a medium bowl. Using an electric mixer, beat butter and both sugars together in a large bowl on medium-high until light and fluffy, about 5 minutes. Add egg and beat to combine, scraping down sides of bowl; beat in vanilla.

3. With mixer on low, add dry ingredients in 3 additions, alternating with milk, and beginning and ending with dry ingredients, beating to combine after each addition. Scrape down sides of bowl as necessary and beat to combine.

4. Toss berries with remaining 2 teaspoons flour until coated; fold berries into batter. Divide batter among prepared muffin cups and bake, rotating tin halfway through, until a toothpick inserted in the center comes out clean, 25 to 30 minutes. Let cool slightly before serving.

NOTE

Muffins will keep, tightly covered at room temperature, for 2 days.

SOME SUGGESTIONS FOR SWAP-INS AND -OUTS	
FLOUR Substitute up to a quarter (that's ½ cup here) of the all-purpose flour for an alternative flour of your choice. Almond flour, spelt, or another flour from ancient grains will work.	**FLAVOR** Add up to 2 teaspoons of dried spices—cinnamon or freshly grated nutmeg; cardamom in small doses—or a teaspoon of finely grated lemon or orange zest.
FOLD-INS 1½ cups of anything that holds its shape can be folded into this batter. That includes most fruits, dried or fresh, as long as they're not too watery. Coarsely chopped nuts (preferably toasted) are excellent, as is a combo of the two.	**TOPPERS** Sometimes I sprinkle quick breads with a layer of sugar before baking. It gives the exterior a crispy sweet crunchy topping. Sprinkle with sugar—raw or granulated—or use this basic ratio for streusel topping: 1 part butter: 1 part sugar: 2 parts flour; squeeze together in your fingers until crumbly and sprinkle on top of muffins before baking.

QUICK BREAD TIPS

BY ALLISON ROBICELLI

Quick breads should be exactly that, quick. And while "quick" is on point, the "bread" part is iffy. In most cases, breads are leavened with yeast and are not too sweet. Quick breads, on the other hand, are chemically leavened and plenty sweet. Seriously, it's just cake in a loaf pan. But you knew that already, didn't you?

Go grab a recipe for quick bread—whatever you're in the mood for—and let's go over some tips.

BANANA

Common knowledge says you should be using ultra-ripe bananas. This is not necessary. As long as it's not on the green side, any banana makes great banana bread.

CARROT

Do not use pre-grated carrots unless you want dry, disappointing bread. Grate them by hand, always.

OIL

If you haven't learned that not all oils are the same, please learn it now. Unless you're making something that specifically calls for a certain type, like olive oil, use a neutral oil with no flavor. Canola, grapeseed, and vegetable are good choices. In fact, make those your only choices unless the recipe says otherwise.

APPLE/PEAR

All that extra liquid when you shred your fruit is no bueno for a good bread. Put the fruit in a strainer and gently press out the excess; measure the drained fruit as instructed. Drink the leftover juice. It's delicious.

NUTS

Even though they'll be baked in the bread, the batter won't allow them to get hot enough to toast for the fullest flavor. Give 'em a quick toast beforehand, OK? And let them cool completely before you stir them in.

NOW LET'S BAKE

1. You can do this in a mixer, but it's just as easy to do by hand. With a wooden spoon, mix up your fruit with your sugars until it's smooth. It'll draw out all the natural liquids of your fruit and end up looking like very expensive cat food.

2. Next, in another bowl, whisk your eggs until they're totally smooth, then mix in the oil. Pour it into the fruit, and stir until combined.

3. Sift your flour, leavening, and spices together, and dump it all into the bowl. Stir until just combined. Don't keep stirring after it comes together. If you've ever had gummy bread, it is because it was stirred excessively. Stop right now.

4. Bake as directed, and contain yourself for at least 10 minutes before you dive in. If you can manage to hold out even longer, you'll learn that quick breads tend to get better the next day. Maybe make yourself two or three, just to be safe.

WHAT'S THE DIFFERENCE BETWEEN BAKING SODA AND BAKING POWDER?

If you've ever tried substituting baking powder for baking soda, you've discovered that you can't use the two interchangeably. Baking soda and baking powder are easily confused, as they have similar names and look exactly alike, and both break down in moisture and/or heat to help baked goods rise instantly without yeast, but they have completely different chemical compositions. Here's your cheat sheet.

BAKING SODA

Baking soda is an alkaline base with only one ingredient: sodium bicarbonate.

When baking soda is combined with an acidic ingredient (like buttermilk, yogurt, chocolate, or lemon juice) it produces carbon dioxide gas to leaven baked goods.

Baking soda spreads, so adding more does not mean more lift. It can leave a metallic, soapy taste if it's not balanced with enough acid, or if you use too much.

BAKING POWDER

Baking powder is basically baking soda with an acidic element already built in, usually in the form of cream of tartar and a little bit of cornstarch.

It's available as both single-acting and double-acting powders. Single-acting powders include either slow-acting acids or fast-acting acids. Double-acting powders have both acids and their effects come into play at two different stages throughout the baking process.

When you're using baking powder, try to avoid overmixing the batter. You want to incorporate the dry ingredients into the wet just enough without letting too many bubbles escape from the mixture.

THE MILLION-DOLLAR QUESTION STILL REMAINS: CAN YOU USE BAKING SODA INSTEAD OF BAKING POWDER, AND VICE VERSA?

Not exactly. If you swap baking powder for baking soda, expect the taste of your baked goods to change for the worse. Baking soda is much stronger than baking powder, so you'll have to triple the amount of baking powder to meet the amount of baking soda that's required. To make your own baking powder at home, use a 2:1 ratio of cream of tartar to baking soda. (In general, though, it's much better to run to the store and grab the right one.)

Sausage and Cheese Biscuit Pull-Apart Bread

If a sausage, egg, and cheese sandwich hooked up with warm, buttery biscuits, their children would be this pull-apart bread. Premade biscuit dough provides a base for this easy-to-tear loaf before it's loaded with cooked sausage. And feel free to have fun with the flavors. Here we've used classic country sausage, sharp cheddar, and salty Parmesan, but why not change it up? Try spicy chorizo with Monterey Jack and cotija, or chicken-apple sausage with yellow cheddar and grated Manchego.

1 (16.3-ounce) can refrigerated biscuits

¼ cup unsalted butter, melted

8 ounces mild country sausage, cooked and crumbled

2 ounces sharp cheddar cheese, shredded (about ½ cup)

2 ounces Parmigiano-Reggiano cheese, shredded (about ½ cup)

½ teaspoon kosher salt

¼ teaspoon black pepper

1. Preheat oven to 325°F. Lightly grease a 9- x 5-inch loaf pan with cooking spray. Set aside.

2. Place biscuit dough rounds on a work surface. Using your hands or a rolling pin, press or roll 1 biscuit to ¼-inch thickness. Brush with a small amount of melted butter, and sprinkle with 1 tablespoon of the sausage and about 1 tablespoon each of the cheddar and Parmigiano-Reggiano. Press or roll a second biscuit to ¼-inch thickness, and place on top of sausage and cheeses. Lightly press biscuit to compress stack. Brush biscuit with a small amount of melted butter, and sprinkle with about 1 tablespoon each of the cheddar and Parmigiano-Reggiano. Pick up biscuit stack by 2 opposite edges, and place in prepared loaf pan, folding edges of stack up into a taco shape. Repeat procedure with remaining biscuits and additional butter, sausage, and cheeses.

3. Sprinkle the top of the loaf with remaining sausage and cheese, and bake in the preheated oven until golden brown and a thermometer inserted in the center of the loaf registers 190°F, 30 to 35 minutes. Remove from the oven, and cool 10 minutes before serving.

ONCE YOU KNOW HOW TO MAKE BRIOCHE, ALL THINGS ARE POSSIBLE

BY ALLISON ROBICELLI

If you've always thought you couldn't make brioche, you were probably right. It is a bit challenging and your lack of confidence can result in a self-fulfilling prophecy. That changes today. I shall sherpa you through the brioche recipe of your choice, showing you where you might err and pulling you out the other side to victory. And if it still gets screwed up? Just slice that sucker and dry it out for brioche French toast. No one will be the wiser.

By the way, we're using a stand mixer, because that's the finest of all the ways in my opinion. You can also use a food processor with a dough blade.

POOLISH TIME

Poolish is another name for a starter, but more fun to say. "Starter" is a concentrated dynamo of yeast and flour that's getting itself ready for a Big Bang–worthy explosion of flavor.

The ingredients for poolish are yeast, warm milk or water, some form of sugar, and flour. Mix together the specified amount of the first three things with a fork, then add some of the flour you've measured out a spoonful at a time until you get a relatively thick slurry. Do not add the salt here, because that will kill the yeast. If salt is in your recipe, wait to add it until the yeast has stopped bubbling.

Let the poolish sit for a few minutes to get bubbly, then pour the rest of the flour on top of it and cover the bowl with plastic wrap. Let this sit in a warm place for at least an hour to let that yeasty flavor start to develop. You'll see it start to rise up and bubble through the flour. That means your yeast is strong and ready to take no prisoners.

GET MIXING

Use the dough hook to mix this up a bit by hand first; you want to make sure to pull the poolish up from the bottom so mixing goes quicker. Put the hook on the mixer and turn it to medium until you get a smooth dough. Increase the speed to medium-high and add the eggs; mix for a minute. Stop the mixer and pull the dough off the sides with the hook, folding the dough into the center a few times. Put the hook back on and continue on medium-high until the dough is pulling up on the hook and trying to climb its way out of the bowl.

Cut off small pieces of softened butter and throw them in one at a time. The dough will get smooth and shiny and possibly sticky, but don't fret. Lightly oil a large bowl, scrape the dough into it, cover with plastic wrap or a clean towel, and let rise until doubled.

Using a rubber spatula, fold the dough on itself a few times to deflate and come together in a ball. Cover again, and put it into the fridge for a "slow ferment." Let this rest for an hour, let it rest for a day or two. You can rest, too.

TIME TO GO BRIOCHIN'

Now shape the dough however your recipe directs. If you've got a specialty mold, great, but if not you can use other pans. No one will complain about the shape, and if they do, banish them from your house.

Let your brioche rise, and bake as instructed. The best way to know it is done is with an instant-read meat thermometer, which should read 190°F when inserted into the center of the bread. When it's ready, let it sit for at least 20 minutes so it can set up completely, then go to town on that sexy beast.

HOW TO MAKE BRIOCHE ROLLS

1 dissolve yeast in warm milk; let stand 5 minutes. add flour, sugar, and eggs

2 using a paddle attachment, beat until smooth. replace with a dough hook, beat at low speed 5 minutes

3 add cubes of butter, one at a time, mix until dough is smooth and elastic

4 place dough in large bowl coated with cooking spray; cover and let rise in warm place until doubled in size

5 form into a ball; cover, and refrigerate

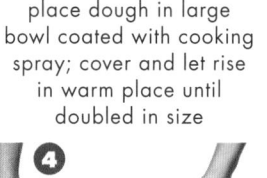

6 divide dough into 4 equal portions

7 cut each portion into 6 equal pieces

8 roll each piece into a 1½-inch ball. repeat for remaining dough

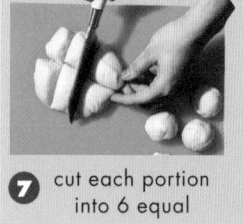

9 place rolls in greased muffin cups

10 brush rolls with egg mixture

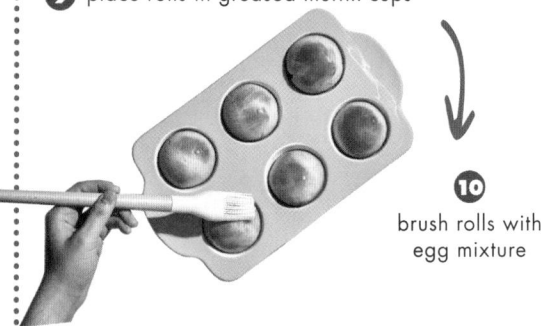

11 bake until golden; brush melted butter on top

12 done

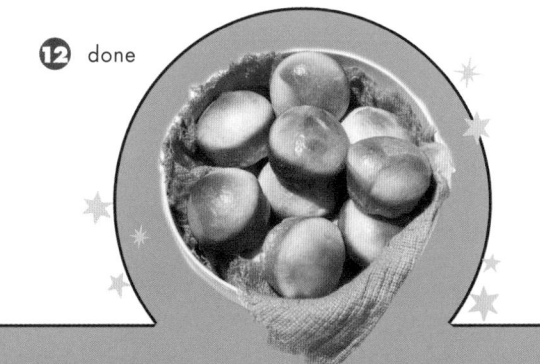

Apple and Date Strudel with Tahini-Honey Glaze

Tart and soft, and just a little sweet, this strudel is one of those pastries you'll make once, and then likely once a week for the rest of fall. We think a sour Granny Smith is the best baking apple, but if you like them sweet, go for Gala.

FOR THE STRUDEL

½ cup finely diced pitted Medjool or Deglet Noor dates

¼ cup bourbon or apple cider (or 2 tablespoons each)

2 large Granny Smith apples

2 tablespoons lemon juice

2 tablespoons honey

1 tablespoon brown sugar

2 tablespoons all-purpose flour, plus extra for work surface

½ teaspoon allspice

1 sheet frozen puff pastry, thawed

2 tablespoons melted butter

2 tablespoons granulated sugar, crushed shortbread cookies, or ground walnuts or almonds

1 large egg

1 tablespoon turbinado or granulated sugar

FOR THE GLAZE

¼ cup room-temperature tahini

3 tablespoons melted coconut oil

2 tablespoons room temperature honey

Powdered sugar, optional, for serving

1. Prepare the Strudel: Put the dates into a small bowl and cover with bourbon or apple cider. Let the mixture soak for 8 hours, or heat in the microwave for 1 minute, then soak for 10 minutes. Drain the dates; discard the liquid.

2. Preheat the oven to 375°F and line a rimmed baking sheet with parchment paper.

3. Peel, core, and thinly slice the apples. Toss the apples in a large bowl with lemon juice, honey, brown sugar, flour, allspice, and the soaked dates.

4. Unroll the thawed puff pastry on a lightly floured work surface. Roll it out into a 16- x 12-inch rectangle, and position it vertically. Brush the pastry with melted butter. Sprinkle the bottom third of the pastry, leaving a 1-inch border, with granulated sugar, crushed cookies or nuts. This will keep the apples from soaking through during baking.

5. Using a slotted spoon, spoon the apple mixture on top of the sugar-covered area of the pastry.

6. Fold over the puff pastry edges on the bottom and sides to cover the apple mixture. Then carefully roll the pastry up, jelly roll-style. Using 2 bench scrapers or spatulas, lift and place the strudel, seam-side down, on the prepared baking sheet.

7. Mix 1 egg with a tablespoon of water and brush it over the top of the strudel; sprinkle with turbinado sugar. Using a sharp knife, make 4 (2-inch) slits across the top of the pastry—this ensures steam will escape during baking and the pastry will get crisp. Bake the strudel for 15 minutes, then rotate the baking sheet. Bake for another 15-20 minutes, or until golden brown.

8. Take the strudel out of the oven and let it cool for at least 20 minutes.

9. Prepare the Glaze: Whisk together the tahini, melted coconut oil, and honey until smooth. Just before serving, drizzle the glaze liberally over the cooled strudel, and add powdered sugar if you feel the urge.

DIY Toaster Strudel

While we can't deny that store-bought Toaster Strudels are great when devoured in two bites, they also kind of taste like chemicals. So here's how to make them yourself. If you want to make your own icing piping bag (and you definitely should want to), just fill a sandwich bag with a glaze of a few tablespoons powdered sugar and 1 tablespoon milk. Snip off a corner of the bag and go wild.

1 large egg
1 box of thawed phyllo
   dough

About half a stick of salted
   butter, melted
1 (8-ounce) block of cream
   cheese

Suggested fillings: jam,
   cinnamon sugar, fruit
   butter, peanut butter,
   optional

1. Beat the egg well with about 2 tablespoons of water to make a very runny egg wash.

2. Lay out a single sheet of phyllo dough and lightly brush with melted butter. Fold in half, gently pressing the two long sides together. Again, brush lightly with butter.

3. Mentally divide the dough into 4 quadrants. In the second quadrant, lay out some thin slices of cream cheese, leaving 1 inch on both the top and bottom un-cheesed.

4. Top with whatever else you want: such as a schmear of jam, a sprinkle of cinnamon sugar, a squiggle of peanut butter, a drizzle of honey.

5. Brush all the exposed phyllo with egg wash. Fold the first quadrant over the cream cheese quadrant, and press the top and bottom edges together. Now brush it again with a little bit more egg wash.

6. Gently fold the filled section over onto the third quadrant. Repeat with the egg wash. Fold the top and bottom edges onto the toaster strudel, like a burrito. Brush the folded parts with egg wash. Bring the fourth and final quadrant over the filled part and gently smooth it all out. Repeat with more sheets of phyllo dough until you're sick of making these.

7. Preheat your oven to 350°F. Brush a baking sheet with butter, then lay out the strudels. Brush the tops with more melted butter. Bake for about 15 minutes until nice and golden brown. Cool completely.

8. Once cool, package them in a way they won't get destroyed in your freezer. To reheat, microwave for 1 minute, then cook in a toaster oven until they reach your desired level of toastiness.

Pop-Tart Haus

To anyone who's tried to make a gingerbread house from homemade cookies, I salute you. To anyone who's resorted to gluing graham crackers to an old milk carton after failing to make a gingerbread house, I'm right there with you. This year, however, there will be no crumbling gingerbread, because this year, a toaster pastry house will be the centerpiece of your holiday table.

Here's how to make one: Buy as many boxes of Pop-Tarts as you plan to make houses (you'll need one box per house, plus maybe a few extras in case of mistakes, or if someone wants to make a mansion). Next, make a huge batch of super-sturdy icing—bakers will recognize it as essentially Royal Icing, which hardens as it sets thanks to whipped egg whites (here we use meringue powder). Gather up all the colorful cereal you can find, as well as candies for decoration and shredded coconut for snow. Use the empty Pop-Tart box as the inner support for your house and stick toaster pastries to it to make the walls.

FOR THE ROYAL ICING

1 (1-pound) box powdered
  sugar

¼ cup meringue powder

½ cup water

8 assorted prepared
  breakfast toaster pastries
  (such as Pop-Tarts)

Assorted cereals, cookies,
  and candies

1. Prepare the Royal Icing: Add sugar and meringue powder to the bowl of a stand mixer fitted with a paddle attachment, and beat on low until incorporated, about 1 minute. While machine is running on low, slowly add water until desired stiff, spackle-like texture is achieved.

2. Build the Haus: Cut the bottom off an empty toaster pastry box, leaving the top flaps and about 3 inches of the box. The top flaps will become support for the roof. Spread the icing onto the backs of the toaster pastries and stick them horizontally to the box sides to form the walls of the house. Start with 4 pastries for the walls, then use 2 pastries for the open gable roof. Use the icing as you would mortar, to hold the structure together. Cut 2 pastries in triangles to fit below the roof and add extra icing to attach. Let dry overnight at room temperature.

3. Decorate the cottage with assorted cereals, cookies, and candies, creating a chimney, door, and siding, as desired. Use more cereal to create a landscape, if desired.

NO BAKING
REQUIRED

MAKE SCONES, STAY INSIDE, REMAIN COZY

BY ALLISON ROBICELLI

If you know anything about British or Irish cuisine, you know they have at least 40 baked goods that are technically scones but with different names in hopes they'll trick you. It's a lovely enough item that by just tinkering with it a wee bit—a dash of oat flour here, a few blueberries there, a spot of cream—it can reinvent itself over and over again. As long as you know the basics of how things go together, you can tackle any scone/biscuit/shortcake/etc. recipe that comes your way, whether it's sweet, savory, or little bit of both. Not only that, you will not be restrained by them.

FLOUR

There are plain scones, oat scones, potato scones, but everything starts with a bit of plain all-purpose flour, which holds it together.

EGG OR NO EGG?

Purists insist that scones should be dry, buttery, and crumbly, which you get with the "no egg" method. Adding one egg to the liquid might technically put it in biscuit territory, but who the hell cares? One egg whisked into your liquid component will result in a softer scone that is enjoyable without clotted cream.

LIQUID

Cream scones rely on heavy cream, which might scare you off. But know that Queen Elizabeth eats these every single day (I fact-checked), and she's not dead yet!

Buttermilk makes a very nice scone, but if your recipe doesn't call for it, you'll have to adjust your leavening. Baking powder is meant to rise when there's nothing acidic in your batter. Buttermilk is acidic so you'll need to swap out some of the baking powder for baking soda.

BUTTER

It. Must. Be. Cold. If it's warm it'll just melt into a puddle in the oven, then solidify into a brick. Use a food processor or grate frozen butter on a cheese grater. Then work quickly to make sure it has no time to soften before baking (and if it does, pop it in the freezer for a few minutes).

FILLINGS

The best time to add fillings is before you add the liquid ingredients. It gives you enough time to evenly distribute things without overworking the dough. If you want to add things like blueberries, keep them frozen and toss them with flour before adding.

SHAPE

Some people are traditionalists and like patting their scones into a disc before cutting into triangles. Some like a scone that resembles a drop biscuit. Some have so much money they buy $60 specialty scone pans to make perfectly uniform wedges. Honestly? It doesn't matter. The dough is going to bake and taste the same regardless. Go whichever way you like. Just keep your eye on them to make sure they don't overcook. The Queen would not be amused.

BAKING SUBSTITUTIONS CORNER

Sometimes you have stuff, and sometimes you don't. This page is for those times when you're about to start baking something, and you realize you're out of one crucial ingredient. And you can't go to the store because it's closed, or there's a blizzard, or you've been blacklisted for over-sampling, or you just don't feel like it. Fear not, and use one of these substitutions.

BUTTERMILK

What are buttermilk pancakes without their title ingredient? There's a quick way to mimic the sour liquid: Mix 1 tablespoon lemon juice or white vinegar per cup of milk, then set aside for 5 to 10 minutes to let the acid in the juice or vinegar quickly curdle the milk. For a cup of thicker faux buttermilk, mix ¼ cup of water with ¾ cup of unsweetened yogurt, or use equal parts water and sour cream.

BROWN SUGAR

Brown sugar is just regular old granulated sugar that's been processed with molasses, so all you have to do to make brown sugar is add 2 tablespoons of molasses to every cup of white sugar. You can either dump the ingredients into a food processor or blender to get the right, sticky consistency, or you can just mix with a spoon. No molasses? Blend 2 tablespoons of maple syrup or agave nectar per cup of granulated sugar.

BAKING POWDER

As mentioned earlier, use only in case of emergency: ½ teaspoon cream of tartar + ¼ teaspoon baking soda = 1 teaspoon baking powder.

CREAM CHEESE

If you're looking for a sweet cream cheese substitute, try mascarpone cheese, which is naturally sweet with a smooth texture. You can also use a high-quality ricotta cheese, though it will have a more grainy texture than standard cream cheese.

EGGS

Flaxseed and water create the fluffy, fatty texture of a fresh egg, helping pancakes and muffins rise just as tall as ever. To make one flax egg, mix 1 tablespoon of flaxseed meal and 2½ tablespoons of water, then let the mixture sit for 5 minutes to gel. No flaxseed? Use chia seeds instead.

CORNSTARCH

You likely already have one cornstarch substitute in your kitchen: flour. For every 1 tablespoon of cornstarch needed, use 3 tablespoons of flour instead. If you're in need of a gluten-free cornstarch substitute, try tapioca flour (great for pie fillings) or arrowroot flour (perfect for acidic sauces, like those with a tomato base).

Doughnut Hole Croquembouche

The classic French croquembouche is a cone-shaped pile of cream puffs bound together with threads of caramel. Making one from scratch requires lots of time and skill that, hey, you may or not have—we don't know your life. You could be Paul Hollywood, and if you are, thanks for reading, and will you blurb our next book? Big fans. But if you're a novice baker with 30 minutes to throw together a croquembouche or croquembouche-adjacent dish, make this.

3 thick-cut bacon slices

1 cup packed light brown sugar

½ cup unsalted butter

¼ cup whole milk

1 tablespoon bourbon

50 prepared glazed doughnut holes

1 (9-inch) Styrofoam cone

Powdered sugar

1. Cook bacon in a large skillet over medium until crispy, 4 to 5 minutes per side. Transfer to a plate lined with a paper towel. Break into bite-size pieces.

2. Combine brown sugar, butter, and milk in a medium saucepan over medium-high. Bring to a boil, and cook, stirring often, until sugar is dissolved, about 2 minutes. Remove from heat, and stir in bourbon. Set aside.

3. Use toothpicks to hold doughnut holes onto Styrofoam cone, starting at the base and building to the top, placing one doughnut at the tiptop. Place bacon in gaps between the doughnuts. Drizzle caramel sauce over doughnut cone. Dust with powdered sugar. Serve immediately or at room temperature.

Cinnamon Roll Babka Buns

Morning is not the optimal time for complex decision-making. Anything you need should be obtainable with a gesture and a grunt. OJ? Ungh. Coffee? Ungh! Roll, babka, or sticky bun? Ungh? Choose? This cinnamon, nutmeg, Nutella, and hazelnut treat is gloriously sweet, gooey, and just spicy enough (especially if you opt for Saigon cinnamon) to give your mouth a little wakeup thrill. No need to say thanks—that smile on your face comes through loud and clear.

⅓ cup warm whole milk (about 110°F)

2½ teaspoons active dry yeast

¼ cup granulated sugar, divided

1⅔ cups all-purpose flour

1⅔ cups bread flour

5 large eggs

1¼ teaspoons table salt, divided

2¼ cups unsalted butter, softened at room temperature, divided

4½ cups packed light brown sugar, divided

½ cup honey

½ cup heavy cream

½ cup tap water

¼ cup ground cinnamon

1 teaspoon ground nutmeg

1 cup chocolate-hazelnut spread (such as Nutella)

1¾ cups finely chopped hazelnuts, divided

1 cup hot water

1. Whisk together milk, yeast, and 1 tablespoon of the granulated sugar in the bowl of a stand mixer fitted with a dough hook. Let stand 5 minutes. Add all-purpose flour, bread flour, eggs, 1 teaspoon of the salt, and remaining 3 tablespoons sugar. Beat on low speed until combined, 2 to 3 minutes, stopping to scrape down bowl as necessary. Continue to beat on low speed until dough is loose and sticky, 3 to 4 minutes. With the mixer running on low speed, add 1 cup of the softened butter, 2 tablespoons at a time, beating just until blended after each addition. Stop the mixer occasionally to scrape down the bowl. Increase speed to medium, and beat until dough is sticky and soft, 15 more minutes. (Dough will be glossy, shiny, and elastic.) Increase speed to medium-high, and beat until dough has formed a ball and comes away from bowl cleanly, about 1 more minute. Place dough in a large bowl coated with cooking spray. Loosely cover with plastic wrap, and let rise in a warm place (80° to 85°F), until doubled in size, 1½ to 2 hours.

2. Melt ¾ cup of the butter in a skillet over medium. Stir in 2 cups of the brown sugar, and cook, stirring constantly, until sugar melts, 4 to 5 minutes. Remove from heat, and stir in honey, cream, water, and remaining ¼ teaspoon salt. Set aside.

3. Place remaining 2½ cups brown sugar in a bowl. Stir in cinnamon and nutmeg until combined.

4. Place remaining ½ cup softened butter in a microwave-safe bowl, and microwave on HIGH until melted, 20 to 30 seconds. Very gently divide dough in half, and place 1 half on a floured surface. Wrap remaining dough half with plastic wrap, and chill until ready to use.

5. Roll dough on floured surface into a 16- x 12-inch rectangle with 1 long side facing you. Brush dough with half of the melted butter. Sprinkle with half of the brown sugar-cinnamon mixture, and lightly press to adhere. Starting at long edge farthest from you, roll firmly, jelly-roll style, into a log. Using a sharp knife, cut into 16 (1-inch) rounds.

6. Place 2 rounds, cut side up and with edges touching, on lightly floured surface. Press rounds into a 4- x 5½-inch rectangle with 1 long side facing you. Repeat with remaining 14 rounds, to create 7 more rectangles. Dot 1 tablespoon of the chocolate-hazelnut spread evenly over each rectangle. Sprinkle each with 1 tablespoon of the hazelnuts. Starting at long side farthest from you, roll each rectangle firmly, jelly-roll style, into a log. Using a sharp knife, cut 1 log in half lengthwise. With cut edges up, twist pieces together, forming a 5½-inch-long twisted braid. Wrap braid around itself, tucking loose ends under. Repeat with remaining logs.

7. Repeat Steps 5 and 6 with remaining melted butter, dough half, brown sugar-cinnamon mixture, chocolate-hazelnut spread, and ½ cup hazelnuts.

8. Divide cooled brown sugar-butter mixture between 2 (9- x 13-inch) baking dishes. Sprinkle evenly with remaining ¾ cup hazelnuts. Place 8 braided rounds, about ¾-inch apart, in each prepared dish.

9. Cover baking dishes with plastic wrap, and chill 6 hours or overnight. Remove from refrigerator, and let stand at room temperature until dough is very puffy and buns are touching, 1 to 2 hours.

10. Preheat oven to 350°F with 1 rack in upper third and 1 rack in lower third of oven. Place an ovenproof skillet on bottom rack. (Do not remove skillet while oven preheats.) Add hot water to preheated skillet on bottom oven rack. Remove and discard plastic wrap from buns. Place baking dishes on rack above skillet. Bake buns until tops begin to brown, 25 to 30 minutes. Cool in baking dishes on wire racks 10 minutes before serving.

Shibuya Honey Toast

Every loaf of bread wishes it could grow up to be Shibuya Honey Toast. It's the monarch butterfly of all bread-based breakfasts. Popular in Japan, Taiwan, and Singapore, it's essentially a toasted, hollowed-out bread bowl filled with fruit and ice cream. The best part is how fun it is to eat: Simply drop it on the table along with a pile of forks and tell your friends to dig in. What could be better?

1 pain de mie loaf, or unsliced Pullman white bread loaf

6 tablespoons unsalted butter

4 tablespoons honey, divided, plus more for garnish

½ teaspoon kosher salt

¼ cup fresh raspberries

¼ cup fresh blueberries

¼ cup fresh blackberries

¼ cup sliced fresh strawberries

¼ cup granulated sugar

Vanilla ice cream

Cinnamon

1. Preheat oven to 325°F. Slice loaf into 3 (5-inch) sections; reserve end slices for another use. Place middle section, cut side down, on a cutting board. Use a serrated knife to cut out a cube from center of bread section, leaving a ½-inch border around crust. Gently remove center cube from bread. Cut center cube into small cubes.

2. Melt butter and 3 tablespoons of the honey in a nonstick skillet over medium, stirring until combined. Pour mixture into a small bowl; reserve. Add bread cubes and 2 tablespoons of the melted butter mixture to skillet; sprinkle with salt. Cook, stirring and turning often, until golden and crisp on all sides, 3 to 4 minutes.

3. Brush interior and exterior of hollowed-out bread with reserved melted butter mixture. Place on a baking sheet, and bake in preheated oven until golden brown, 20 to 23 minutes. Meanwhile, combine berries, sugar, and remaining 1 tablespoon honey in a small saucepan. Cook over medium, stirring often, until sugar dissolves and berries begin to burst, 2 to 3 minutes.

4. Place bread "cup" on a serving plate. Spoon about ¼ cup berry mixture into bread cup. Layer with about ¼ cup croutons, continue layering with more berries and croutons until bread cup is filled. Top with vanilla ice cream, cinnamon, honey, and remaining fruit.

MAKE YOUR HOUSE SMELL LIKE A FOOD COURT

BY DAWN PERRY Cinnamon rolls were in regular rotation when I was growing up. There was no clearer sign of Sunday morning than the assertive pop of a vacuum-packed canister being split open. They would swell and snuggle in the oven, their giraffe-like pattern of flaky cinnamon topping melting to cover the rolls in a layer of perfectly engineered sweet spice. They were more biscuits than "rolls"—with a questionable ingredient list and wartime-appropriate expiration date—but these were the cinnamon rolls of my youth. And I loved them.

I'll admit I dabbled with the 'Bons, their irresistible scent luring my tween posse toward a random alcove of the mall. But as I grew older I started to find the icing too sweet and the size intimidating. But that aroma, even after all these years, is still intoxicating.

I wanted to create a sweet treat that would still make the house smell like a food court without sending me into an extended sugar coma. I came up with cinnamon rolls of a more manageable size, swapping some of the sugar for maple syrup and sticky sweet dates to offer complexity. Make no mistake, these cinnamon rolls are indulgent, but they're homemade so it's cool, right? These aren't necessarily good for you, but they're good for you.

Sticky Toffee Cinnamon Rolls

FOR HOMEMADE DOUGH

1½ cups warm water (100° to 110°F)

1 tablespoon granulated sugar

2 (¼-ounce) packets active dry yeast

4 cups all-purpose flour, plus more for work surface

2 teaspoons kosher salt

FOR THE TOPPING

½ cup packed light brown sugar

4 tablespoons butter

2 tablespoons maple syrup

½ cup chopped pecans, almonds, or walnuts (or a combination)

FOR THE FILLING

8 tablespoons unsalted butter

8 ounces Medjool dates, pitted and chopped

⅔ cup packed light brown sugar

½ teaspoon kosher salt

4 teaspoons cinnamon

1. Prepare the Dough: Combine warm water and sugar in a medium bowl. Sprinkle yeast over top and set aside until foamy, about 5 minutes. Add 4 cups flour and salt, and stir with a wooden spoon until a shaggy dough forms. Turn out onto a lightly floured surface and knead until dough comes together, about 10 times. Lightly oil a medium-size bowl. Add dough and turn to coat. Cover with plastic wrap and set aside until doubled in size, about 90 minutes.

2. Meanwhile, Prepare the Topping: Combine brown sugar, butter, and maple syrup in a 10-inch skillet, preferably cast iron. Cook, stirring often, until sugar dissolves and mixture is evenly bubbling across the surface, 2 to 3 minutes. Let cool slightly, then sprinkle with nuts. Set aside. (If you don't have a 10-inch skillet, you can do this in whatever skillet you have and then swiftly transfer the toffee mixture to a 10-inch cake pan.)

3. Preheat oven to 350°F. Prepare the Filling: Combine butter, dates, brown sugar, and salt in a medium saucepan and place over medium-high. Cook, stirring often, until butter melts. Continue to cook, stirring and mashing to help break up

dates, until mixture comes to a boil and dates are broken down, about 4 minutes. Let cool to room temperature.

4. Once the dough has doubled in size, turn out onto a lightly floured surface. Divide dough in half (this will make it easier to work with). Working with one at a time, roll each piece into a 12- x 16-inch rectangle. Divide date mixture between the two pieces of dough, spreading all the way to the edges. Sprinkle each piece evenly with 2 teaspoons cinnamon. Starting from the long end, roll up dough and place seam-side down. Cut dough crosswise into 2-inch spirals. Transfer rolls, cut sides down, to prepared skillet or cake pan, arranging snugly to fit. Bake until golden and risen, 30 to 35 minutes. Let cool 5 minutes before inverting onto a rack. Let cool slightly before eating.

NOTE

You can make your own dough for these, but a couple of balls of prepared pizza dough also work just fine.

Strawberry-Rose Cream Cheese Danishes Are Your New Superpower

BY CAROLINE LANGE Making Danishes is the ideal sort of party trick to whip out for a brunch. The fillings can largely be made ahead, and the puff pastry dough (which you can buy frozen, as I do) just needs to thaw. That means you can pull it out of the freezer and pop it in the fridge before you go to bed, and it will be ready to use by the time you're sipping your first mug of coffee in the morning.

These Danishes have a good smear of cream cheese enriched with an egg yolk, which makes the resulting filling custardy and almost fluffy. I do not sweeten it because I like the slight savoriness of it with the sweet fruit, but you can add a little sugar or honey if you'd like.

But the special ingredient here is rosewater. Strawberries are a part of the rose family, and the flavors sing together. You won't taste it much in the final Danish, but it lends a floral quality that feels summery to me. And no, it's not absolutely necessary, but rosewater is inexpensive, widely available—especially at Middle Eastern groceries—and you'll find lots of uses for it, like adding it to icings, rice pudding, or a smoothie.

But don't let me forget to talk about the pastry itself. Find the best-quality puff pastry you can, roll it very thinly to ensure crispy, flaky layers, score around the edge to give the pastry a guideline for puffing up and taking shape, and keep the dough as cold as you can. When the cold butter in pastry hits the hot oven, it will turn to steam, and that's what makes pastry light and delicious. Don't skip the freezer time before baking the pastries because it helps them maintain their shapes.

- 3 tablespoons honey
- 1 pound strawberries, stemmed and halved lengthwise
- 2 long strips lemon zest (use a vegetable peeler)
- Pinch kosher salt
- ¾ teaspoon rosewater
- 8 ounces cream cheese, room temperature
- 1 egg yolk
- 1 (14-ounce) package frozen puff pastry, thawed overnight (or at least 2 to 3 hours) in the refrigerator
- 1 large egg
- Splash water or milk

1. To make the strawberry-rosewater filling, combine the honey, half the strawberries, strips of zest, and a pinch of salt in a medium saucepan over medium heat about 20 minutes, stirring regularly, until the strawberries have become a fairly smooth sauce. Add the rest of the strawberries and simmer gently about 5 minutes, until softened but still holding their shape. Remove from the heat, stir in the rosewater, and set aside to cool to room temperature.

2. To make the cream cheese filling, beat together the cream cheese and the egg yolk. Set aside.

3. Line 2 baking sheets with parchment paper. Unfold the puff pastry and cut it into 8 equal pieces on a clean work surface. Carefully set 7 of the 8 pieces on a dish and keep them in the fridge while you work with the first one. The colder you can keep your puff pastry before it bakes, the better—you don't want the butter in it to melt while you're working it.

4. Roll the first piece of puff pastry into an approximately 4- x 9-inch rectangle on a sheet of parchment. Use a 4-inch-wide cookie cutter, bowl, or ramekin as a stencil for the Danishes; you will be able to get two Danishes out of each eighth of pastry. Use a small sharp knife to cut out the circles and set them on the parchment-lined sheet trays. Repeat, working as quickly as possible, until the first baking sheet is full, leaving about an inch between circles.

5. Lightly score a circle ⅓ inch in from the edge of each pastry circle. Dollop a scant tablespoon of cream cheese filling into the center of each pastry circle. Put the entire tray into the freezer for 20 minutes while you preheat the oven to 400°F and whisk together the egg and water with a fork.

6. Remove the very cold pastries from the freezer and brush the edges lightly with egg wash. Spoon a very heaping teaspoon or so of strawberry filling into the center, on top of the cream cheese. Bake the pastries 15 minutes at 400°F, then reduce the heat to 375°F and bake 10 minutes more, until the pastries are deeply golden. Remove the pastries to a wire rack and let cool. Repeat the above process until all of the dough has been used.

Strawberry and Prosecco-Glazed Granola Coffee Cake

There's nothing not to love about a bottle of bubbles that makes day drinking not just acceptable, but extra festive—so why not maximize your sparkling wine intake, and drizzle it all over your breakfast? This gorgeous cake gets heft from rich sour cream, but the extreme genius comes in the form of a prosecco and strawberry glaze topped with a cardamom-kicked granola and—get this—prosecco-soaked strawberries so you can have your prosecco and eat it, too.

FOR THE TOPPING

2 cups prosecco

2 cups small strawberries

½ cup granola, for sprinkling on top

FOR THE STREUSEL

⅓ cup (about 1½ ounces) all-purpose flour

¼ cup packed light brown sugar

1½ teaspoons ground cardamom

3 tablespoons (1½ ounces) unsalted butter, chilled and cubed

1 cup granola

FOR THE CAKE

2½ cups cake flour

2 teaspoons baking powder

½ teaspoon baking soda

¾ teaspoon kosher salt

1½ cups granulated sugar

¾ cup (6 ounces) unsalted butter, softened

3 large eggs

1 teaspoon pure vanilla extract

1¼ cups sour cream

FOR THE GLAZE

1 quart strawberries, hulled

1½ cups light corn syrup

1 cup prosecco

1 tablespoon cornstarch

1. Prepare the Topping: Combine strawberries and prosecco in a medium bowl. Cover and chill until ready to use.

2. Prepare the Streusel: Stir together the all-purpose flour, brown sugar, and cardamom in a small bowl. Add chilled butter, and, using your fingers or a fork, work mixture together until loose crumbs form. Stir in granola. Set aside.

3. Prepare the Cake: Preheat oven 350°F. Stir together cake flour, baking powder, baking soda, and salt in a medium bowl. Combine granulated sugar and softened butter in the bowl of a heavy-duty electric stand mixer fitted with the paddle

attachment. Beat on medium-high speed until fluffy. Reduce speed to medium-low, and add eggs, 1 at a time, beating until fully incorporated after each addition. Beat in vanilla. Reduce speed to low. Add cake flour mixture to granulated sugar mixture alternately with sour cream, beginning and ending with cake flour mixture, beating just until incorporated after each addition.

4. Coat a 12-cup Bundt pan with baking spray. Scrape half of batter into prepared pan. Set aside 2 tablespoons streusel; top batter evenly with remaining streusel. Top evenly with remaining batter, and sprinkle with reserved 2 tablespoons streusel. Bake in preheated oven until a wooden pick inserted in center of cake comes out with moist crumbs, 45 to 50 minutes.

5. Cool cake in pan on a wire rack for 15 minutes. Invert cake onto a serving plate and cool completely, about 1 hour.

6. Prepare the Glaze: Combine strawberries, corn syrup, and prosecco in a small saucepan. Bring to a simmer over medium-high, stirring often. Reduce heat to medium, and simmer, whisking occasionally, until thickened and strawberries have broken down. Stir in cornstarch, and simmer 1 minute. Remove from heat, and cool slightly, 12 to 15 minutes.

7. Spoon glaze evenly over the cake. Remove topping from the refrigerator, and top the cake with 8 of the prosecco-soaked strawberries and ½ cup granola. Serve the cake with remaining prosecco-soaked strawberries.

Pomegranate Pavlova

Pavlova has a strange history. It's named after a Russian ballerina. Australia and New Zealand both like to say they invented it. A hotel restaurant in each country has laid claim to it, and to this day no one's backing down. (We flipped a coin, and we're team New Zealand.) No matter where it came from, this pomegranate version is airy, simple to make, and perfect in every way.

4 large egg whites

2½ cups sugar, divided

2 teaspoons cornstarch, sifted

1 teaspoon pure vanilla extract

2 navel oranges

¼ cup pomegranate juice

1 (16-ounce) container heavy cream, divided

1 cup pomegranate seeds

1. Preheat the oven to 180°F.

2. Place the egg whites in the bowl of a stand mixer with a whisk attachment. Mix over high speed for 2 minutes, or until egg whites are foamy and beginning to stiffen.

3. Slowly incorporate 2 cups sugar while still mixing on high speed. Mix for 3 to 4 minutes more, or until stiff peaks form. Fold in cornstarch and vanilla until just combined.

4. Spoon mixture onto a baking sheet lined with parchment paper and form into a 9- to 10-inch circle. Bake for 1 hour and 30 minutes, and then turn off the oven. Whatever you do, DO NOT OPEN THE OVEN DOOR. Let the pavlova sit in the oven for 1 hour before removing.

5. Meanwhile, segment the oranges over a bowl to catch any juice that falls. Reserve the segments and squeeze the remaining juice out of the oranges before discarding.

6. Combine the orange juice, pomegranate juice, and ¼ cup plus 2 tablespoons sugar in a small saucepan. Cook over medium until the sugar is dissolved and mixture begins to thicken. Turn off the heat and stir in 1 to 2 tablespoons of heavy cream. Reserve sauce.

7. Place the remaining heavy cream and remaining 2 tablespoons sugar in the bowl of a stand mixer. Using the whisk attachment, mix over high speed for 8 to 10 minutes or until stiff peaks form.

8. Remove the pavlova from the oven and spread whipped cream over top. Top with sauce, reserved orange segments, and pomegranate seeds.

CHAPTER FIVE

ADVANCED

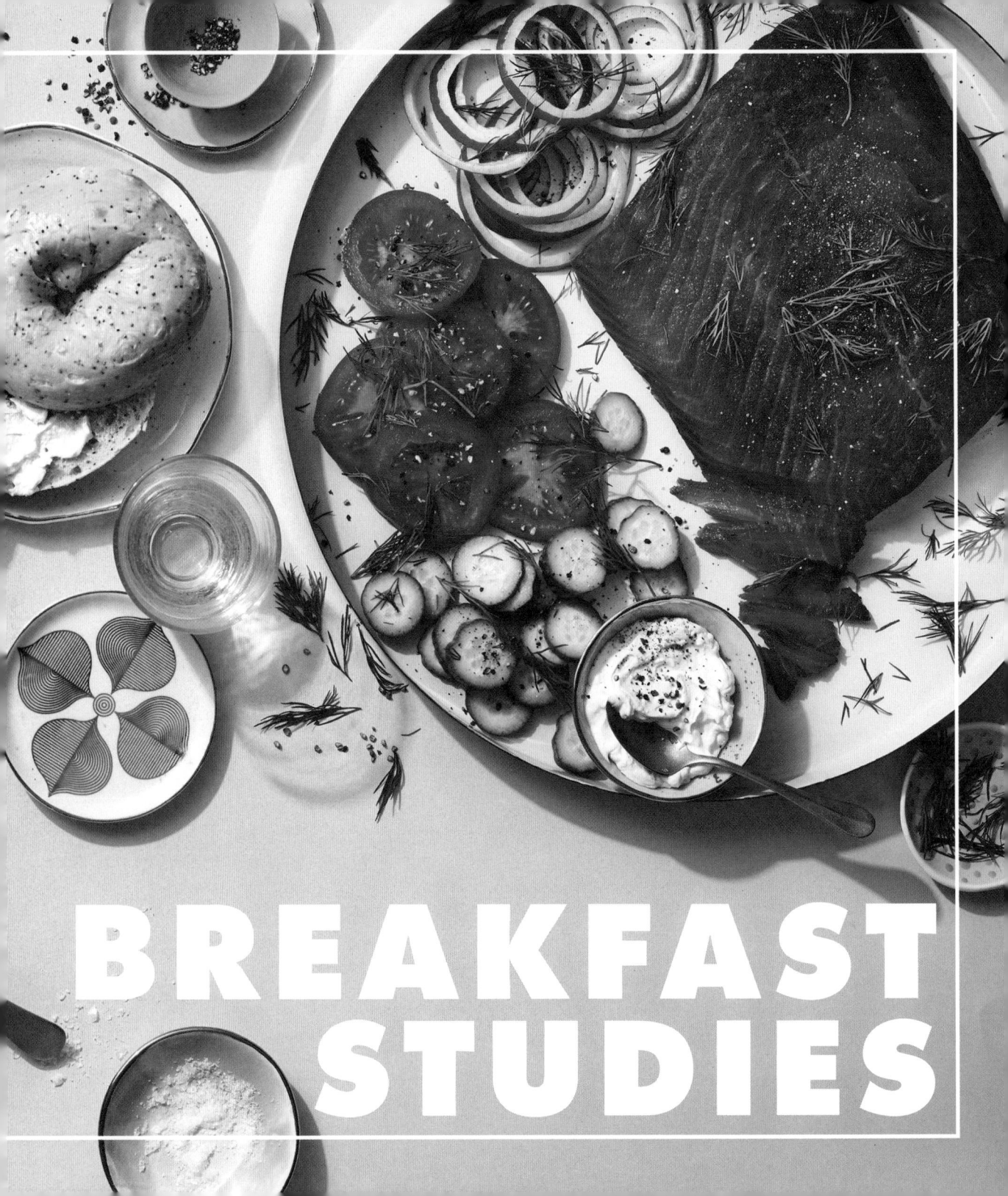

BREAKFAST STUDIES

Scotch Eggs for Normal People

BY ALLISON ROBICELLI While I'll never turn down the opportunity to order a Scotch egg, it disappoints me when a gastropub serves me a comically large softball of sausage, split directly in half to reveal the hard-boiled egg inside. These two gaping Scotch egg halves are usually arranged side by side on a threadbare carpet of wilted mixed greens, finished off with a drizzle of some mystery substance mixed with jarred mayo and re-christened to sound fancy. I will still eat and thoroughly enjoy it because eggs plus sausage plus deep-frying could never possibly be wrong. But still, I pine for a Scotch egg that's constructed within the bounds of sanity. That means one with a near equal sausage-to-egg ratio that's large enough to satiate, yet small enough to store in your pocket for an impromptu snack.

Scotch eggs keep well in the fridge for quite a few days, so it's best to make a dozen or so if you're putting in the effort. Who's going to do all this work for one egg? That's ridiculous. Twelve eggs in a carton, two pockets in your pants. That's nearly an entire week of meals in one go. [Editor's note: Extra Crispy does not endorse this as a safe food-handling strategy.]

12 large eggs

1½ pounds loose sausage meat of your choice

1 cup all-purpose flour

Salt and pepper, to taste

3 additional large eggs

2 cups panko or crushed saltines

Vegetable oil, for frying

1. Soft-cook 12 eggs for 6 minutes before shocking them in ice water. Allow to sit in the water for 5 minutes before peeling.

2. Put a piece of plastic wrap out on the counter, and pat out a bit of sausage meat to make a rectangle-ish strip of meat about 8- x 4-inches. It can be as thick as you'd like, but I think ½ inch is ideal.

3. Stand the egg up in the middle of the sausage strip. Lift up the plastic to easily wrap the sausage around the egg, gently pressing to evenly pack it on. Remove any sausage meat that you find to be excessive. It's not an exact science, but you'll get the hang of it quickly.

4. Roll the sausage-coated egg in a bit of flour that's been seasoned with salt and pepper. Whisk the 3 additional eggs with 2 tablespoons of water. Dip the Scotch eggs into the egg wash, then roll in panko. Refrigerate for at least 30 minutes or longer—at this point, the eggs can be held raw for up to 2 days.

5. When you're ready to cook, heat the vegetable oil to 350°F. Using a spider strainer, carefully drop in the eggs and fry until deep golden brown and crisp, about 5 minutes. Remove to a paper towel to drain. Serve warm or at room temperature.

Onion Strings Make Everything Extremely Fancy

Deep-fried frizzled onions are the shaved white truffles of us normal folk. Stack these fried onion strings mile high on your average burger and, like magic, you've transformed it into a luxe item. Scatter onion strings atop canned green beans, and you've gone from depressing TV dinner side to beloved holiday classic. Why not bring fried onion strings to breakfast? How about atop your schmear on a French onion bagel, and then gild that lily with some lox? What about a nice over-easy egg slipped between the halves of a toasted English muffin, stuffed with onions, and slathered with a tomato-based condiment? Keep onion strings in baggies to stuff in a drive-thru breakfast burrito. The process for making fried onion strings is easy, but make sure you have all your stuff together before you start. Otherwise you're going to end up running around your kitchen with flour-caked hands and watery eyes, screaming about third-degree burns.

Lots of canola oil or other high-heat oil

6 onions

All-purpose flour

Salt and pepper

And, if you dare, another spice. Garlic, paprika, cumin—go wild.

1. First, get your oil ready for deep-frying. Tell me you already know how to do this. I can't hold your hand right now.

2. Slice those onions nice and thin—we're talking ⅛ inch or less. Anything larger would be an onion ring, which is a totally different project. (It will be the same exact direction, except you slice the onions thicker.)

3. Put them in the bowl and separate them into individual rings. Once separated, add flour ½ cup at a time while continually tossing until they're all completely coated. Doing it this way keeps you from ending up with wasted excess flour and gluey, stuck-together onion bits.

4. When the oil is hot, about 350° to 370°F (this is what a thermometer is for), gently shake off some onions and gingerly plop them in. Let

them frizzle, stirring occasionally, until they're browned to your liking. This won't take too long so you really don't need to time it.

5. Remove the onions to the sheet pan that's been lined with paper towels, then hit it immediately with salt, pepper, and other spices. Toss them around a bit to coat, then spread them out to cool. The spreading is key, since if they're left in a pile they'll steam, and then they'll be soggy and gross.

6. Repeat over and over until everything is fried and your house smells like onions.

7. Once the onions are completely cool, you can move them to a sealed container; put a crumpled-up paper towel in there to absorb any extra moisture that may sneak inside. They should last a few days, though they'll probably be gone within 15 minutes.

Texas Red Chili and Eggs

BY MARGARET EBY Making chili is a meditative act. It fills your house with the aroma of spices and browned beef, and it promises a warm belly at the end of a long day of work. There are all kinds of chili, but my favorite all-day chili is one that I make every year for the Super Bowl, a classic bowl of red. You may know the dish by other names—Texas chili, Texas-style chili, chili con carne, or Texas red—but the rules are more or less the same. No tomatoes, no onions, no beans. Just beef and spices braised long and slow until they're coaxed into a spicy, thick bowl of chili.

I'm not from Texas, so this chili doesn't qualify as authentic. Think of it as a loving cover band tribute to a recipe from Frank X. Tolbert, a Texan journalist who, by all accounts, was a wizard when it came to his bowls of red. Over many Super Bowls, I've tweaked the original recipe into something that's extremely delicious. The best part of this chili is it's even better the day after you make it. In fact, it's exceptionally good as a breakfast on, say, the cold grim Monday after the Super Bowl. Top it with a runny egg or two, add some cornbread, and it's a brunch feast.

- 3 to 4 pounds of chuck roast or chuck steak
- 1 tablespoon vegetable oil
- 4 to 6 dried ancho chile pods
- 3 to 6 fresh jalapeños (depending on how hot you like your chili)
- 3 to 4 dried guajillo peppers
- 2 cloves of garlic, minced
- 1 tablespoon cumin
- 2 to 3 tablespoons masa harina, divided
- 1 quart beef broth
- Tabasco, to taste
- 1 tablespoon white vinegar
- 1 tablespoon brown sugar
- 1 to 2 runny eggs, scallions, cilantro, or limes, for topping

1. Roughly cut the chuck roast or steak into 2-inch cubes. In a large pot, heat the vegetable oil over medium. Brown the chuck in batches, just until the outside of the chunks develops a sear. Don't worry about cooking it through, and don't clean out the pot between batches (just add a bit more oil if the chuck starts sticking to the pot between batches).

2. Soak the dried ancho chiles in hot water for about 10 minutes, until they've plumped. Drain, reserving a cup of the water. De-stem, de-seed, and chop the reconstituted peppers, trying to avoid washing away the flesh inside. Do not touch your eyes while handling hot peppers—use gloves if you need.

3. De-stem and de-seed the jalapeño peppers, and roughly chop them. Place them with the dried ancho chiles and guajillo peppers and the minced garlic in the bowl of a blender, and pulse until a thick paste forms. If the paste isn't quite coming together, add a tablespoon or so of the reserved pepper liquid to smooth it out.

4. In the bottom of the pot, which should still be crusty from cooking the beef in it, place all the chuck along with the blended pepper paste. Add cumin and 1 tablespoon of the masa harina, and stir.

5. Add the beef broth and reserved pepper liquid. The goal is to have liquid just slightly cover the beef. You can add more water or broth if needed.

(I make this chili gluten-free, but if that's not a concern, you can add beer.)

6. Bring the pot to a boil and then reduce to a simmer. Leave the pot simmering for about 2 hours, checking on it often until the meat breaks apart easily with a fork.

7. Once the meat is tender, taste. If it's not hot enough for you, add Tabasco. Add the vinegar and brown sugar and the other tablespoon of masa harina, stir, and let simmer for 10 minutes.

8. If the chili gravy isn't thick enough, turn off the heat and let the chili settle for about ½ hour. The meat will reabsorb some of the liquid, making for a thicker chili. You can also add more masa harina or ground-up corn tortillas.

9. Serve in a bowl with accompaniments, like scallions, sour cream, shredded cheese, or limes. Top with a sunny-side up egg or two. And you can't go wrong with a side of cornbread. Or Fritos.

YES, YOU CAN MAKE THOSE LITTLE JAPANESE OMELETS AT HOME

BY JAMIE FELDMAR When I visited Japan, I did what many tourists do on a bleary-eyed morning there: I went to the Tsukiji Fish Market. The inner market is famous for its pre-dawn tuna auction, but what fewer people talk about is the outer market: the ring of pickle shops, kitchenware stands, and produce vendors lining the perimeter of the fish market itself. It's where many locals grab a quick breakfast on the go. Street food in general isn't huge in Tokyo, but the outer market has several *tamagoyaki* stalls, which I quickly zeroed in on.

Tamagoyaki is a Japanese omelet that's typically made by rolling several thin layers of egg (mixed with soy, mirin, sugar, and sometimes dashi, in which case it's called *dashimaki*) on top of each other while they cook in a small rectangular pan designated solely for this purpose. They can skew savory or sweet, and some of the vendors near Tsukiji bolster theirs with seafood or seaweed, though plain is the most common. Neatly pressed yellow slices of tamagoyaki show up all over the place in Japanese cuisine: in bento boxes, sushi restaurants (in *Jiro Dreams of Sushi*, an apprentice goes through 10 years of preparation before being allowed to make it), and sometimes with breakfast.

I'd had tamagoyaki before, but never seen it made, and I stood rapt while vendors tilted their *makiyakinabe* pans over an open flame, carefully sending thin streams of egg batter across the surface, then using oversized chopsticks to elegantly roll each cooked layer into a neat rectangle. I'm not squeamish about eating mackerel for breakfast, but in those first early-morning hours at Tsukiji, I could think of nothing I wanted more than tamagoyaki. Served hot, it almost melts in your mouth; when cool or at room temperature, the eggs settle, becoming dense, soft, and deeply satisfying. I wolfed down an entire tray of the stuff on the street, like a lady.

Tamagoyaki isn't hard to find in Japanese restaurants where I live, in New York, but too many versions are chalky and dry, lacking the silky-smooth texture and nuanced salty-sweet flavor I'd fallen hard for in Japan. I wanted to make my own, but I don't have room in my tiny apartment for single-use kitchen items like makiyakinabe pans; plus, I doubt my abilities to roll such perfect and neat little egg layers. I needed to find another way.

This is where Yuji Haraguchi, the owner of Okonomi restaurant and Osakana fish market in Brooklyn, steps in. Haraguchi has been serving traditional Japanese breakfasts to New Yorkers since Okonomi opened. Okonomi's tamagoyaki tastes different—fresher, softer, lighter—than anyone else's I'd eaten here, and it looks different, too: a perfect, shiny-smooth cube of yellow egg cake, with a burnished brown top, and no folded egg layers in sight. I had to find out how he made it.

Turns out, Haraguchi had many of the same concerns as me when developing his tamagoyaki recipe: namely, a lack of space and a lack of the desire to spend hours carefully rolling thin sheets of egg just so ("The traditional technique is hard!"). He developed a technique for baked tamagoyaki that's simpler, lighter, and arguably tastier than the traditional stovetop method.

Haraguchi's method is to blend together eggs with sugar, white soy sauce, dashi, mirin, and soy milk creamer, then pour the mixture into a baking sheet and cook it in the oven. "When we first made it, I have to say, it was really bland," says Okonomi's head chef, JT Vuong. "But we've found the perfect amount of sugar and salt, while still keeping the flavor straightforward." The finished product is at once creamy, custardy, delicate, and delicious.

Baked Tamagoyaki

12 large eggs

¼ cup plus 3 tablespoons dashi

⅔ cup soy creamer

3 tablespoons brown sugar

2 tablespoons white soy sauce

2 tablespoons mirin

1. In a large mixing bowl or container, combine all ingredients and blend thoroughly, either using an immersion blender or whisking well by hand. Try to avoid incorporating too much air into the mixture, as it will lead to unattractive bubbles in the tamagoyaki.

2. Chill the mixture overnight in the refrigerator to allow flavors to meld.

3. The next day, preheat the oven to 300°F and remove the egg mixture from the refrigerator. Line a 9- x 9-inch baking sheet with parchment paper with walls at least ¼-inch high. Gently re-whisk the eggs for a few seconds to re-incorporate all ingredients, then pour the eggs through a strainer into the baking sheet.

4. Bake at 300°F for 10 minutes, then lower the temperature to 200°F and continue baking for 1 hour and 15 minutes. The tamagoyaki is done when it's set along the edges and still jiggling ever-so-slightly in the center, and the top has become an even golden-brown color.

5. Allow tamagoyaki to cool at room temperature, then cut into square or rectangular slices using the tip of a very sharp knife. The remaining tamagoyaki can be sealed in plastic wrap in the refrigerator for 2 to 3 days.

Ramen Carbonara Will Cure Your Soul-Splitting Hangover

BY STACEY BALLIS A good carbonara is a thing of beauty: a tangle of noodles slicked with a creamy cheese-forward sauce, little nuggets of salty pork cheeks. When done well, it is glorious and rich. Carbonara should be the perfect food for a challenging morning: carbs to settle the stomach, protein to bolster the spirit, bacon, because, well, bacon. It is comfort food on various fronts. The problem with morning carbonara is that it cannot be made well when bleary-eyed unless you are a chef or an Italian nonna.

But I am here to save your morning, with a technique that gets you all the good stuff you need in carbonara, made easy enough to be cooked while you're operating at less than 100 percent capacity. First off, it is a one-pan wonder. Second, it uses ramen noodles, so it comes together super fast. And whereas in a normal carbonara you dread the formulation of the egg curds, here, being breakfast and all, you are looking for that to happen, making it a carbonara with scrambled eggs.

I'm giving you a recipe that serves two, in case someone else is on the premises. I recommend you serve this right in the pan with a couple of forks, and return directly to bed.

6 slices bacon, chopped into lardons

3 tablespoons butter

1 cup grated Parmesan, divided

2 packages ramen noodles, seasoning packs discarded

4 large eggs, beaten

2 scallions, sliced

Freshly ground black pepper

1. In a large saucepan over medium high heat, cook the bacon until it is rendered and browned. Remove to a plate with paper towels to drain. Blot the residual bacon fat out of the pan with a paper towel, but leave any crispy bits that might be stuck.

2. Add 2 cups of water, the butter, and ½ cup of the Parmesan cheese to the pot. Heat over medium-high heat, stirring constantly, until you have a creamy looking broth, being sure to scrape the bottom to get those bacon bits added to the mix. Add the 2 squares of noodles in to cook, stirring frequently, until they are softened. Keep stirring until the noodles are al dente and the sauce is thickened, about 3 to 4 minutes. Pour off the excess broth into a

small bowl, leaving the noodles a bit soupy but not swimming. Essentially you want the broth to come up halfway of the depth of the noodles. You should have about ½ cup of reserved broth. Keep stirring until the sauce reduces a bit and just coats the noodles, maybe another minute.

3. Push the noodles to one side of the pan and add the eggs in the space you create, stirring them inside that hole until they begin to form large curds, then mixing the eggs in with the noodles. Add the bacon bits, and remaining cheese, and the reserved broth stirring all the time until you get a pile of noodles and sauce with egg curds. Top with sliced scallions and a good grinding of black pepper.

Nothing Clears a Crisper Drawer Like Green Shakshuka

Classic shakshuka is a Tunisian dish made of eggs gently poached in thick, spicy tomato sauce. You may have also heard of Eggs in Purgatory, its Italian counterpart. Consider this version to be Eggs in the Crisper Drawer, because it uses up all the extra green things in your fridge.

- 3 tablespoons olive oil
- 1 large white onion, roughly chopped
- 2 large garlic cloves, minced
- 5 tomatillos, diced
- 1 green bell pepper, thinly sliced
- 1 jalapeño, minced and seeded
- 1 small fennel bulb, thinly sliced, optional
- Kosher salt and black pepper
- 1 teaspoon za'atar
- 1 teaspoon cumin
- 1 to 3 bunches leafy greens like kale, Swiss chard, collards, mustard greens, radish tops, spinach, etc.
- 1 cup salsa verde
- 8 to 10 large eggs
- Pita bread or naan, avocado, chopped herbs, crumbled feta or goat cheese, for serving

1. Drop a wide skillet on your stove and heat olive oil over medium. Toss onion and garlic into the pan.

2. Once the onions are translucent, stir in the tomatillos, green pepper, jalapeño, and, if using, fennel. Add a few good pinches of kosher salt, a few grinds of black pepper, za'atar, and cumin.

3. Next, wash and chop the leafy greens. Greens have this magic ability to shrink down to the size of whatever pan they're cooked in, so whether you have half a bunch of lacinato kale or the entire contents of your local farmers' market's greens table, you can make it work. Pile the greens into the pan and top with a lid to help the vegetables wilt. If you're using more

than 4 cups of greens, do this in shifts. Once the greens are mostly wilted, stir in 1 cup salsa verde.

4. Lower the heat and make a bunch of wells in the mixture (as many wells as eggs you plan to cook). Crack eggs into the wells and replace the lid on the pan. Let the eggs steam for 5 to 7 minutes, or until the yolks are cooked to your preference. Meanwhile, toast some bread or naan, slice an avocado, and roughly chop any fresh herbs you have hanging around.

5. When the eggs are cooked, scoop shakshuka into shallow bowls (ladle it directly over the toast or naan if you know what's good for you) and top with additional chopped herbs, sliced avocado, and crumbled feta or goat cheese.

INSTANT POT
BREAKFAST RATATOUILLE
FOR LAZY PEOPLE

BY KAT KINSMAN

Shakshuka will save your soul and your sanity; that's been well established. Sauté some aromatics, tomatoes (canned, even), and possibly some peppers, plop some eggs in there and you're pretty much breakfasted up. But as long as tomatoes, eggplants, sweet peppers, and zucchini are within your grasp, consider rotating ratatouille into your morning repertoire. This way you'll start the day with a full serving of life-awesomeing vegetables and go about your business in a confident, well-fed fashion.

No, you're not crafting this ratatouille the morning-of. You'd have to crawl out of bed at, like, 4 a.m. and contend with sharp objects, and that seems like a recipe for pain and sadness. Stay in bed, knowing that you have this glorious mélange lurking in your fridge or freezer, ready to deploy at a moment's notice.

Not gonna gloss over it—classic ratatouille takes time, but should you care to streamline the process and have access to an Instant Pot, the road to breakfast ratatouille can be considerably shortened. (Note: If you have a pressure cooker, this basic method will adapt as well.)

Assemble your ingredients. The vegetables listed above are pretty standard, and you don't need to be fastidious about the amount or ratio. If you like zucchini, skew heavily that way. If it's tomatoes you favor, have at it. Peel or don't peel—your choice. Add olives or capers if you like. Cut all these into ½-inch chunks, and feel free to pulverize or even blend the tomatoes. Set them aside. It's fine if they're all in the same bowl, because they're about to get to know one another extremely well. Season the whole mess with salt and pepper.

Then have a short reckoning with yourself about herbs. Basil and thyme are boon companions to these vegetables, but if you've got an excess of another you like, invite it into the mix. Do all the requisite de-stemming, chiffonading, and whatnot to remove any stems or woody bits. Let those hang tight for a moment.

Grab a few onions, cloves of garlic, shallots, or even leeks, and mince them. Then fire up the Sauté

function of the Instant Pot, pour in a sloppy quantity of olive oil, and once it starts to shimmer, add these alliums. Stir and stir and stir them into a golden mess, then add the herbs and stir some more, making sure that nothing is sticking and burning onto the bottom. Once that's thoroughly gloppy and glorious, shut off the heat.

Those vegetables you chopped and seasoned—they've been working during this time, casting off water. Pour out any excess from the bowl, pushing and squeezing if that feels reasonable to you. Pat the vegetables as dry as you can, then add them to the Instant Pot along with even more olive oil. (There's no need to add additional liquid because the vegetables will give off plenty of water.)

Seal the Instant Pot, press the Meat/Stew button, and go wash your dishes and tidy up. You've got 35 minutes, plus the time it takes to get to high pressure. When that's finished, release the Instant Pot manually and carefully (it's hot) peer inside to see how things are going. Stir, pour off any excess liquid, and add more oil if needed. Then reseal and hit that Meat/Stew button again. Develop a 35-minute hobby, or clean out your fridge a little.

Then manually release the pressure again, and gaze upon what you have made. If things are still a little watery, pour off what you can, hit that Sauté button and keep stirring (and oiling) until the mixture is thick and makes a satisfying sluck-sluck sound.

You can eat what you'd like, but make sure to leave a good helping in the fridge for breakfast. When you awake, plop a quantity of the now thoroughly melded ratatouille into a deep skillet and warm it evenly throughout over low heat. Then crack eggs into cups, make little divots in the ratatouille, and slide an egg into each. Then cover and cook over medium for about 10 minutes, or slide the whole skillet into a warm oven until the eggs are set. Then eat.

Excess ratatouille will keep in the fridge for 3 to 4 days, or frozen in a ziplock bag with the air pressed out for a few months.

Persian Kuku Sabzi Is the Easiest Way to Get Those Greens

This is a safe space to admit that green juices are basically liquid masochism. No one's arguing that they're not chock-a-block with nutritional benefits, but if you're going to be pounding all those greens and herbs, they may as well taste as good as they are for you, and that comes in the form of a kuku sabzi. This Persian version of a frittata is a crisply-crusted, tender-centered cake that can be served warm, room temperature, or cold.

2 bunches green chard, washed

1 large leek

Extra-virgin olive oil

Salt

7 tablespoons unsalted butter, divided

4 cups roughly chopped cilantro leaves and tender stems

2 cups roughly chopped dill leaves and tender stems

8 to 9 large eggs

1. Preheat the oven to 350°F. Strip the chard leaves: Gripping the base of each stem with one hand, pinch the stem with the other hand and pull upward to strip the leaf. Reserve the stems. Remove the root and top inch of the leek, then quarter it lengthwise. Cut each quarter into ¼-inch slices, place in a large bowl, and wash vigorously to remove dirt. Drain. Thinly slice the chard stems, discarding any tough bits at the base. Add to the washed leek and set aside.

2. Gently heat a 10- or 12-inch cast-iron or nonstick frying pan over medium and coat the bottom of the pan with oil. Add in the chard leaves and season with salt. Cook, stirring occasionally, until the leaves are wilted, 4 to 5 minutes. Remove the chard, set aside and allow to cool.

3. Return the pan to the stove and heat over medium. Add 3 tablespoons of the butter. When the butter begins to foam, add the sliced leeks and chard stems, along with salt. Cook until tender and

translucent, 15 to 20 minutes. Stir from time to time, and if needed, add a splash of water, reduce the heat, or cover with a lid to trap steam.

4. In the meantime, squeeze the cooked chard leaves dry, discard the liquid, then coarsely chop. Combine in a large bowl with the cilantro and dill. When the leeks and chard stems are cooked, add them to the greens. Mix everything up evenly. Taste and season generously with salt, knowing you're about to add a bunch of eggs to the mixture. Add the eggs, one at a time, until the mixture is just barely bound with egg—you might not need to use all 9 eggs, depending on how wet your greens were and how large your eggs are, but it should seem like a ridiculous amount of greens.

5. Wipe out and reheat your pan over medium-high and add remaining 4 tablespoons of butter and 2 tablespoons of oil, then stir to combine. When the butter begins to foam, carefully pack the kuku mixture into the pan.

6. To help it cook evenly, use a rubber spatula to gently pull the edges of the mixture into the center as they set. After about 2 minutes of this, reduce the heat to medium and let it continue to cook without touching it.

7. Because this kuku is so thick, it'll take a while for the center to set. Do not let the crust burn before the center sets. Peek at the crust by lifting the kuku with a rubber spatula, and if it's getting too dark, reduce the heat. Rotate the pan a quarter turn every 3 or 4 minutes for even browning.

8. After about 10 minutes, when the mixture is no longer running and the bottom is golden brown, prepare to flip the kuku. Tip out as much of the cooking fat as you can to prevent burning yourself, then flip the kuku onto the back of a cookie sheet or into another large frying pan. Add 2 tablespoons olive oil into the hot pan and slide the kuku back in to cook the other side. Cook for another 10 minutes, rotating the pan every 3 or 4 minutes.

9. If something goes awry when you try to flip, don't freak out! Just do your best to flip the kuku, add a little more oil into the pan, and get it back into the pan. If you prefer not to flip, then slip the whole pan into the oven and bake until the center is fully set, about 10 to 12 minutes. Check for doneness using a toothpick, or shake the pan back and forth, looking for a slight jiggle at the top of the kuku. When it's done, carefully flip it out of the pan onto a plate. Blot away any excess oil. Serve.

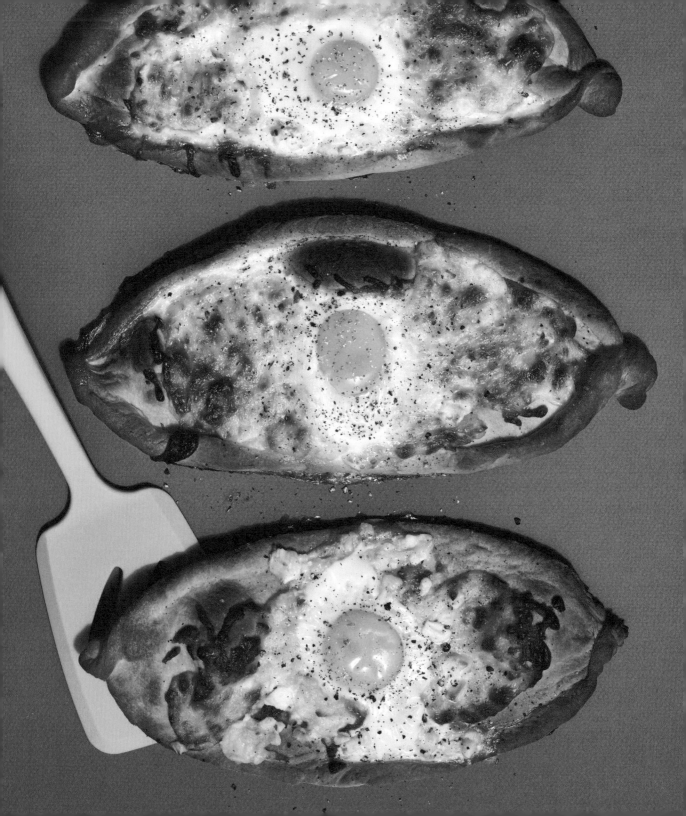

Khachapuri Is a Boat-Shaped Wonder

Think of khachapuri as a breakfast boat you take through the sea of cheese, and then dock at a blissful afternoon nap. These dense egg-and-cheese pies are a staple in Georgia, the country. Usually they get their gooeyness from sulguni, a salty and sour Georgian cheese, but here we're using a combo of mozzarella, feta, and cottage cheese. If you can get sulguni, by all means use it.

- 1 cup whole milk
- 2 (¼-ounce) packages active dry yeast
- 2 tablespoons plus 1 teaspoon granulated sugar, divided
- 3¼ cups all-purpose flour, plus more for dusting
- ½ cup unsalted butter, cubed and softened
- 2 teaspoons kosher salt, divided
- 1½ tablespoons olive oil
- 12 ounces mozzarella cheese, shredded (about 3 cups)
- 6 ounces feta cheese, crumbled (about 1½ cups)
- ½ cup cottage cheese
- Cooking spray
- ½ cup unsalted butter, melted
- 6 large eggs
- 1 teaspoon black pepper

1. Heat milk in a saucepan over medium to 115°F; pour into a bowl. Sprinkle with yeast and 1 teaspoon of the sugar. Let stand 1 minute; stir. Let stand until foamy, about 10 minutes.

2. Combine flour, softened butter, 1 teaspoon of the salt, and remaining 2 tablespoons sugar in the bowl of a heavy-duty electric stand mixer fitted with the dough hook attachment. Beat on low speed until butter is incorporated. With mixer running, add yeast mixture. Increase speed to medium, and beat until a supple dough forms, about 10 minutes.

3. Turn dough out onto a work surface; shape into a ball. Place oil in a large bowl. Place ball in bowl; turn to coat completely with oil. Cover bowl loosely with a clean towel; place in a dry, warm place. Let stand until dough has doubled in size, about 1 hour.

4. Turn dough out onto a work surface, and divide into 6 even portions. Roll each portion into a ball. Place balls on a baking sheet, and let stand in a dry, warm place until slightly springy, about 20 minutes.

5. Preheat oven to 425°F. Stir together mozzarella, feta, and cottage cheese in a large bowl.

6. Lightly dust a work surface with flour. Working with 1 ball at a time, roll into an oval shape with a maximum length of 10 inches and maximum width of 4 inches. Spoon ½ cup cheese mixture into center of oval, leaving a 1-inch border. Roll dough borders up and toward center of oval, and pinch dough together at ends to create a canoe shape. Repeat with remaining dough balls and cheese mixture.

7. Line 2 baking sheets with parchment paper, and coat with cooking spray. Place 3 khachapuri on each prepared baking sheet. Brush crusts evenly with ⅓ of the melted butter. Bake in preheated oven 15 minutes.

8. Remove sheets from oven. Break an egg in the center of each khachapuri. Brush crusts with ⅓ of the melted butter. Return to oven; bake until dough is golden brown and egg whites are set. Remove from oven. Sprinkle with pepper and 1 teaspoon salt; brush with remaining butter. Serve immediately.

WE TASTED 11 FANCY BUTTERS TO FIND THE BEST ONE

BY MARGARET EBBY

There are two kinds of butter. There are the workhorse butters, the ones you can buy in sticks for less than $5 per pound and store in your freezer for bursts of baking inspiration. And then there are the fancy butters, which I reach for when I have a particularly nice crusty bread or a biscuit just dying for a smear. Fancy butter adds something more than just luscious fattiness to a dish. A good fancy butter reminds you that it came from somewhere specific. Like wine, it has a terroir. But which is the best fancy butter? Which is the block of butterfat that's worth dropping extra cash on?

THE METHODOLOGY

First, Extra Crispy Culinary Editor Rebecca Firkser and I sourced 11 fancy salted butters available via both regular and specialty grocery stores. We aimed for things that you could obtain without bribing anyone to fly over from France with a cooler. Then we sat down with the inimitable John Winterman, Managing Partner at Bâtard, and noted butter enthusiast, who agreed to serve as our *maître de beurre*. Each butter was tasted on sourdough bread and on a radish.

11	**PLOUGHGATE CREAMERY CULTURED SALTED BUTTER**	I am a fan of Ploughgate's maple butter, so I was excited to try the straight-up cultured salted butter. Unfortunately, it wasn't a favorite. The further into high-end cultured butter you get, the more the gap between cheese and butter closes. This butter reminded me of that—it tasted very cultured, with almost a yogurty tartness to it, and a strong funky note. It was good with radishes, but too assertive for bread. It's butter that challenges you, which is interesting, but not exactly what I was looking for in a fancy butter.
10	**LES PRES SALES BUTTER**	This butter is sort of fudgy in texture, though it has a good distribution of salt and a smooth aftertaste. It wasn't the best, it wasn't the worst. Our *maître de beurre* noted that it would probably go especially well with scrambled eggs or over popcorn.
9	**BEURRE D'ISIGNY**	This kind of butter is why the phrase "smooth like butter" exists. It has a nice cultured taste, a slight tanginess that doesn't overwhelm the butter's essential fatty, butteriness, but balances it. It would be just the thing on toast, or balanced with something sweeter like jam. Unsurprisingly it performed best with the bread, rather than the radish, but it has a nice, clean mouthfeel with both.
8	**BEPPINO OCCELLI**	This is a show-off butter. It comes in waxed paper and every pat has an embossed design on top. It tasted really good, too—light and mellow and creamy, a little sweet, and would be insanely good on a blueberry muffin. If you put it out at a dinner table, instead of hoarding it all for yourself, people would be impressed. It reminded Senior Food and Drinks Editor Kat Kinsman of a milkshake—smooth buttery goodness.

7	**PAYSAN BRETON**	Another butter that's a bit of a show-off, this has lovely fluted sides inside its foil package. Also, it tastes very good. It's very salty at first bite and then mellows out into something that's a little bit sweet and a little bit tangy. "I feel like I can taste that this creature ate grass," Kat Kinsman noted. It feels like it came to you from a glorious place with nice grass and sunny skies and good hot toast.
6	**ÉCHIRÉ**	This butter is one that French butter fiends freak-out about and chefs love. (Apparently there's a whole shop in Tokyo that exclusively sells Échiré.) You can understand why when you taste it. It's not a showstopper like the Beppino Occelli, but it's an understatedly elegant butter. It's got a great balance and is just salty enough. It's the kind of butter that would play well with others but can hold its own in the spotlight, too.
5	**COLLIER'S WELSH BUTTER**	Collier's wraps its butter in black foil featuring a man who appears to be a coal miner. Obviously, this immediately endeared it to me, and even more exciting is how incredibly delicious it is. This butter is bright, clean, and a little sweet. It's even-handed with the salt, and has a great aftertaste. It's excellent. Congratulations to the country of Wales.
4	**KERRYGOLD**	I grew up visiting Ireland and eating an incredible amount of Kerrygold on toast, scones, and soda bread. This is where my love of butter came from, and it was nice to see how well it held up to other contenders. "Talking about how good Kerrygold is like talking about how good *Casablanca* is," John Winterman said. He's right. It's a classic for a reason. If none of the other butters are in your price range, know that you can pick up Kerrygold and still have some of the tastiest butter ever made.
3	**DOUBLE DEVON CREAM BUTTER**	Double Devon Cream Butter was not an entry that I expected to be a heavyweight, but it is very good. It is steadfast and true, bright and just salty enough. It's just a hair above Kerrygold in terms of its buttery pleasingness. And given his choice of butter to take home, John Winterman took this one.
2	**VERMONT CULTURED SALTED BUTTER**	This butter is not subtle. It is a rush of tangy, salty, buttery goodness and demands to be noticed. It is a different kind of treat from the other contenders, a sort of over-the-top buttery butter. It's a Beyoncé kind of butter. It's a star, is what I'm saying.
1	**BORDIER BUTTER**	Bordier butter is the one with the biggest cult following, the one that is hardest to find outside of France, and the one that most lists like this cite as the number one, best of all time. *We'll see about that*, I thought. Stacked up against all these offerings, is Bordier really all that special? Friends, I need to inform you that it is…spectacular. It's a butter with such complexity of flavor that it's insane that all these butters have exactly the same two ingredients: cream and salt. It's perfectly balanced, sweet and salty, a tiny bit tart, and incredibly harmonious. If you're someone who cares about fancy butter, who cared enough to read this list, then at some point in your life, you need to taste it.

10-Minute Asparagus Brunch for Fancypants People

BY CAROLINE LANGE I am not someone with addictive tendencies—in fact, I'm an exceedingly, sometimes overly moderate person. I like lots of different things all the time, and not too much of any one thing ever. The exception to this is when asparagus swings into season at the farmers' market. I just about ran home from the market with the first asparagus of the season, steamed it in a pan, and then consulted my very odds and ends-filled refrigerator.

Knowing how much asparagus loves cheesy, salty, funky, richness (think asparagus in quiches or eggs Benedict.) I emerged with a tub of miso and the butter dish. Mashed together and tossed with the hot asparagus, the miso butter makes a salty, savory sauce, and it really is just the thing for the very green, very demure on its own asparagus.

Another reason I love asparagus: It is totally kosher to eat it with your fingers. This is even true when it is dripping with butter. If you add eggs to the equation, you have to add the fork back in, but you get a really lovely brunch, one that feels a little fancy. It is very easily batchable, making it an ideal choice if you're having a crowd over.

1 tablespoon unsalted butter, room temperature

1½ teaspoons white or yellow miso, plus more to taste

½ pound asparagus, ends trimmed (I do this by simply bending the stalk gently about an inch above the base and waiting for it to snap off)

As many eggs as you like

Freshly ground black pepper, to taste

1. Set aside just a bit of the tablespoon of butter—you'll use it for greasing the pan.

2. Mash the rest of the butter together with the miso in a small bowl. Set aside.

3. Set the asparagus in a frying pan that has a tight-fitting lid. Add a splash of water, set on the lid, and turn the heat to medium-high. Let the asparagus steam until bright green and tender; the exact time will depend on how thick your asparagus stalks are, about 3½ to 4 minutes. Shake the pan occasionally and keep checking—you'll know when they're done.

4. Drain off all but about a tablespoon of water (or, if the water's gone, add a tablespoon) and turn the heat to low. Drop in the miso butter and swirl, gently tossing the asparagus in the butter to coat. It should look slightly saucy. Set the asparagus on the serving plate and cover so they stay warm.

5. Add the butter you set aside before to the pan and cook the eggs as desired: fried, scrambled, poached, or soft-boiled. Set the cooked eggs over the asparagus. Season to taste with salt and pepper.

Cilbir with a Fried Egg

Yogurt is a no-brainer at breakfast. Scoop it into a bowl, cover it with fruit and granola, and you've basically made an a.m. sundae. But sometimes your cravings may skew more savory, and that's where cilbir comes in. This Turkish delight melds creamy garlic and herb-kicked yogurt, a spice-spiked butter, and the sloppy pleasure of a golden yolk.

2 cups Greek yogurt

2 tablespoons lemon juice

1 garlic clove, grated

3 tablespoons chopped dill, plus more for garnish

1 tablespoon chopped parsley, plus more for garnish

Salt, to taste

2 large eggs

3 tablespoons butter, melted

2 teaspoons crushed red pepper

½ teaspoon sweet paprika

Coarse sea salt

1. Stir together Greek yogurt, lemon juice, garlic, dill, parsley, and salt in a bowl. Refrigerate while preparing the rest of the dish.

2. Fry the eggs. You already have your favorite method for this.

3. Spice up the butter. Heat a saucepan over medium. Melt the butter with crushed red pepper and paprika, stirring frequently.

4. Assemble it. Divide the yogurt between 2 bowls. Top with a fried egg, drizzle with spiced butter and sprinkle with coarse salt, dill, and parsley.

CROSSHATCHELBACK POTATOES

BY KAT KINSMAN

Throughout 2014 and 2015, it seemed as if the entire food-related internet was one giant Hasselback potato. In case you've mentally blocked out that particular culinary era, Hasselback potatoes—named for the hotel in Stockholm where the recipe was developed—are potatoes that have been evenly sliced from tip to tip, while remaining attached at the bottom. The result is a fanned-out potato that crisps marvelously on its radical expanse of exposed surface area and provides plenty of slim pockets in which to slip herbs, cheese, bacon, chives, sour cream, and anything else that might delight you.

That surely deserves an "A" for effort, but why not go for the extra credit? Just rotate the potato 90 degrees and slice to create a crosshatched Hasselback that's not entirely unlike a blooming onion—minus the batter and deep fry.

(Though hey, if the oil is hot, no one would dream of foiling your fun.) The crosshatched Hasselback potato takes a little more patience than a standard one, but pays off in double the crisp, and a ridiculous amount of glee.

If you're a little nervous about your knife skills, just work slowly, and use a serrated blade and a sawing motion to keep yourself on task. To prevent the potato from rolling or a slice going all the way through to the cutting board, place it in a channel between two low, flat surfaces (cookie sheets and plastic cutting boards work well) so the knife will automatically stop.

Brush or roll the potatoes gently in oil or melted butter, making sure that it gets into the crevices, and season however pleases you. Roast until crisp, and then revel in the compliments.

YES, YOU CAN MAKE BEET-CURED LOX AT HOME

BY JAMIE FELDMAR In the olden days, lox was made only with the belly of a salmon. It was cured with salt and perhaps a bit of sugar, and that's it. But as lox has evolved, so too has its flavor, which today might include everything from orange zest and ginger peel to pastrami spices and brown sugar. One of the more eye-catching lox variants to hit New York City in recent years can be found at Black Seed Bagels. Baker Dianna Daoheung developed a recipe for a beet-and-horseradish lox that's become something of a signature. The fish is stained a deep ruby-red, and when thinly sliced, nearly melts into the bakery's wood-fired bagels. It's beautiful to behold, and, most importantly, delicious to eat. It's also easy to make at home.

Now, let's take a moment to discuss terminology. Lox is sometimes referred to as cured salmon, meaning it's covered in salt and seasonings to draw out moisture, but not actually cooked or smoked. Lox is rich, silky, and borderline-translucent when thinly sliced; and today it's made more often from a salmon fillet than belly. Lox is not smoked salmon. Smoked salmon is also cured but then either cold- or hot-smoked. Gravlax is lox, Scandinavian-style, cured with less salt and more herbs like dill and juniper, plus alcohol for good measure. Nova is cold-smoked salmon from Nova Scotia. Got that? We could go on, but those are the basics, so let's move along to how to make lox.

"Making beet-cured lox is an extremely easy process," says Daoheung, even for the curing neophyte. The hardest part of the whole thing is, arguably, waiting three to four days for the cure to complete. The basic cure for a 1½ pound piece of fresh salmon is 1 cup of kosher salt mixed with ¼ cup of granulated sugar. "We keep it simple, but you could add peppercorn, mustard seeds, or caraway seeds here if you'd like," Daoheung says.

She pats the salmon dry and coats both sides of the fillet heavily with the salt-sugar mixture. Salt has been used for centuries as a preservation technique, inhibiting the growth of spoilage-causing microbes by absorbing water. In other words, so long as you're using high-quality salmon to begin with, there's little to worry about in the lox-making process; while the fish isn't technically cooked, when properly cured it's safe to eat "raw."

From there, Daoheung smothers the salmon with a few cups of grated raw beets and a cup of grated fresh horseradish root. "The beets are really more for color than flavor, but the horseradish gives you that great earthiness," she says. "You could also add ginger root, lemon zest, or orange zest here if you're into experimenting." From there, the salmon is topped with fresh dill fronds, then placed in the refrigerator for three to four days to cure. After the second day, Daoheung will remove the salmon and rinse the cure and beet-horseradish mixture off, then re-coat the fillet with a second batch for extra color, though this step isn't necessary for home cooks.

After three days, begin to check the firmness of the salmon, which will indicate its doneness. It should spring back gently when you touch it (too hard and the salmon is overcured; too soft and you probably need to leave it in for another 12 to 24 hours). Toss any leftover cure or veggies and give the salmon a final rinse before serving. Slice it very thin from a high angle to show off your handiwork and the salmon's beautiful jewel-toned hues.

Beet-Cured Lox

**1½ pounds skin-on salmon
fillet (ideally, a thick
center-cut)**

1 cup kosher salt

¼ cup granulated sugar

**3¾ cups grated beet
(from about 3 medium
beets)**

**1 cup grated fresh
horseradish**

1 bunch dill

1. Lay out a piece of plastic wrap approximately 3 times longer than the salmon. Place the salmon, skin-side down, on top of the plastic.

2. In a small mixing bowl, combine the salt and sugar. Using your hands, rub the salt mixture across all sides of the salmon, evenly coating every part of its surface with a thick layer of salt.

3. In a small mixing bowl, combine the grated beet and grated horseradish. Generously coat all sides of the salmon with an even layer of beet mixture.

4. Scatter a handful of fresh dill fronds across the top of the salmon. Cover salmon loosely with

plastic wrap and place in the refrigerator. After 3 days, check for doneness, and cure for an additional day if necessary.

5. When salmon is fully cured, rinse excess cure and pat dry. Slice very thinly, from a high angle with a very sharp knife, and serve with bagels, cream cheese, and sliced vegetables.

Cauliflower Hash Browns

Do you ever wake up and think, *I'd straight up murder someone for some hash browns right now*? Well, please don't ever do that. We can get through this. Do you...have some potatoes? No? Hm, what about cauliflower? Yes? OK, cool. Everyone be cool. Take a deep breath and follow these instructions. You'll have hash browns soon enough, you sweet, sweet creature.

4 cups riced cauliflower (about 16 ounces)

2 large eggs, beaten

4 ounces sharp cheddar cheese, shredded (about 1 cup)

⅓ cup finely chopped white onion

¼ cup chopped fresh chives

2 tablespoons all-purpose flour

1 teaspoon kosher salt

1 teaspoon black pepper

¼ cup salted butter, divided

Sour cream

Sliced scallions

1. Stir together cauliflower and beaten eggs in a medium bowl. Stir in cheese, onion, chives, flour, salt, and pepper.

2. Melt 2 tablespoons of the butter in a large cast-iron skillet over medium. Scoop ⅓ cup of the cauliflower mixture into your hand, and press firmly to form a 3-inch-wide patty. Cook 4 patties until well browned on bottom and set, 4 to 5 minutes. Carefully turn patties, and cook until browned on bottom, 3 to 4 minutes. Transfer to a plate. Repeat with the remaining cauliflower mixture and butter to make 4 more patties. Serve immediately with sour cream and sliced scallions.

Basic Slow-Cooker Strata

BY STACEY BALLIS I used to only make strata when we had weekend houseguests. You can put it together the day before and let it hang out in the fridge and toss it in a hot oven in the morning, thus eliminating the stress-inducing conversations about how everyone likes their eggs and praying no one wants theirs sunny-side up or over easy. Then it hit me: What would happen if I didn't let it sit at all and just cooked it low and slow all night while I slept?

Magic, that's what happens, people. Layer the ingredients in a slow-cooker pot, mix a custard, and pour it over. Then cook it on low overnight and wake up to delicious brunch-worthy breakfast without going full-Martha.

The word *strata* means layers, and those layers can be anything you want. Part of an artisanal loaf slightly past its prime? Glorious. English muffins, bagels, or frozen waffles are fair game; just use what you've got. Now, you need fillings. Shred up those last two pieces of chicken from dinner. Any vegetables floating around in your crisper drawer—chop 'em up and layer them in. You just want to avoid packing too tightly, because you want holes and nooks and crannies for the custard to flow into. Any cheese you like is great in this, shredded or crumbled over the first layer of filling, then the second layer of bread, and repeat.

You can even make a sweet version with cinnamon raisin bread or leftover croissants. Layer that with dollops of cottage cheese, or ricotta and chopped fruit, a sprinkle of warm spices, and a bit of sugar and vanilla, and a healthy plop of sour cream added to the custard.

Speaking of custard, add in a tablespoon of something extra: Dijon mustard, miso paste, or tahini if you're craving Middle Eastern flavors. The strata lends itself to garnishing. Maybe fried onions or chopped nuts. And don't be shy about sauces if you like them, a splash of hot sauce or a drizzle of maple syrup—you do you at breakfast.

8 slices breadstuffs (or 4 English muffins, 4 bagels, 8 frozen toaster waffles, 8 crumpets, 4 croissants, etc.) torn into large pieces and tossed with 2 tablespoons melted butter

3 cups total filling items (some of my faves: onion/spinach/ Gruyère/moo shu pork/ scallions/chorizo/black bean/cheddar/ Bolognese/ zucchini/ricotta)

8 large eggs
2 cups milk (or a combo of milk and half-and-half or cream)

Layer half the bread followed by half your chosen filling items in a well-greased slow-cooker pot, season, repeat. Mix the eggs with the milk and season as desired, adding any bonus item you like. Pour slowly over the strata and press on the top to help soak the bread. Refrigerate until right before you go to bed, then cook on low for 8 hours. Garnish as desired (fried onions, chopped nuts, or toasted, buttered breadcrumbs), slice, and serve.

NOTE

I make this in a 4-quart cooker, which makes for a nice thick circular strata. If you have a larger oval one, you will end up with a little less loft, but no less deliciousness.

Turn Your King Cake into French Toast

If you have the good fortune to have a King Cake in your house, you probably don't need any help disposing with it. King Cakes—those cream cheese icing slathered, cinnamon-y rings of joy that mark the Carnival season—are one of those baked goods that disappear quickly. "Oh, I'll just have a sliver," you say, and five slivers later you're deep in a sugar coma. But if that King Cake has gotten just a wee bit too stale, then the solution for you is simple. Turn your King Cake into French toast.

The principle of King Cake French Toast is the same as regular old French toast, with a couple caveats. Because frying the icing on top of a King Cake, though probably delicious, would ruin the whole look of the thing, you only soak the bottom half of the King Cake in your French toast custard, and crisp up the un-icinged side of the cake in the skillet. You could add maple syrup to it, should you want, but the sweetness from the icing and colored sugar on the cake make it not totally necessary. Also? Be prepared to share, since the smell of King Cake being cooked up in a skillet is a dang delight. Don't forget to fish out the plastic baby, either! And if you run out of King Cake, sprinkle DIY colored sugar on everything, and pretend.

3 eggs

1 cup half-and-half

1 teaspoon salt

6 to 8 slices of King Cake, ideally slightly stale

Butter

1. Whisk together eggs, half-and-half, and salt until thoroughly blended. Place slices of King Cake in a baking dish or similar pan, frosting-side up, and pour egg mixture in about halfway up the height of the cake. (Since the slices won't be flipped, to preserve the frosting, only the bottom half gets soaked and cooked.) Cover and let the slices chill in the refrigerator for 2 hours, then drain the liquid from the pan and let the slices chill and further drain for 1 more hour.

2. Melt your desired quantity of butter (only you know your soul) in a skillet over medium-low and when it has stopped foaming, place the soaked slices frosting-side up in the pan and cook to

desired doneness. If desired, to cook the sides more thoroughly, either use tongs to slightly tilt the slices into the butter, or draw it up the sides with a spatula, taking care not to melt the icing. Work in batches if needed, wiping out and re-buttering the skillet as needed. Serve hot.

NOTE

For DIY colored sugar, place ½ cup sugar in a ziplock sandwich bag. Slowly add 8 drops of liquid food coloring and seal the bag, pushing out extra air. Shake until combined, breaking up any clumps. Once the color is evenly distributed, pour the sugar onto a baking sheet until dry, about 1 hour.

This Magical Yogurt Bowl Is Caffeinated, Sweet, and Healthy Enough

Yogurt works hard, man. Not only is it busy being all kinds of delicious and tricking brains into thinking we're scarfing down ice cream (once we tart it up with toppings), but it's also working all sorts of gut-friendly jazz. But—and yes, being selfish here—can't it get us all wired, too? This recipe takes a tip from the classic espresso-and-gelato dessert: affogato, with a little extra go-go-go, thanks to the addition of chocolate-covered espresso beans, and crunchy cocoa nibs. Save any extra coffee syrup to sweeten your drinks, drizzle on ice cream and baked goods, or eat by the spoonful when you need to pull an all-nighter.

1½ cups granulated sugar

1 cup brewed dark roast coffee

1 cup vanilla yogurt

¼ teaspoon orange zest

3 tablespoons chocolate-covered espresso beans

1 tablespoon cocoa nibs

3 to 4 orange segments

1. Bring sugar and coffee to a boil in a saucepan over high. Cook, stirring occasionally, until syrupy, 6 to 8 minutes. Remove from heat, and cool slightly, about 20 minutes.

2. Stir together yogurt and zest in a bowl. Top with espresso beans, cocoa nibs, and orange segments. Drizzle with ¼ cup of the coffee syrup. Serve immediately.

HOW TO LIVE THAT YOGURT BARK LIFE

BY MAXINE BUILDER AND REBECCA FIRKSER

If you dream of eating Popsicles for breakfast every single day, you've flipped to the right page. Welcome to Planet Yogurt Bark. Yogurt bark is basically yogurt that's been frozen into a slab, and then broken into smaller pieces. It's like a frozen parfait, and it might be the easiest way to eat yogurt when you're on the move. Because it's frozen solid, you don't need any utensils, and there's no risk of spilling.

It's also super-easy to make, with no baking required. Really, the whole process of making yogurt bark takes less than 15 minutes. All you have to do is line a rimmed baking sheet with wax or parchment paper. Then take your yogurt, any type and any flavor, and pour it out onto the sheet. Cover it with your toppings of choice, and pop the whole thing in your freezer for at least three hours, or until frozen. Then break it into pieces and enjoy.

Once you've got the technique down, you should play around with ingredients. This is where yogurt bark gets really fun. Yogurt is basically a blank canvas, and you can use any flavor with any combination of toppings. And you don't have to make a ton of yogurt bark at once. Yogurt bark is a great way to use up leftover yogurt; just use a smaller pan or even line a shallow plate with wax paper instead of a full-size baking sheet.

Yogurt bark is also a great way to use up whatever fruit you have in the fridge or nuts and granola you have in the pantry. Just plop those goodies on top of your yogurt, pop the whole thing in the freezer, and eat what's basically a Popsicle for breakfast.

If you're looking for some inspiration to get started on your yogurt bark journey, here are six easy recipes with just four ingredients.

6 EASY 4-INGREDIENT YOGURT BARK RECIPES

Line a baking sheet with wax or parchment paper. Pour yogurt, then cover with toppings. Place in freezer for at least three hours, or overnight, until solid. Then break into chunks and enjoy.

UNICORN YOGURT BARK
Vanilla Yogurt + Raspberry Jam +
Blueberry Jam + White Chocolate Chips

COCONUT YOGURT BARK
Dairy-free Coconut Yogurt + Coconut Flakes +
Crystallized Pineapple + Macadamia Nuts

GRANOLA YOGURT BARK
Plain Yogurt + Blueberries + Granola +
Slivered Toasted Almonds

PB & CHOCOLATE YOGURT BARK
Banana Yogurt + Mini Pretzels +
Chocolate Chips + Peanut Butter Chips

GORP YOGURT BARK
Vanilla Yogurt + Peanuts + Raisins + M&M's

CHERRIES & CHOCOLATE YOGURT BARK
Vanilla Yogurt + Dried Tart Cherries +
Walnuts + Dark Chocolate Chips

Fruit Curd, Y'heard?

BY MARGARET EBY I am a compulsive purchaser of lemons. Every time I return from the grocery store with a fresh bag of lemons, I usually find another three or four already rolling around in the fridge. It's a sad thing to watch those sunny orbs wither into uselessness, so when my lemon count has reached an untenable level, I make fruit curd.

Fruit curd is not a sexy-sounding substance. You've probably most often heard of the cheese variety, or of curds in the context of Little Miss Muffet's dietary habits. But don't be deceived: Fruit curd is jam's more indulgent cousin. It's a luscious, tart spread that can be used on scones or dolloped in yogurt or baked into a crazy-good pie.

Lemon is the primary flavor for my curd, but you could easily use grapefruit, orange, or lime, too. I've heard passion fruit, mango, rhubarb, raspberry, and blueberry are also great. All you really need is fruit juice. Fresh is best, but in a pinch, whatever you've got. (If using grapefruit, reduce the juice first to give it a tangier bite, or leave it as is for something milder.) The real trick about curd is that you need to watch it closely as it congeals at a low temperature on the stove. Do not multitask or you will end up with lemon-sugar scrambled eggs. Many curd recipes call for the butter to be added slowly and then the whole curd strained through a sieve at the end of the process. I've found that if you cream all the ingredients together before you put them in the pot, you can skip the sieving process entirely. My recipe is inspired by David Lebovitz's Meyer Lemon Curd and Lemon Tart, though I've learned to adapt the sugar levels to the sweetness of the juice.

One cup fruit juice or puree (fresh is ideal, but we don't really live in an ideal world)	**⅔ cup sugar** (⅓ cup less if you prefer things very tart or if the juice is mild, ⅓ more if you like it sweet)	**4 whole large eggs and 4 egg yolks** **12 tablespoons butter**

1. Cream together the juice, sugar, eggs, and butter with a hand or stand mixer. It'll look a little separated at this point, but that's OK.

2. Transfer the mixture into a small to medium saucepot over low.

3. Let the mixture warm slowly over low, and stir it 7 to 10 minutes (but your cooking vessels and stovetop may vary). The curd is done when it's

thickened to the point that it coats the back of a spoon.

4. Transfer the curd to a jar or bowl, stirring occasionally to allow steam to escape. If flecks of egg white appear, strain through a fine wire-mesh strainer to remove them.

5. Let cool in the refrigerator for at least an hour. The curd will thicken further as it cools.

MAKE THE PORRIDGE YOU WANT TO SEE IN THE WORLD

BY CAROLINE LANGE

Porridge is the kind of thing you might eat when you're very small, sick, or cold. That does not sound at all glamorous, and yet today there are nearly 1.1 million posts on Instagram tagged #porridge. But porridge is an excellent place to play. There's a lot of fun in finding the pairings that express most emphatically oats' creaminess, rice's sweetness, or farro's nuttiness.

A FEW THINGS TO NOTE

You can cook porridge from raw grains, but I don't love the idea of waiting 45-plus minutes for my farro to cook down. I think that the porridge is better if you start with cooked farro to which you add more liquid and cook further. This will be true of most longer-cooking grains (like farro, rice, or barley), whereas quick-cooking grains (like oats, quinoa, or groats) can go from zero to porridge just fine.

I like the "pasta" method of cooking for nearly all grains, including rice: Just fill up a pot of water, bring it to a boil, dump in however much grain you'd like, let it cook until just tender, then drain. The cooking time will depend on the grain.

The exception to this is cornmeal, which plays by its own rules. For that, you'll want a 4:1 ratio of liquid to grain, and it's really best served right after you make it (though you can reheat it, slowly, in a pot or the microwave, mashing it as you do with a fork or a wooden spoon). Think grits.

When it comes to making the porridge, I like a 2:1 ratio of liquid to grains. So, for example, simmer ⅔ cup liquid with ⅓ cup raw oats—or ⅔ cup liquid with ⅓ cup cooked farro. Stir regularly, over relatively low heat, until the grains are tender and your preferred level of mush. Add a little salt. Your canister of oatmeal says it's optional, but it really isn't.

Go wild! Combine grains with similar cook times in the same pot.

TRY THESE FLAVOR COMBINATIONS

Oats + oat milk + pinches of cinnamon and nutmeg + cream

Quinoa + whole milk + ginger powder and chopped pears + toasted sunflower seeds + sliced pears and honey

Cornmeal + equal parts buttermilk and water + lemon zest + toasted sliced almonds + blueberries and lemon curd + dollop of yogurt

Farro + a combination of water, apple cider, and milk + pinch cinnamon + toasted pumpkin seeds + sliced apples sautéed with a little maple syrup + salted butter or a drizzle of olive oil

Barley + hemp milk + sliced banana and toasted cashews + coconut oil and a sprinkle of flaky salt

Rice (brown or white) + coconut milk + toasted sesame seeds + coconut flakes + tahini

Mix of grains or buckwheat groats + almond milk + flax seeds + poppy seeds + roasted fruit or squash + dollop of crème fraîche

DIY Dinosaur Eggs Oatmeal

Has there ever been a better group of mad geniuses than the junk food developers of the '90s? They gave us mass-produced classics like Dunkaroos, Bagel Bites, Uncrustables, and the Ecto Cooler. The '90s was a simpler, stupider time. People feared fat, not sugar. We wanted food to be cheap and didn't care how processed and removed from actual food it was. And if food looked like things that weren't food, like animals' body parts, that was OK with everyone. Exhibit A: Cheetos Paws. Because, sure, a snack that resembles the hand of a cool but probably sociopathic cheetah should exist. Exhibit B: Dinosaur Eggs Oatmeal, which came on the scene in the late '90s and confused parents everywhere while keeping kids' attention for at least 90 seconds. You can still buy these at the store, but where's the fun in that? Slip in your Gin Blossoms CD, put on a dolphin necklace, and make this oatmeal that's kinda gross but also kinda rad—just like the '90s were.

1 (2-ounce) white chocolate baking bar, chopped

Dinosaur sprinkles

1¾ cups water

⅛ teaspoon kosher salt

1 cup uncooked regular rolled oats

1 tablespoon light brown sugar

¼ teaspoon ground cinnamon

2 tablespoons heavy cream

2 tablespoons powdered sugar

1. Microwave white chocolate in a small microwaveable bowl on HIGH until melted, about 1 minute and 30 seconds, stirring every 30 seconds. Transfer melted chocolate to a small piping bag fitted with a fine writing tip or ziplock plastic bag with a small hole cut from 1 corner of the bag. Line a baking sheet with parchment paper. Pipe 20 small egg shapes. Place 1 dinosaur sprinkle on each egg, and pipe chocolate over dinosaurs to cover completely. Transfer baking sheet to freezer, and freeze until hardened, about 5 minutes.

2. Bring water and salt to a boil in a medium saucepan with lid over medium-high. Stir in oats. Reduce heat to medium-low, and simmer, covered, 3 minutes. Remove lid, and cook, stirring occasionally, until oats are tender and water is almost absorbed, about 2 minutes. Stir in brown sugar and cinnamon. Remove from heat, and stir in cream. Divide oatmeal evenly between 2 bowls.

3. Combine powdered sugar and eggs in a small ziplock plastic bag. Seal bag, and shake to coat. Pour egg mixture through a fine wire-mesh strainer over a trash can to remove excess powdered sugar. Top oatmeal evenly with eggs. Dinosaur eggs will "hatch" when stirred into warm oatmeal.

This Baked Oatmeal Has a Secret (the Secret Is Sweet Potatoes)

Come fall, when the heat starts to kick on in the morning and the leaves streak with red and orange, I want pumpkin pie for breakfast. But then I think, no, I should probably just have oatmeal. And that is why I started making orange baked oatmeal. Halfway between a smooth pumpkin pie and a proper breakfast of porridge is a fat square of sweet potato baked oatmeal. I find that sweet potato tastes more like the fall pie of nostalgia than pumpkin. Sure, you can make this recipe with pumpkin puree (either canned or the real deal) but pumpkin tends to be a bit less sweet than sweet potatoes, so if you do that, bump up the brown sugar to ⅓ cup, or add a heavy pour of maple syrup. Taste as you go, and you will prevail.

1 medium-size sweet potato

2 cups uncooked regular rolled oats

1 teaspoon baking powder

½ teaspoon kosher salt

1 teaspoon ground cinnamon

½ cup pepitas, sunflower seeds, chopped walnuts, almonds, or a blend of your favorite nuts and seeds, optional

2 cups milk or preferred non-dairy milk

¼ cup light brown sugar

2 tablespoons melted butter, plus extra softened butter for baking dish

1 teaspoon pure vanilla extract

1. Preheat the oven to 400°F. Scrub the sweet potato, dry, and place it on a parchment-lined baking sheet. Use a paring knife or a sturdy fork to prick holes all over the potato. Bake the potato until a paring knife will easily slide all the way through, 35 minutes to 1 hour, depending on the thickness of the potato and strength of your oven.

2. When the potato is done, let it cool on the baking sheet for at least 15 minutes. You can also do this step the night before you plan to serve your baked oatmeal. (Just wrap the cooled potato in foil and refrigerate until you're ready to move on to the next step.)

3. Scoop the flesh from the sweet potato into a food processor or blender. Pulse until the mixture gets very smooth, adding a tablespoon of milk along the way to help it blend if it's having trouble. Alternatively, you can mash the sweet potato with a fork, but it won't get as smooth and fluffy. Scoop out ½ cup of the puree.

You won't need the rest, unless you'd like to double the recipe. Store the potato puree in the fridge in an airtight container and use it as an egg replacer in pancakes or quick breads (¼ cup puree = 1 egg), or just top it with a bit of maple syrup and presto: instant snack.

4. Preheat the oven to 375°F and butter an 8-inch square baking dish.

5. In a medium bowl, mix together rolled oats, baking powder, kosher salt, and ground cinnamon. Mix in nuts or seeds if using.

6. In a small bowl, whisk together the ½ cup of sweet potato puree, milk, light brown sugar, melted butter, and vanilla extract until smooth.

7. Sprinkle the oat mixture into the prepared baking dish, then pour the sweet potato mixture over oats. Tap the baking dish a few times on the counter to make sure the liquid reaches all the dry mixture. Bake for 35 to 40 minutes, or until the top is set and golden.

Cornmeal Pancakes with Mascarpone and Jam Because Why Not

We've got nothing but love for a standard short stack, especially when it's drenched with butter and real maple syrup. But every once in a while, it's fun to put our pinkies all the way up and get fancy with the flapjacks. These sweeter, smaller corncakes take on layers of slightly savory mascarpone and luscious preserves or jam (cherry and blueberry, respectively, top our list, but you do you) to make a plate that's not just ridiculously delicious, but also oh so wham-bam Instagram-friendly.

1 cup all-purpose flour	¼ teaspoon kosher salt	Cooking spray
1 cup medium-grind cornmeal	1⅓ cups whole buttermilk	⅓ cup blueberry jam
1 tablespoon granulated sugar	2 tablespoons unsalted butter, melted and cooled	⅔ cup mascarpone cheese
¾ teaspoon baking powder	2 large eggs	⅓ cup cherry preserves
¼ teaspoon baking soda	1½ tablespoons canola oil	⅔ cup fresh blueberries

1. Sift together flour, cornmeal, sugar, baking powder, baking soda, and salt in a small bowl. Stir together buttermilk, butter, and eggs in a large bowl. Stir flour mixture into milk mixture.

2. Heat ½ tablespoon of the oil in a large nonstick skillet over medium. Coat inside of a 3-inch round cookie or biscuit cutter with cooking spray. Place in hot skillet; spoon 1½ tablespoons of batter into cookie cutter. Cook until just set, 45 seconds to 1 minute. Remove cookie cutter. Cook pancake until golden brown on the edges; turn pancake, and cook another 90 seconds. (You can do up to 4 at a time. As soon as you remove the cookie cutter, start on the next pancake.) Place cooked pancakes on a baking sheet, and keep warm in a 225°F oven. Repeat process with remaining oil and batter, to make 32 pancakes.

3. To assemble the stacks, place 1 pancake on each of 8 plates. Layer each with 2 teaspoons of the blueberry jam, 1 pancake, 2 teaspoons of the mascarpone, 1 pancake, 2 teaspoons of the cherry preserves, 1 pancake, and 2 teaspoons of the mascarpone. Top each with about 3 blueberries.

The Best Part of Waking Up Is Campbell's Chicken with Rice in Your Cup

BY HEIDI JULAVITS

I grew up in a cold house. I don't mean that metaphorically. Our thermostat, in the winter, was set at 53°F. This was the 1970s; however, this was Maine. Given the cost of fuel, the gas shortage, and the fact that Maine, during that period, attracted from beyond its borders a certain highly educated (and often, though not always, and definitely not in the case of my parents, self-hating independently wealthy) person looking for a simpler way of life, cold houses were the norm in my neighborhood. Our house, a two-family Victorian built in 1888 sat atop a hill atop a promenade. We could stare a hundred miles across the state to New Hampshire and Mount Washington on clear days, and were, to put it mildly, exposed to wind and snow and rain and other more regularly scheduled forms of weather-like abuse. We lived under the flight path of the airplanes landing at the Portland International Jetport, so we were also exposed to the shaking caused by their passing close overhead. Hurricane-force gusts from the jet engines struck the windows that rattled maniacally even when you walked past them wearing multiple pairs of socks.

Instead of relying on our furnace, my parents thought they'd be so much more environmentally savvy by burning coal. Yes, coal. In their defense, we found a ton of coal in our basement when we moved into the house, and my parents thought, thriftily, since it was already out of the ground and going to waste, "Let's burn it!" So we bought a coal stove from Scandinavia, and around this stove, which was roughly two feet wide and four feet long, we huddled. I did my homework there, I read books there, and most crucially because the house was coldest in the morning, I ate breakfast there.

Breakfast was never any big thing in our house. Mothers were supposed to provide breakfast (again the '70s), but my mother taught high school English and was often grading papers and getting her lesson plans in order. She did not have time to make us pancakes or bacon. I didn't like cereal, or rather cereal with cold milk on a cold morning was the last thing I wanted to put in my mouth. Ditto yogurt, ditto orange juice. Toast immediately returned to room temperature (53°F) and became a giant crouton. I was a lover of soup, however, and I was handy with a can opener, and I could turn on the stove burner. One particularly cold morning I thought, "Why not soup?" My favorite childhood picture book was *Soup for the King* by Leonard Kessler. The book was about a king who loved soup. I can't, as a 47-year-old adult, really remember what else happened in this book, so I asked a friend who had a copy to remind me. She wrote:

The king loves soup for every meal, breakfast, lunch, and supper. The queen is sick of soup but the king won't give it up. So the queen bugs the royal cook, who quits. The palace holds soup auditions throughout the land. A poor tailor is sick of soup, too. His wife sends their son out with their pot of soup to see if they can sell it and buy meat. Of course, the tailor's son accidentally enters the soup auditions with his mother's soup. And he wins, with his cold potato soup. So the king's men come and fetch the boy's mother, who thinks her son is in trouble, but instead they make her the royal cook. And now the king gets to eat soup every day again, and the tailor gets to eat a lot of non-soup dishes, and no one follows up on the queen, WTF Leonard Kessler.

As usual, one's own myths never quite hold up to inspection. Cold soup won the king's heart! Still, the point is that the king loved soup so much he was willing to risk his marriage in order to always be eating it.

This is the kind of monomaniacal loyalty soup inspires. I also had loyalty toward soup: Campbell's Chicken with Rice soup. No other soup was acceptable. I ate a can of Campbell's Chicken with Rice soup every morning before school, before leaving my cold house to enter the even colder outdoors where my braids, still wet from washing, froze.

I remember, too, experiencing a little bit of shame about my breakfast. I pretended I ate "normal" breakfasts (in the same way I pretended we had a shower in our bathroom—we didn't, only a bathtub), and when at other people's houses for sleepovers, I would push scrambled eggs around a plate and feign happiness over the mother-cooked breakfast food. So delicious! My breakfast soup habit indicated, I feared, some deeper form of deviance or misfittedness that would only intensify over time. Who knows what kind of lonely, queen-less weirdo I'd eventually be. And though I'd long outgrown this worry by adulthood, I recall, as a twenty-something grad

MY BREAKFAST SOUP HABIT INDICATED, I FEARED, SOME DEEPER FORM OF DEVIANCE OR MISFITTEDNESS THAT WOULD ONLY INTENSIFY OVER TIME. WHO KNOWS WHAT KIND OF LONELY, QUEEN-LESS WEIRDO I'D EVENTUALLY BE.

student in New York, stopping by a Philippine restaurant near my apartment for coffee, and looking at the menu, and seeing that they served for breakfast a dish called congee—rice porridge cooked in chicken broth. Congee is eaten all over Asia, in very hot countries, not cold ones, but still. Though I was no longer self-conscious about my morning soup habit, I remember feeling a powerful sense of redemption. There was a cultural precedence for my choice! A whole freaking continent eats what I ate!

But in Maine, in the '70s, what did we know about Asian breakfast traditions? I am now a parent of two kids. Without any prompting from me, save that I don't make breakfast for them, they both started eating soup in the morning when they were very young. They were early adopters. Survivalists, some would say. Eat soup or die. Our singsongy bedtime ritual involved them yelling, after they said goodnight, "LEAVE OUT SOUP!" Because they were too young to open tin cans but not too young to press a button on the microwave, in which bowls of soup awaited. Soup, maybe, is not about warmth or comfort but is instead about seizing power when powerless. It's about developing self-reliance and the ability to strongly, and even tyrannically, desire and demand what is not, in your culture, the norm. Eat soup in the morning and you are, until the bowl is empty, a king.

A SINDHI BREAKFAST, JUST LIKE MAMA USED TO MAKE

BY POOJA MAKHIJANI On and off during my childhood, I lived in a multi-generational, Asian-American household. My paternal grandparents, who became U.S. citizens in the 1970s, traveled back and forth between New Jersey where I lived, and Pune, their hometown in western India. On weekends, my paternal grandmother, who I call "Mama," made hearty Sindhi breakfasts like *loli*, a jaggery-filled whole-wheat flatbread that she sprinkled with sugar for me; and *saiyoon*, sweet vermicelli with fried potatoes, served with papadam and pickled mangoes. I recoiled from many of these breakfasts.

My only favorite was *dal pakwan*, a treat served on rare Sundays. "This is the king of breakfasts," Mama explained. She lovingly fried the pakwan, a caraway-seed-flecked, deep-fried, crispy flatbread, and simmered and stirred the nutty dal, a slightly sour lentil stew seasoned with tamarind pulp. She served the pakwan and dal with two chutneys—fiery mint and sweet date-and-jaggery—along with sliced, raw onions. Dal pakwan is a mélange of flavors and textures. I loved the sweet, sticky chutney and stirred it into the creamy dal before scooping it up with the crunchy pakwan.

Years later, as an adult, I embrace a cuisine whose secrets have been long kept in the kitchens of a community-dispersed Partition, which cleaved the subcontinent. I venture to Mumbai's Sindhi enclaves, Chembur and Ulhasnagar, when on holiday, eating at Guru Kripa, the oldest eatery in Sion, which serves simple Sindhi meals—including my now-beloved dal pakwan. In Singapore and New York City, I turn to Kailash Parbat, an international chain whose Sunday

menu carries Sindhi delicacies. Here, the pakwan is flavored with sharp and slightly bitter carom seeds—a more traditional preparation of the flatbread.

When trying to recreate the recipes of my ancestral cuisine in my kitchen, I realize how utilitarian these breakfast meals were. They used ingredients commonly found in a family's pantry, and made excellent use of leftovers. I make a stack of four pakwan and a bowl of mild dal (omitting the chiles) for my five-year-old daughter. She takes a few bites of the pakwan. "This is crispy," she says. She calls me "Mama."

Dal Pakwan

FOR THE PAKWAN

1 cup all-purpose flour

¼ teaspoon salt

½ teaspoon coarsely-ground black peppercorns

½ teaspoon caraway seeds

2 tablespoons ghee (clarified butter)

Vegetable oil (for deep-frying)

FOR THE DAL

1 cup dried split lentils or chickpeas

2 tablespoons ghee (clarified butter)

2 medium onions, finely chopped

1 teaspoon ginger, minced

1 teaspoon garlic, minced

4 green chiles, finely chopped

½ teaspoon turmeric powder

½ tablespoon cumin powder

½ tablespoon coriander powder

Pinch asafoetida

½ teaspoon salt

2½ cups water

1 large tomato, blanched, peeled, and diced

4 tablespoons tamarind pulp

FOR TEMPERING

1 tablespoon ghee

1 teaspoon cumin seeds

FOR GARNISH

2 tablespoons chopped coriander leaves

1. Prepare the Pakwan: Sift together flour, salt, and spices. Fold in ghee.

2. Add water to form a pliable dough. Divide dough into fourths, and roll each portion into a 6-inch round. Prick each round with a fork to prevent them from puffing up while frying.

3. Over high heat, bring oil to 320°F. Fry, one at a time, until crisp and golden.

4. Prepare the Dal: Soak lentils for 1 to 2 hours. Drain and rinse.

5. Heat ghee in a heavy-bottomed pan over medium. Sauté onions, ginger, garlic, and chiles for 10 minutes, or until onions are translucent.

6. Add lentils, spices (turmeric powder, cumin powder, coriander powder, asafoetida, and salt), and 2½ cups water to pan. Bring to a boil. Reduce heat to low and simmer for 30 minutes, or until lentils are soft.

7. Add tomato and tamarind pulp and cook for an additional 5 to 10 minutes. Remove from heat.

8. In a small pan over a low flame, heat ghee. Add cumin seeds. They will splutter! When they stop, pour tempering mixture into lentils.

9. Garnish with coriander leaves. Serve with pakwan.

CHAPTER SIX

FRANKEN-FOODS

& MASHUPS

Egg-in-a-Doughnut

Toad-in-the-road, egg-in-a-hole, baby-bird-in-bread, frog-in-a-bog—call it what you will, frying an egg inside toast is always a good idea. But what if you could make it better? Listen, we're not here to denigrate egg-in-a-hole or toast itself. We love toast and have written about the wonders of making toast, and we'll continue to do so until our executive overlords say, "Hey Extra Crispy, cut out all the toast stuff, OK?" But there's a wide world out there, and sometimes you might want an egg in a doughnut instead of toast. If you feel that way, don't let anyone stop you. Be the change you want to see in the world of breakfast, and fry an egg inside a doughnut.

2 round cake-style doughnuts (at least 1-inch-thick)

1 tablespoon unsalted butter

2 large eggs
Salt and pepper, to taste

1. Enlarge the hole in the center of each doughnut using a 1½-inch biscuit cutter or round cookie cutter.

2. Melt the butter in a large skillet over medium. When it starts foaming, place the doughnuts in the pan and carefully crack an egg into each hole.

3. Cook for 2 minutes, then carefully slide your spatula under the egg and flip. Don't hesitate, just do it.

4. Only cook the egg for a couple more minutes. If you're not into that sort of thing, just keep it on the heat until the yolk meets your standards. Season with salt and pepper to taste.

THERE ARE AT LEAST 66 DIFFERENT NAMES FOR EGG-IN-A-HOLE

BY KATE WELSH

I was recently with my boyfriend's family at the beach. His mom very kindly made us breakfast, and one morning, she made what she called a Marty Wilson. A what? Apparently, that's what she grew up calling what I have always known as toad-in-a-hole: that delicious dish of an egg fried in bread. And those names? They are so, so far from the only ones for this breakfast dish.

The first time a recipe for the dish appeared in print, in Fannie Farmer's *Boston Cooking School Cookbook*, it was named "egg with a hat," calling for the bread's center cutout to be served on top of the egg, as its "hat." And it's popped up again and again in popular culture: in the movie *Moonstruck*, where it's called *uova nel cestino*, or "egg in a trash can;" in the film *Moon Over Miami*, in which it's called "gashouse eggs" (which may come from the German *gasthaus*, or "guesthouse"); and in the movie *V for Vendetta*, they called it "egg-in-the-basket."

For those of you keeping score, that's six different names already. And we're just getting started. I scoured the internet for all the different names people have for the dish, including going through nearly 350 comments on a *Serious Eats* thread, 171 comments on a *New York Times* Cooking recipe, and already compiled lists by *HuffingtonPost* and *Chicago Foodies*. I only included names that had more than one nod. Ready?

Here is (almost) every single thing you could call eggs fried in bread:

EGG-IN-A-HOLE • EGG-WITH-A-HAT • EGG-IN-A-TRASH CAN • EGG-IN-THE-BASKET • EGG-IN-A-NEST • EGG-IN-THE-MIDDLE • EGG-IN-A-CAGE • EGG-IN-A-WINDOW • EGG-IN-A-POCKET • EGG-IN-A-WELL • EGG-IN-A-BOAT • EGG-IN-A-FRAME (OR FRAMED EGG) • EGG-IN-A-BLANKET • EGG-ON-AN-ISLAND • EGG-IN-JAIL • BIRD'S NEST • BIRD DROP • BIRDIE-IN-A-BASKET • TOAD-IN-A-HOLE • TOAD-IN-THE-ROAD • FROG-IN-THE-POND • BULL'S EYE • OX EYE EGG • CAMEL'S EYES • ELEPHANT TRACKS • MARTY WILSON • BETTY JANE • MARY JANE • ADAM AND EVE ON A RAFT • THE POPEYE • ONE-EYED SUSIE • ONE-EYED JACK • ONE-EYED PETE • ONE-EYED PIRATE • LAZY-EYED PIRATE • ONE-EYED EGYPTIANS • ONE-EYED TEXANS • A MAN IN A RAFT • FIREMAN'S TOAST • COWBOY EGGS • HOBO TOAST • ROCKY MOUNTAIN TOAST • POLISH EGGS • LIGHTHOUSE EGGS • BIRMINGHAM EGGS • HOT HOUSE EGGS • GUESTHOUSE EGGS • GASHOUSE EGGS • GASLIGHT EGG • KNOT-HOLE EGGS • GOLDMINE EGG • CIRCUS TOAST • SUNSHINE EGGS • HOL[E]Y EGGS • HOLE-IN-ONE • HOCUS POCUS EGG • PEEK-A-BOO EGGS • BREGG • TOAST TITS • SPIT IN THE EYE • CARTWHEEL • DIAMOND TOAST • BABY IN A BUGGY • DOUGHNUT EGG • TOAST WITH A TUMMY (OR BELLY-BUTTON EGG) • MOON OVER MIAMI EGGS

Cauliflower "Chicken" and Waffles

Chicken and waffles is a classic—if indulgent—combo of batter-coated, savory, succulent fried bird, crisply-griddled waffles that give way to a pillowy heft, and ideally, a generous drizzle of real maple syrup. That's all fine and dandy until the vegetarian at the table starts giving you the puppy dog eyes. Why should the carnivores have all the brunchy fun? This cauliflower swap-in delivers all of the glorious crunch, plus a sassy little thrill of hot sauce swirled into the mix. It's been clucking nice knowing you, chicken, but we're dunzo.

6 cups water

2 tablespoons apple cider vinegar

16 ounces cauliflower florets, cut into bite-size pieces

1¾ cups self-rising flour

¼ cup plain yellow cornmeal

1¾ cups whole milk

1 large egg

1 tablespoon plus ½ teaspoon granulated sugar, divided

Canola oil

1 cup all-purpose flour

¼ teaspoon black pepper

¼ teaspoon cayenne pepper

1¼ teaspoons kosher salt, divided

½ cup whole buttermilk

½ cup pure maple syrup

1 tablespoon hot sauce (we like Cholula for this)

1. Preheat oven to 200°F. Bring water and vinegar to a boil in a large saucepan over high. Add cauliflower, and cook until almost tender, about 2 minutes. Using a slotted spoon, transfer cauliflower to a wire rack on a baking sheet. Place baking sheet in refrigerator, and chill until cool, about 15 minutes.

2. While cauliflower cools, heat a waffle iron to medium-high. Whisk together self-rising flour, cornmeal, whole milk, egg, and 1 tablespoon of the sugar in a large bowl until smooth. Pour batter into waffle iron, and cook according to manufacturer's instructions. Transfer cooked waffles to a wire rack on a baking sheet, and keep warm in preheated oven.

3. Pour oil in a medium Dutch oven to a depth of 2 inches. Heat oil over medium-high to 350°F. Whisk together all-purpose flour, black pepper, cayenne, ¾ teaspoon of the salt, and remaining ½ teaspoon sugar in a medium bowl. Place chilled cauliflower in a separate medium bowl. Pour buttermilk over cauliflower, and toss to coat. Add coated cauliflower to flour mixture, and toss to coat. Fry in hot oil, stirring occasionally to prevent clumping, until golden and crisp, about 5 minutes. Transfer to a wire rack, and sprinkle evenly with remaining ½ teaspoon salt.

4. Whisk together maple syrup and hot sauce in a 1-cup glass measuring cup. Microwave on HIGH until warm, 15 to 20 seconds. Place 1 waffle on each of 4 plates; top evenly with fried cauliflower. Drizzle evenly with syrup mixture.

Waffle-Crusted Buffalo Chicken Tenders

Chicken and waffles are a ridiculously effective combination. Buffalo chicken is also a brilliant thing. In these head-spinning, heart-racing times of large, televised sports events, political apocalypse, and *The Bachelor*, it just makes sense to consolidate as many good things as possible and stuff them into our mouths to maximize pleasure. That's why I made Waffle-Crusted Buffalo Chicken Tenders with Spicy Maple Syrup for you.

Toss the chicken in a marinade of buttermilk and Frank's and turn some frozen waffles into coating crumbs and fry away to a happier place. Oh, and the dipping sauce is so dementedly good that I licked the bowl after I made it. I am not ashamed to admit that.

1 pound boneless, skinless chicken thighs

¼ cup Frank's RedHot sauce (or your favorite brand)

1 cup buttermilk

Salt

Frozen waffles

1 cup all-purpose flour

Salt and pepper

2 large eggs, beaten

Oil for frying

FOR THE SAUCE

½ cup Frank's RedHot sauce (or your favorite brand)

¼ cup melted butter

¼ cup maple syrup

1. Slice the chicken into evenly-sized strips/chunks and place in a lidded container. Mix hot sauce, buttermilk, and a hefty pinch of salt, and pour over chicken. Cover and chill for 4 hours or overnight, shaking a few times to ensure the chicken is evenly covered.

2. Bake frozen waffles at 325°F for about 20 minutes, flipping halfway through. Bake as long as needed for the waffles to completely dry out. Note: Frozen waffles also vary widely in size, but figure on using around 5 to 6. Break the cooked, cooled waffles into pieces into a food processor and pulse until you have a mixture of fine crumbs and larger shards. You can also make waffles from scratch and do this, but really just follow your bliss.

3. Add oil to a deep fryer and heat it to 350°F. (Note, you can also pan-fry in an inch of oil in

a heavy, deep vessel.) Set out 3 bowls and fill with half the flour (seasoned to taste with salt and pepper), egg, and half the waffle crumbs. Dredge the buttermilk-covered chicken pieces in flour, then egg, then waffle crumbs, and set aside until you have enough to fill a fryer basket with pieces without crowding. Top up the dry ingredients in the bowl as you go, if they get too damp and gross.

4. Fry the chicken for 3 minutes, pull from the oil to make sure that they are not overbrowning, and fry for an additional 3 to 4 minutes. Let the hot strips rest and drain onto a paper towel-lined baking sheet or plate.

5. Whisk together hot sauce, butter, and syrup, adjusting the ratio for your personal taste.

6. Serve the chicken with a side of sauce while it's all still hot. Know joy.

9 NEW FRANKENFOODS TO MAKE AT HOME

BY MARGARET EBY AND REBECCA FIRKSER

Yeah, yeah, we all know about the Cronut. But the famous croissant-doughnut hybrid only scratches the surface of possibilities for frankenfoods. If you have two foods you love, why not try combining them? Some things might not be a great match (we cannot in good faith recommend garlic milk), but you'd be surprised by how compatible some of your favorite breakfast flavors are. If you think it would taste good mixed on a plate, it'll probably taste good prepared together as a mashup. Try some of our equations and see.

COLD BREW

LIME JUICE

+ SIMPLE SYRUP

COFFEE LIMEADE

For a genius, refreshing summer drink, mix one part limeade (also known as lime juice and simple syrup) and one part cold brew. Serve the coffee over ice, and add a splash of sparkling water if you're looking for some fizz.

SLICED ONIONS

+ PANCAKE BATTER

PANCAKE ONION RINGS

Dunk thickly sliced white onions into a batch of pancake batter, then fry 'em up. Whether you want to serve them with maple syrup or hot sauce is ultimately your call (or check out our frankenfood equation below for an even better idea).

MAPLE SYRUP

+ HOT SAUCE

HOT MAPLE SYRUP

Too good to be true? Nah. For that sweet-hot mixture of maple syrup and hot sauce, just make a mixture of four tablespoons of maple syrup and one tablespoon of your favorite hot sauce.

GREEK YOGURT

LEMON JUICE

CRUSHED BAGEL CHIPS

LOX

CAPERS

+ SCALLIONS

BAGEL PARFAIT

Savory yogurt might not be your go-to, but just think about how good a dollop of sour cream is on, say, a taco. Mix scallions, lemon juice, salt, and black pepper into a serving of Greek yogurt and top with crushed bagel chips, capers, and a few pieces of torn lox.

INSTANT RAMEN
SCRAMBLED EGGS
SCALLIONS
TORTILLA
+ HOT SAUCE

RAMEN BREAKFAST BURRITO

For mornings when carbs on carbs is the only answer, start with a batch of instant ramen. Drain the broth, then scramble an egg into the hot pan with the noodles. Scoop the mixture into a warm tortilla with a handful of scallions and a squirt of hot sauce, and fold it into the coziest burrito imaginable.

SCRAMBLED EGGS
BACON
PEPPER JACK CHEESE
+ CORN TORTILLAS

BACON, EGG, AND CHEESE TAQUITOS

Layer scrambled eggs, crumbled bacon, and a pile of pepper jack cheese into small corn tortillas. Roll them up, then fry a batch of BEC taquitos in an inch of vegetable oil.

WATERMELON
STRAWBERRIES
BLUEBERRIES
APPLE
GRAPES
FRESH OJ
+ PROSECCO

MIMOSA FRUIT SALAD

Make a mimosa with ¼ cup orange juice and ¼ cup sparkling wine (prosecco, cava, Champagne—whatever you've got) and pour the cocktail over sliced watermelon, berries, apple, and grapes. Then invite pals to your fruit party.

FRENCH TOAST
CHEDDAR CHEESE
CRUMBLED CANDIED BACON
+ REDEYE GRAVY

FRENCH TOAST DISCO "FRIES"

Cut a few slices of French toast into strips and bake until crispy. Scoop the French "fries" into a bowl and top with shredded cheddar cheese and a mountain of crumbled candied bacon (regular bacon works fine, too if you're short on time). Finish these breakfast disco fries with a dollop of redeye gravy.

CRUSHED TOMATOES
HOT SAUCE
HORSERADISH
WORCESTERSHIRE
CELERY SALT
VODKA
+ EGGS

BLOODY MARY SHAKSHUKA

Get your tomato sauce drunk. Cook crushed tomatoes with hot sauce, horseradish, Worcestershire, celery salt, and—wait for it—a three-second pour of vodka. Simmer until the flavors meld together, then poach a few eggs in the sauce. Your shakshuka has never had so much fun.

Make Cereal Popsicles When You Just Can't Deal with Bowls and Spoons

In sitcoms, people always seem to walk downstairs in the morning and sit down to an elaborate breakfast feast that they barely touch. There's cereal, orange juice, waffles, eggs, bacon, sausage, coffee—basically everything the props department could think of to fill the table. Your life is probably much different. If you have time to sit down and slowly enjoy a bowl of cereal before going to work, bless you. If you find yourself eating a banana and a KIND bar in your car every day, and you hate it, we feel you. Our advice is basically what a prehistoric human might tell you: Try putting your food on a stick.

2 cups milk

1 cup cereal

Chopped berries, bananas, or chocolate chips, optional

1. Evenly disperse the milk among six ice pop molds. If you don't eat dairy, go for coconut, soy, or almond milk. Feel like getting fancy? Use strawberry or chocolate milk.

2. If you're using extra ingredients, mix them with the cereal in a bowl.

3. Add the mixture to each mold until the milk reaches the top. Add another sprinkling of cereal for good measure.

4. Freeze 4 to 6 hours.

5. To serve, run the molds under hot water to release the ice pops.

Mojito Pancakes Are Fluffy, Boozy, and Perfect in Every Way

BY JUSTIN WARNER The first time I was on a competition cooking show, I had to create a restaurant in 24 hours. As I had never cooked professionally, I wanted to focus on a simple food that could be presented in many creative ways. I, of course, went with pancakes. So now I present you with mojito pancakes. Boozy pancakes are not just a good idea because booze + pancakes = hell yeah, although that's certainly part of it. The rum evaporates at a lower temperature than milk does, giving the pancakes some extra leavening in the form of alcohol vapor bubbles. This yields Mickey D's-level fluffy pancakes that are screaming for some minty butter and limed-up maple syrup.

FOR THE BUTTER

1 bunch mint leaves

1 stick butter, softened

Zest of one lime

FOR THE PANCAKES

2 cups unbleached all-purpose flour

2 tablespoons granulated sugar

2 teaspoons baking powder

½ teaspoon baking soda

½ teaspoon table salt

Zest of one lime

1 tablespoon lime juice

1¼ cups milk

¼ cup rum

3 tablespoons unsalted butter, melted and cooled slightly

1 large egg

2 teaspoons vegetable oil

FOR THE SYRUP

1 cup maple syrup

2 tablespoons limeade concentrate

2 tablespoons rum

1. Prepare the Butter: Chiffonade the mint, add the softened butter, and lime zest and mix it with a fork. Set aside.

2. Prepare the Pancakes: In a large mixing bowl, combine the dry ingredients and lime zest for the pancakes.

3. In a separate bowl, combine the lime juice, milk, rum, and melted butter.

4. Combine the wet with the dry, add the egg, and whisk briefly. Lumps are cool. Set the batter aside.

5. Prepare the Syrup: Add 1 cup maple syrup to a sauté pan and heat over medium high until bubbly.

Add the limeade concentrate. Then, carefully add the rum, stand back, and ignite with a long barbecue lighter. Be careful! Have a pan lid handy to put out the flames if you are scared, or omit the rum in the syrup.

6. In another skillet over medium, add the oil and allow it to heat up, swirling it around the skillet.

7. Make pancakes. Add a quarter cup of batter or so at a time, flip once bubbles appear in the center.

8. Make as many pancakes as you can, then top with the butter and drizzle with the syrup. Get crunk at breakfast.

Everything Bagel Seasoning and Lox Nigiri Sushi

BY JUSTIN WARNER I worked for a long time in sushi joints in Colorado. Believe it or not, because of Denver International Airport and rich-people ski towns, the landlocked state has a thriving sushi scene. I used to be a total purist. I'd never be caught dead ordering a California roll, let alone its cream cheese-laden cousin, the Philadelphia roll. Eventually, I realized that "fun" is just as important as "fine" when it comes to food, so I sought out to confront my Phillyphobia by crafting one of the finest bites of breakfast sushi imaginable. Here, the breakfast classic of bagels and lox transforms into breakfast sushi. A sliver of smoked salmon is anchored to caper-brined sushi rice with a dab of wasabi cream cheese. Homemade everything bagel seasoning seals the deal. You may be shocked at how good caper-brined sushi rice is; I use it for all my sushi needs.

FOR THE RICE

2 cups sushi rice

¼ cup caper brine

¼ cup sugar

2 tablespoons unseasoned rice wine vinegar

FOR THE WASABI CREAM CHEESE

2 tablespoons wasabi powder

2 tablespoons water

4 ounces cream cheese, room temperature

FOR THE BAGEL SEASONING

2 tablespoons poppy seeds

1 tablespoon pretzel salt

1 tablespoon white sesame seeds

2 teaspoons dried minced onion

1 teaspoon dried garlic flakes

1 (8-ounce) package lox

1. Prepare the Rice: Put the rice in a fine wire-mesh strainer and rinse it under cold running water, rubbing it together with your fingers, until the water runs clear. Allow the washed rice to drain.

2. Cook the rice in a rice cooker with the amount of water specified by your cooker. (I used 3 cups of water for this amount.) I've never, ever screwed up rice in a rice cooker so long as I cover the rice with about an inch of water. If you don't have a rice cooker, follow the directions on your rice package.

3. Combine the caper brine, sugar, and vinegar in a measuring cup.

4. When the rice is done, use a bamboo paddle or spatula to gently spread portions out around the inside of a large bowl. Removing it in portions exposes more surface area and allows for quicker cooling. Once all the rice is in the bowl, dribble the vinegar mixture onto the paddle while moving it back and forth a few inches above the rice, so as to thinly and evenly distribute it. Use the paddle to gently break up any chunks of rice in "slicing" motions. When the clumps are broken and cease to re-form, all the rice has been seasoned. The rice should glisten and feel warm, but not hot.

5. Wet your hands with water (the rice is very sticky) and gently return the rice to a cooler or to a wooden bowl. Cover the rice with a clean, moist towel until ready to use, or up to 2 hours. If you use a cooler, close the lid. If using a wooden bowl, cover with plastic wrap.

6. Prepare the Wasabi Cream Cheese: Mix the wasabi powder and 2 tablespoons water in a bowl until dissolved. Add the cream cheese to the bowl and use a rubber spatula to fully incorporate the wasabi.

7. Prepare the Bagel Seasoning: Combine all the ingredients in a small pan. Toast until fragrant. Transfer to a small plate to cool.

8. Prepare the Nigiri: Wet your hands with water. With your dominant hand, grab less than a ping-pong ball's worth of rice. Gently squeeze it. Too much squeezing makes the rice like clay, too little and it falls apart. Once the rice ball is formed, pick up a slice of lox with your non-dominant hand. With your dominant pointer finger, swipe a little wasabi cream cheese onto the fish. Gently press the rice ball onto the cream cheese–smeared fish. Flip the nigiri fish-side-up, and gently apply pressure with two fingers of your dominant hand and a cupping motion with your non-dominant hand. Rotate the fish and rice ball 180 degrees and repeat, to round off the corners and adhere the fish to the rice ball.

9. Gently press the top of the fish into the seasoning.

10. Continue forming nigiri, rewetting your hands to keep the rice from sticking to them.

Your Quiche Is Missing a Tater Tots Crust

We've found the solution to feeling meh about quiche: Make the crust out of tater tots. This quiche starts out as many quiches do: eggs, mushrooms, leeks, Gruyère. But then the filling gets ladled into a crispy crust made of salty tots. After a quick trip in the oven, the end result is the best riff on eggs and potatoes you've ever had.

4 cups frozen tater tots

¼ cup unsalted butter

½ teaspoon kosher salt, divided

½ teaspoon black pepper, divided

4 thick-cut bacon slices, chopped

8 ounces sliced cremini mushrooms

1 large leek, white and light green parts only, thinly sliced

¾ cup heavy cream

3 large eggs

2 ounces Gruyère cheese, shredded (about ½ cup)

1 teaspoon fresh thyme leaves

1. Preheat oven to 400°F. Place tater tots in a large microwavable bowl. Microwave on HIGH until warmed through, about 3 minutes. Add butter and ¼ teaspoon each of the salt and pepper; mash with a fork until tater tots are broken up and mixture sticks together.

2. Press potato tot mixture onto bottom and up sides of a 9-inch pie pan. Bake in preheated oven on middle rack until browned, 25 to 30 minutes. Remove from oven, and cool completely, about 20 minutes.

3. Meanwhile, cook bacon in a large skillet over medium, stirring occasionally, until bacon is crisp and fat has rendered, 8 to 10 minutes. Using a slotted spoon, transfer bacon to a plate lined with paper towels to drain, reserving drippings in skillet. Increase heat to medium-high, and add mushrooms.

Cook, stirring occasionally, until mushrooms are golden brown and tender, about 8 minutes. Add leek and remaining ¼ teaspoon each salt and pepper; cook, stirring occasionally, until leeks begin to brown and have softened, about 3 minutes. Remove from heat, and set aside.

4. Whisk together cream and eggs in a medium bowl or measuring cup until combined. Spread mushroom mixture in an even layer in prepared crust; sprinkle evenly with bacon. Carefully pour egg mixture evenly into crust. Top evenly with cheese, and bake at 400°F until golden and bubbly and eggs are cooked through, 25 to 30 minutes. Remove from oven, and cool slightly, about 10 minutes. Sprinkle with thyme, and cut into 8 slices. Serve warm, at room temperature, or cold.

A QUICHE FOR THE REST OF US

BY ALLISON AND MATT ROBICELLI Quiche, by nature, is fancy. It is for prim ladies in floral dresses, their delicate hair tucked under wide-brimmed straw hats, lounging on wicker furniture. It is for garden parties where everything is served on antique bone china, garnished with a light smattering of freshly minced herbs, and eaten with very small forks that aren't quite miniature but certainly not designed for the monstrous paws of the plebes who weren't invited. Quiche is something you eat half a portion of, declare, "Oh my heavens, it is just so rich we simply cannot bring ourselves to eat another bite!" and then spend the remaining hours sating yourself with lemon water and the wafting scent of your uneaten lunch.

We do not get invited to these parties. We don't own any floral dresses, but we do have yoga pants that are wearing out in the crotch that we refuse to throw away because the ventilation they're providing in this humidity is utterly fantastic. We once tried to be one of those ladies who could pull off a straw hat, but our cat decided he needed to use it as a bed for an entire week, then peed in it to let us know we look stupid in hats. We've never found quiche so rich that we couldn't eat an entire slice—or, for that matter, the entire pan in one sitting.

Yet its elegance cannot intimidate us, turning us away from its creamy, cheesy, eggy splendor. Once the delicate crust, daintily trimmed herbs, and antique bone china are stripped away, you find that quiche is not much more than a bacon, egg, and cheese that went to Princeton.

There's no reason that folks like us, with our holey-crotch yoga pants and cat-pee hats, can't have a quiche of our own. Something that makes us feel we are grabbing a slice of the good life of those society types, while keeping one foot in the gutter where our hearts truly lie. Our quiche may have gotten rejected from Princeton, but Daddy called in some favors and managed to get our sweet baby into Notre Dame.

It's a scientific fact that any pedestrian bacon, egg, and cheese sandwich can instantly be elevated to Michelin standards by adding some ketchup and a crushed-up 50-cent bag of Doritos. So logically, building a quiche based on this principle will result in something akin to the Mona Lisa of brunch. Since pie dough doesn't need to rely on gluten to hold its form, we can replace the majority of the flour in a standard pâte brisée with "house-ground Doritos flour"—an ingredient we've managed to find many uses for in our kitchen and bedroom. Baked with a traditional quiche filling swirled with crispy bacon and cheddar cheese, we cover it in a tangy tomato glacé (read: ketchup), then gild the lily with a crown of roughly crushed Doritos for extra crunch and so all the other quiches know not to fuck with it. (Turn the page for the recipe.)

We're not remotely concerned with whatever nutritional damage our tremendously awesome upgrade may cause, because truthfully, even without our interference, quiche is legitimately one of the most unhealthy things you could possibly eat. It's primarily butter, filled with half-and-half, fatty pork, and cheese. Even if you added spinach or fancy herbs there is no saving you here, so just own that and embrace the insanity. Breezy floral dresses are excellent at covering up Doritos gut.

THIS RECIPE IS IN NO WAY SPONSORED OR CONDONED BY DORITOS. WE JUST LIKE THEM.

Doritos Quiche

FOR THE CRUST

1 large bag of Doritos

½ cup all-purpose flour

1 stick frozen butter, cut into small pieces

1 large egg

2 tablespoons cold water

FOR THE FILLING

4 large eggs

2 cups half-and-half

Salt and pepper

8 ounces cooked bacon, chopped

6 ounces shredded sharp cheddar cheese

⅔ cup ketchup

1 small bag of Doritos

1. Prepare the Crust: In a food processor, grind the large bag of Doritos until completely pulverized. Measure out 2 cups and reserve the rest. Return to the food processor, along with the flour, and process on low for 30 seconds.

2. Add frozen butter cubes, and pulse until it resembles coarse meal, about 20 seconds.

3. Stream egg into the food processor while continuing to pulse. The dough should just barely come together. If it appears too dry and falls apart when you pinch some between your fingers, add a bit of water while pulsing.

4. Press dough mixture into sides and bottom of a 9-inch pie plate. Refrigerate for a minimum of 1 hour.

5. Place a sheet pan or cookie sheet in the oven, and preheat to 375°F.

6. Prepare the Filling: Whisk eggs well so they turn pale yellow. While continuing to whisk, slowly pour in half-and-half until mixture is uniform. Add a pinch of salt and a few grinds of black pepper. Put the custard into a large liquid measuring cup, or another container with a pouring spout.

7. Scatter cooked bacon pieces and cheddar cheese evenly over the bottom of the crust. Without removing from the oven, place the pie plate on the preheated cookie sheet, then slowly pour the filling evenly over the crust. Bake for 50 to 55 minutes, until it appears just barely set in the center and is still slightly jiggly, tenting with foil after 30 minutes if crust is becoming too brown. Cool for a minimum of 20 minutes if you'd like to serve it warm—otherwise, refrigerate until you are ready to serve.

8. Using a small spatula, frost the quiche with ketchup. Roughly crumble the small bag of Doritos and sprinkle over the top.

9. Serve on a platter garnished with additional Doritos flour at any temperature you damn well please. Quiche is cool like that.

Note

If you have problems keeping the dough together, add a little water, knead it in, and try again. If worse comes to worst, pick the dough up piece by piece and patch it together in the pie plate. No one can see the insides, anyway.

Velveeta Chex Mix Nacho Dirtbag Casserole

BY KAT KINSMAN AND MARGARET EBY Chex Mix, Velveeta, Doritos, Fritos, Kraft Singles, chorizo, salsa, Budweiser, and eggs. That might sound like an unholy combination, but it's probably a list of ingredients you might have all or most of after, say, a Super Bowl party. There's a hard time limit on how long you want that half-bag of a snack food to hang out. But a not-so-secret secret is that, with enough cheese and a few eggs to use as a binder, you can turn dang near anything into a casserole, including Chex Mix.

This is far, far from actual chilaquiles, but thanks to the salsa-soaked chip crumbles, the casserole does have a note of that classic Mexican hangover dish, plus some beer tang from the Budweiser, and so much glorious cheese. Velveeta is best for its gooeyness factor, but in a pinch you can use any other yellow cheese, including and especially Kraft Singles. You can also substitute whatever other chips or crackers you have on hand for the Chex Mix, and whatever cheap beer you have for the Budweiser. This casserole is not about being fussy. It's about being the best frat house mom you can be to yourself.

Chips, Chex Mix, Fritos, crackers, whatever, crushed

Cheese (we used Velveeta, Kraft singles, and a shredded Mexican blend)

Salsa

Sour cream

6 large eggs

¼ cup milk

Sliced chorizo

Beer

Hot sauce

1. Preheat oven to 375°F. Grease a casserole pan or baking dish in whatever manner you see fit. Lay down a thick layer of crushed chips, Chex Mix, what have you. Cover that with cheese, ideally Velveeta, but feel free to deploy Kraft Singles, shredded cheese, pimento cheese, or any other cheese-like substance you have available. If you have sour cream or salsa on hand, that's great! Dollop 'em in there.

2. Whisk together 3 eggs and milk, and pour over the layers evenly. Crush up crackers and Chex mix, and layer those on, then more cheese, sliced chorizo, and salsa. Cover with another layer of whatever chips, Chex Mix, etc., you still have left.

Whisk together 3 eggs with however much beer seems reasonable, and pour that over the top. The ethos you're going for is "fraternity house carpet." Another cheese layer? Why not. Cover with foil and bake until the egg is set, about 15 minutes. Remove from oven, cool, and refrigerate for several hours, or overnight to let the flavors meld and the chips soften.

3. Remove from fridge, top with additional cheese, and bake covered with foil in a 400°F oven until the casserole is heated all the way through, 20 to 40 minutes. Remove foil and let the cheese slightly brown. Slice and serve proudly with a crap-ton of hot sauce.

Breakfast Frito Pie Will Leave You With Zero Regrets

BY MARGARET EBY Frito pie is one of the unsung snack heroes of childhood, a self-contained mess of deliciousness that is a staple of many summer camp and diner experiences. Frito pie or a "walking taco" has an incredibly easy premise. Take a bag of Fritos, preferably the snack-size ones you can grab in vending machines. Open it. Dump in a few scoops of chili, maybe some scallions, cheese, sour cream, salsa, or a spritz of lime juice, and dig in. You could use a fork or chopsticks to avoid dropping chili and salsa on yourself, or just dig right in with your hands. Chips count as utensils.

Frito pie is self-contained, requires no cleanup, and is infinitely customizable. If you have vegetarians, you can have veggie chili. Fritos are also gluten-free, though they are processed in the same facility as products with gluten, so if you're extremely sensitive, you might want to swap them out for another option. (Rice crackers are pretty great.) Want to dress it up as brunch? Add a couple poached or fried eggs with the yolk still runny and drop 'em straight in the bag. You can also make a large-format Frito pie using a large bag of Fritos layered with the fixings—guests can just dip in as they want. The possibilities are endless and extremely crunchy.

1 snack-size bag of Fritos per person, or one large bag of Fritos for sharing

Several servings of Texas Red Chili and Eggs (page 180), or chili of your choice

Poached or fried eggs, to taste

Sour cream

Scallions, chopped roughly

1 lime, cut into wedges

Shredded cheese

Slit open Fritos bags. Scoop in chili, runny egg, and whatever toppings you want. Serve.

THE BASTARDIZED ETHNIC RECIPE CORNER

BY JUSTIN WARNER Say you and I are one big dopey family on *Family Feud*. Steve Harvey wants to know the top six things Americans have for brunch. Eggs Benedict takes the top spot, and right behind it is its Mexican cousin, huevos rancheros. This clássico del campo is ubiquitous at brunches all over the U.S., and rightfully so. The OG version consists of warm corn tortillas for sopping up crisp-bottomed sunny eggs, a bright and spicy salsa for booting your hangover, and maybe some slow-cooked beans and seasoned rice to fill the belly. When these components are prepared with care, using ranch-fresh ingredients, huevos rancheros becomes a world-class dish.

In the States, though, you are just as likely to find the eggs scrambled (which defeats the purpose of having the tortillas for yolk soppage) and the corn tortillas made from wheat (adios, sabor). There is also a large number of gabachos who don't think brunch is brunch without meat. Instead of adding chorizo or longanisa, I've seen huevos rancheros with everything from soy bacon to Jimmy Dean's. In its voyage north, huevos has become so bastardized it should join the Night's Watch. But that's not necessarily a bad thing.

I like to celebrate authenticity and tradition as much as I do reinterpretation and progress. That is what's great about America—we don't have to get a state-approved haircut or eat a patriot's brunch if we don't want to. We can call a urinal a water fountain, and even more brazenly, call it art. And so it is in this spirit that I offer Potsticker Huevos Rancheros, a super-bastardized but damned delicious dish.

First comes a high-hatted and super-fresh pico de gallo, with a judicious amount of heat. Then you make the best refried beans of your life, cooking them in chorizo grease until they become the tuba to the pico's mariachi trumpets. You will wantonly abandon tortillas and use wonton wrappers to make tiny bombs of chorizo and cheese. The potstickerization of the chorizo and cheese allows you to freeze and portion out the goods for brunches to come.

To cap it off, a little *pelo del perro* in the form of a pico back, which, to my knowledge, was invented at a place called Chilo's in Brooklyn. It's a shot of tequila with a chaser of pico de gallo liquid. There's something magical in this one-two punch. The pico chaser wipes your taste-memory clean of the tequila like that gizmo Will Smith and TLJ use in *Men in Black*. Consume more than one at your own risk. (Turn the page for the recipe.)

Potsticker Huevos Rancheros with Pico Backs

FOR THE PICO

2 serrano peppers

1 jalapeño pepper

14 ounces grape tomatoes

1 shallot

2 cloves of garlic

4 limes

Finely chopped cilantro, optional

1½ teaspoons salt

FOR THE FILLING

14 ounces Mexican chorizo

1 cup shredded cheese

FOR THE REFRIED BEANS

1 (15½-ounce) can black beans

FOR THE POTSTICKERS

30 round wonton/potsticker wrappers (I like the green ones)

FOR THE REST

2 tablespoons butter

Eggs (at least 2)

3 shots of tequila, optional, but very cool

Sliced scallions, optional, but pretty

Sour cream, optional, but delicious

1. For the Pico: Put some gloves on, or don't complain when you rub your eye and it burns. Slice off the tops of the serrano peppers. Slice them lengthwise. Starting at the narrow end, use your knife to flatten them while cutting out the membrane and seeds. Repeat this process with jalapeño. Cut the serrano peppers into long thin strips by dragging your knife through them, skin side up. Do this with the jalapeño as well.

2. Line up all of the serrano strips and slice them perpendicularly into tiny bits. Place half of the serrano bits into a storage container and set the other half aside. Repeat this process with the jalapeño, but place all of the jalapeño bits into the storage container.

3. Cut the tomatoes into quarters by cutting them in half, rotating and cutting again, and finally cutting perpendicularly to the first two cuts. Add these to the storage container with the peppers.

4. Cut off the top of the shallot (the pointy part). Cut it in half from top to bottom. Lay the flat side of the shallot on your board and carefully cut the shallot horizontally down the middle, parallel to your board. Now, make even, vertical cuts in the shallot. Finally, slice perpendicularly to make a fine mince. Discard the root end. Add these to the container with the tomatoes and peppers. Mince the garlic. Put half of the garlic aside with the other serrano. Put the rest in the container.

5. Use a rasp to zest one of the limes, and add this to the storage container with the tomatoes, peppers, and shallot.

6. Roll the limes on your board to extract a little extra juice, then cut them in half and ream so the juice goes into the storage container. Add some finely chopped cilantro if you are into it, then the salt, and toss to coat. I make this directly into a deli container, put the lid on it, and shake the hell out of it. Keep this in the fridge until you are ready to make the dish. The flavor only gets better in my opinion.

7. For the Filling: Squeeze the chorizo out of its casing and into the pan. Over medium-low, cook the chorizo for about 12 to 14 minutes, while using the slotted spoon to mash up any chunks.

8. Put your cheese into a mixing bowl. Use the slotted spoon to transfer the chorizo to the mixing bowl, trying to leave as much of the chorizo grease behind as can be done.

9. Toss the cheese and the chorizo together. Set this aside until you are ready to make the potstickers.

10. For the Refried Beans: To the chorizo grease, add the reserved serrano and garlic. Over medium-low heat, cook for 1 or 2 minutes until sizzling. Then add the black beans, liquid and all. Trust me.

11. Use the slotted spoon to mash up two-thirds of the beans and cook until thickened, 8 to 10 minutes.

12. Transfer these to a storage container to cool, and then place in the fridge until you are ready to make the dish.

13. For the Potstickers: Place heaping teaspoons of the chorizo-cheese mix in the center of the wrappers. Use your finger to lightly wipe a little water around the edge of the wrapper. Fold the wrapper over and press down gently. Wet the outside edge again and fold the edges over themselves 4 to 5 times. This makes for a real cute dumpling. Repeat.

14. Set these aside on a sheet tray or plate until you've exhausted your supplies. This makes about 28 dumplings if you don't mess up. Place these in the freezer until frozen, then transfer them to a ziplock bag to keep until you are ready to make the dish.

15. Assemble the dish: Over medium high, melt the butter until it's bubbling. Add the dumplings in a ring and cook for about 5 minutes.

16. Crack the eggs into the center of the ring, being careful not to break the yolks. Add two spoonfuls of the beans into the whites between the yolks. When the whites are starting to set, proceed to the next step.

17. From here you can channel your inner me and flambé this bad boy. If that scares you proceed to the next step. Have the lid within reach. In your dominant hand hold the grill lighter and in your non-dominant hand the tequila. Carefully pour in the tequila, stand back, and ignite the sputtering fumes. This will create a fire in the pan. Let it go for about 15 to 20 seconds, or until you are skeered and then put the lid on it to extinguish. (If you chose not to flambé, put the lid on the pan and cook until the yolks are as you would like them.)

18. Remove the pan from the heat, and set on a heat-proof surface. Top with the pico, some scallions if you got them and some sour cream if you dig it. Use a spatula to serve or be like me and just eat it out of the pan while standing in your onesie, impressed with yourself.

19. Toast to your accomplishments by doing a pico back: Drain off a shot of the pico liquid and use it as a chaser to a shot of tequila.

Index